Health at a Glance 2013

OECD INDICATORS

OECD

BETTER POLICIES FOR BETTER LIVES

This work is published on the responsibility of the Secretary-General of the OECD. The opinions expressed and arguments employed herein do not necessarily reflect the official views of the Organisation or of the governments of its member countries.

This document and any map included herein are without prejudice to the status of or sovereignty over any territory, to the delimitation of international frontiers and boundaries and to the name of any territory, city or area.

Please cite this publication as:
OECD (2013), *Health at a Glance 2013: OECD Indicators*, OECD Publishing.
http://dx.doi.org/10.1787/health_glance-2013-en

ISBN 978-92-64-20071-5 (print)
ISBN 978-92-64-20502-4 (PDF)
ISBN 978-92-64-20422-5 (HTML)

Annual: Health at a glance
ISSN 1995-3992 (print)
ISSN 1999-1312 (online)

The statistical data for Israel are supplied by and under the responsibility of the relevant Israeli authorities. The use of such data by the OECD is without prejudice to the status of the Golan Heights, East Jerusalem and Israeli settlements in the West Bank under the terms of international law.

Photo credits: Cover © gunnar3000 – Fotolia.com.

Corrigenda to OECD publications may be found on line at: *www.oecd.org/publishing/corrigenda*.

Foreword

*T*his 2013 edition of Health at a Glance – OECD Indicators *presents the most recent comparable data on key indicators of health and health systems across the 34 OECD member countries. Where possible, it also reports comparable data for Brazil, China, India, Indonesia, the Russian Federation, and South Africa, as key emerging countries.*

The production of Health at a Glance *would not have been possible without the contribution of OECD Health Data National Correspondents, Health Accounts Experts, and Health Care Quality Indicators Experts from the 34 OECD countries. The OECD gratefully acknowledges their effort in supplying most of the data contained in this publication. The OECD also acknowledges the contribution of other international organisations, especially the World Health Organization, the World Bank and Eurostat, for sharing some of the data presented here, and the European Commission for supporting data development.*

This publication was prepared by a team from the OECD Health Division under the co-ordination of Gaétan Lafortune. Chapter 1 was prepared by Gaétan Lafortune, Kees van Gool and Nelly Biondi; Chapter 2 by Franco Sassi, Marion Devaux, Michele Cecchini and Nelly Biondi; Chapter 3 by Michael Schoenstein, Gaétan Lafortune, Gaëlle Balestat and Anne Durand; Chapter 4 by Gaétan Lafortune, Valérie Paris, Gaëlle Balestat, Marie-Clémence Canaud and Jessica Farebrother; Chapter 5 by Kees van Gool, Ian Forde, Rie Fujisawa, Nelly Biondi, Evianne van der Kruk and Niek Klazinga; Chapter 6 by Marion Devaux, Valérie Paris, Gaétan Lafortune, Michael Schoenstein, Tomoko Ono, Michael Mueller, Emily Hewlett and Alessia Forti; Chapter 7 by David Morgan, Michael Mueller and Alan Diener; and Chapter 8 by Francesca Colombo, Yuki Murakami, Marie-Clémence Canaud, Nelly Biondi, Michael Mueller and Martin Salomon. This publication benefited from many comments and suggestions from Mark Pearson (Head of the OECD Health Division).

Table of contents

Follow OECD Publications on:

 http://twitter.com/OECD_Pubs

 http://www.facebook.com/OECDPublications

in http://www.linkedin.com/groups/OECD-Publications-4645871

 http://www.youtube.com/oecdilibrary

 http://www.oecd.org/oecddirect/

This book has...   *StatLinks*
A service that delivers Excel® files from the printed page!

Look for the *StatLinks* at the bottom of the tables or graphs in this book.
To download the matching Excel® spreadsheet, just type the link into your
Internet browser, starting with the *http://dx.doi.org* prefix, or click on the link from
the e-book edition.

Editorial:
From expenditure growth to productivity growth in the health sector

Almost six years since the start of the global financial and economic crisis, economic conditions vary widely across OECD countries, with the United States, Canada and Japan on a path to recovery, while the economic prospects of many European countries remain subdued. After a period in which, as part of the stimulus packages, greater resources were channelled to welfare and social protection programmes, the shift towards restoring sound fiscal conditions has often implied substantial cuts in public spending. Like other government programmes, health care has been the target of spending cuts in many OECD countries.

The crisis has had a profound impact on the lives of citizens across the world, and has tested the resilience of many families as they see their wealth and incomes decline. Millions of people have joined the ranks of the unemployed and millions more are experiencing financial stress. The combined effects of the crisis with the associated recent expenditure cuts as well as health care reforms have led to uncertainty about the impact on the health and well-being of the population. The most recent OECD health statistics, presented in this edition of *Health at a Glance*, provide a comprehensive picture of how health systems have evolved during the crisis and the challenges which lie ahead.

Most OECD countries have moved to lower health spending

Growth in health spending has slowed markedly in almost all OECD countries since 2008. After years of continuous growth of over 4% per annum, average health spending across the OECD grew at only 0.2% between 2009 and 2011. Total health spending fell in 11 out of the 34 OECD countries between 2009 and 2011, compared to pre-crisis levels. Not surprisingly, the countries hit hardest by the economic crisis have witnessed the biggest cuts in health expenditure growth. For example, Greece and Ireland experienced the sharpest declines, with per capita health care spending falling by 11.1% and 6.6%, respectively, between 2009 and 2011. Health spending growth also slowed significantly in Canada and the United States. Only in Israel and Japan has health spending growth accelerated since 2009.

In order to limit or reduce public health expenditures, countries have worked to lower the prices paid for publicly financed health care, including cutting the price of medical goods, particularly pharmaceuticals. Governments have targeted hospital spending through budgetary restrictions and cuts to wages. Several countries including Greece, Ireland, Iceland and Estonia have reduced nursing wages in response to the crisis as well as those of salaried GPs. Expenditure on prevention and public health has also been cut since 2009. Further, in several OECD countries, patients are now expected to assume a greater share of health costs.

The crisis has had a mixed impact on health indicators

What has been the effect of the crisis on health? The results are mixed. For example, while suicide rates rose slightly at the start of the crisis, they appear to have stabilised since then. There are also indications that Greece's infant mortality rate, long in decline, has been rising since the crisis started. Neither is good news. But other health indicators tell a different story: mortality from road traffic accidents, for example, has declined. Such deaths had already been steadily falling in most OECD countries, but the rate of decline accelerated after 2008 in some countries that were hard hit by the recession, likely because less economic activity means fewer cars on the roads, and so fewer accidents.

The crisis may also have led to positive changes in certain health behaviours. In particular, alcohol and tobacco consumption in a number of OECD countries fell in the immediate aftermath of the crisis. This was already a long-standing trend in most countries, but the drop in consumption has accelerated due to the combined impact of lower incomes and more stringent policies around purchasing and use. It remains a question as to whether these gains can be maintained once economic growth and household budgets improve.

As the short-term impact of the crisis on health is both bad (mental health) and good (accidents, alcohol), it is not surprising to find that there is no evidence yet of a widespread health impact in the countries hardest hit by the crisis. As with so many things in health, the pathways by which economic crisis and policies affect health outcomes are complex to evaluate. Moreover, most countries, including those most heavily affected by the crisis, continue to make progress in primary health care and the quality of acute care for life-threatening conditions. There are no signs that the crisis is raising cancer-related mortality rates, for example, and most countries have continued to raise survival rates for cardiovascular disease.

Nevertheless, the direction that policies have taken in some countries raises some concern. For instance, prevention is often a more cost-effective way of improving health than spending money once a disease takes root. However, prevention expenditures have been reduced since 2009 (although they only account for around 3-4% of total health expenditure). One example of the consequences is the dramatic rise in the number of new HIV cases reported since 2010 in Athens, Greece, among injecting drug users. Although opioid substitution and needle exchange programmes have expanded since the start of the outbreak, the initial response fell well short of recommended levels of access, illustrating the potential long-term impact on health and spending when highly cost-effective prevention programmes are not fully implemented. Cuts in spending on preventing obesity, harmful use of alcohol, and tobacco consumption are cases of "penny-wise, pound foolish" thinking.

Likewise, cuts to the supply of health care services and changes in health care financing arrangements are also affecting access to care. After years of steady decline, average waiting times for some operations in Portugal, Spain, England, and Ireland show a small increase. There is evidence that more people in countries such as Greece and Italy are foregoing medical care due to financial constraints, reflecting reduced household incomes, but also perhaps rising out-of-pocket costs. Low-income groups are the worst affected, although they are likely to have the highest health care needs, and they may be foregoing necessary care such as medicines or routine medical check-ups for chronic conditions. This may have long-term health and economic consequences for the most vulnerable groups in society.

Towards affordable, sustainable care

Pressures to reduce public spending are likely to persist well into the recovery phase. Given the large fiscal imbalances built during the crisis, fiscal consolidation required to bring debt-to-GDP ratios back to sustainable levels would have to be pursued for a number of years, as stressed in the 2013 *OECD Economic Outlook*. Countries' main consolidation targets vary but generally focus on inefficient public expenditures and include savings on health care.

In a climate of fiscal restraint and efficiency efforts, health expenditure growth should be more aligned to a country's economic growth and its ability to raise revenue. This was not the case before the crisis, when health care funding outpaced economic growth in many countries. The crisis has pushed many countries to undertake structural reforms of their health systems, aimed at changing the incentives or the way that prices are negotiated. Examples include Greece's introduction of a new output-based hospital funding system, Italy's drive for greater competiveness in the pharmaceutical distribution market, Portugal's investment in health care performance management systems and the centralisation of pharmaceutical purchasing powers in Spain. These reforms could make important long-term contributions to the health systems' productivity and efficiency.

Governments must continue to seek clever ways by which health systems can continue to improve the well-being of patients within the new fiscal environment. Some countries are moving towards greater labour productivity by re-examining the traditional functions of general practitioners, specialists, nurses and allied health professionals. Other countries are also looking at the extent to which medical practice variation points towards ineffective or inefficient care. For example, there is a three-fold difference in the rate of caesarean sections between Iceland and the Netherlands, which have the lowest number of caesareans, and Mexico which has the highest rate. Some of this variation may be justified by clinical need, but it could also mean that women are either having unnecessary operations, or being denied care they should be getting. Evidence-based clinical pathways can improve health care productivity.

While the agenda for quality of care has now been firmly embedded in most health care systems, countries can make further gains in patient safety, thereby reducing the costs and health burdens associated with adverse events. Health care quality can also be improved by strengthening primary care systems to better manage complex conditions. The increasing prevalence of complex chronic diseases is one of the many challenges arising from ageing populations and will require constant vigilance and multidisciplinary care to prevent the onset of costly complications.

Many of the reforms implemented since the start of the crisis have had an immediate impact on public expenditure. Some have been controversial, with considerable unrest and political pressure from industry groups, and some may also have had undesirable consequences for access, outcomes and equity. For example, greater out-of-pocket costs are likely to reduce health care use among those in highest need, leading to greater inequity and inefficiency over the longer term.

In the new, more constrained, fiscal climate, the challenge for health care policy makers is to preserve quality health care coverage for the whole population while converting a system built on notions of unconstrained growth to one that is based on greater productivity and fiscal sustainability. This challenge is not new. Countries have pursued the twin objectives of efficiency and equity in health for decades. The economic crisis means that health care policy makers must swiftly and convincingly adopt a health care productivity agenda.

Stefano Scarpetta
Director for Employment, Labour and Social Affairs

Executive summary

Health at a Glance 2013 presents the trends and influences shaping health status, services and policies in OECD countries and the BRIICS. Although indicators such as life expectancy or infant mortality suggest that things are improving overall, inequalities in wealth, education and other social indicators still have a significant impact on health status and access to health services. These health disparities may be explained by differences in living and working conditions, as well as differences that show up in the health-related lifestyle data presented here (e.g., smoking, harmful alcohol drinking, physical inactivity, and obesity).

Health expenditures show considerable variations across countries, in terms of spending per capita, as a share of GDP and recent trends. On average across the OECD, per capita health spending grew by 4.1% annually in real terms over 2000-2009, but this slowed to 0.2% in 2009-10 and 2010-11 as many countries reduced health spending to help cut budget deficits and government debt, especially in Europe. Countries outside of Europe have continued to see health spending grow, albeit at a reduced pace in many cases, notably in Canada and the United States.

Different areas of spending have been affected in different ways: in 2010-11, spending on pharmaceuticals and prevention dropped by 1.7%, while hospital costs rose by 1.0%.

Life expectancy in OECD countries is rising, but so is the burden of chronic diseases

- Average life expectancy exceeded 80 years across OECD countries in 2011, an increase of ten years since 1970. Those born in Switzerland, Japan and Italy can expect to live the longest among OECD countries.

- Across OECD countries, women can expect to live 5.5 years longer than men. People with the highest level of education can expect to live 6 years longer than those with the lowest level of education.

- Chronic diseases such as diabetes and dementia are increasingly prevalent. In 2011, close to 7% of 20-79 year-olds in OECD countries, or over 85 million people, had diabetes.

There are more doctors per capita in most countries, but twice as many specialists as generalists

- Since 2000, the number of doctors has grown in most OECD countries, both in absolute number and on a per capita basis, with only a few exceptions. There was virtually no growth in the number of doctors per capita in Estonia and France, and a decline in Israel.

- There were two specialists for every generalist on average across the OECD, in 2011. The slow growth in, or reduction of, the number of generalists raises concerns about access to primary care for all the population.

Shorter hospital stays and growing use of generic drugs help to contain costs, but large variations in medical practice point towards overuse

- The length of stay in hospital dropped from 9.2 days in 2000 to 8.0 days in 2011 in OECD countries.

- The market share of generic drugs has increased significantly over the past decade in many countries. However, generics still represent less than 25% of the market in Luxembourg, Italy, Ireland, Switzerland, Japan and France, compared with about 75% in Germany and the United Kingdom.

- Wide variations in the utilisation rate of different diagnostic and surgical procedures cannot be explained by differences in clinical needs. For example, in 2011, caesarean sections made up more than 45% of all births in Mexico and Turkey, triple the rate in Iceland and the Netherlands, suggesting possible overuse.

The quality of acute care and primary care has improved in most countries, but could improve more

- Progress in the treatment of life-threatening conditions such as heart attack, stroke and cancer has led to higher survival rates in most OECD countries. On average, mortality rates following hospital admissions for heart attack fell by 30% between 2001 and 2011 and for stroke by almost 25%. Survival has also improved for many types of cancer, including cervical cancer, breast cancer and colorectal cancer.

- The quality of primary care has also improved in most countries, as shown by the reduction in avoidable hospital admissions for chronic diseases such as asthma and diabetes. Still, there is room in all countries to improve primary care to further reduce costly hospital admissions for these conditions.

Nearly all OECD countries have achieved universal health coverage, but the scope and degree of coverage varies

- All OECD countries have universal (or quasi-universal) health coverage for a core set of health services and goods, except Mexico and the United States. Following the 2004 reforms in Mexico, the proportion of the population covered has grown rapidly to reach nearly 90%. In the United States, where 15% of the population was still uninsured in 2011, the Affordable Care Act will further expand health insurance coverage, from January 2014.

- The burden of out-of-pocket spending creates barriers to health care access in some countries. On average, 20% of health spending is paid directly by patients; this ranges from less than 10% in the Netherlands and France to over 35% in Chile, Korea and Mexico.

- Around 19% of out-of-pocket medical expenditure across OECD countries in 2011 was for dental care, while another 12% was for eyeglasses, hearing aids and other therapeutic appliances.
- People in low-income groups are more likely to report unmet medical and dental needs than people in higher-income groups, and are also less likely to consult a medical specialist or a dentist.

Population ageing increases demand for long-term care and puts pressures on public spending, despite informal care

- The life expectancy of people at age 65 has continued to increase, reaching nearly 21 years for women and 18 years for men across OECD countries in 2011. However, many of these additional years are lived with some chronic conditions. For example, over a quarter of people aged 85 years and older suffers from dementia.
- Across OECD countries, more than 15% of people aged 50 and older provide care for a dependent relative or friend, and most informal carers are women.
- Public expenditures on long-term care grew by 4.8% annually between 2005 and 2011 across OECD countries, higher than the growth in health care spending.

Reader's guide

Health at a Glance 2013 presents comparisons of key indicators of health and health systems across the 34 OECD countries, as well as for key emerging countries (Brazil, China, India, Indonesia, the Russian Federation and South Africa). The indicators presented in this publication have been selected on the basis of their policy relevance as well as data availability and comparability. The data come mainly from official national statistics, unless otherwise indicated.

Structure of the publication

The framework underlying this publication assesses the performance of health systems in the context of a broader view of public health (Figure 0.1). It is based on a framework that was endorsed for the OECD Health Care Quality Indicators project (Kelley and Hurst, 2006; Arah et al., 2006).

This framework recognises that the goal of health systems is to improve the health status of the population. Many factors influence the health status of the population, including a number that fall outside health care systems, such as the physical environment in which people live, and individual lifestyles and behaviours. The performance of health care systems also contributes obviously to the health status of the population. This performance includes several dimensions, including the degree of access to care and the quality of care provided.

Performance measurement also needs to take into account the financial resources required to achieve these access and quality goals. The performance of health systems depends on the people providing the services, and the training, technology and equipment at their disposal.

Finally, a number of contextual factors that also affect the health status of the population and the demand for and supply of health services also need to be taken into account, including the demographic context, and economic and social development.

Health at a Glance 2013 compares OECD countries on each component of this framework. It is structured around eight chapters.

Chapter 1 on Health Status highlights large variations across countries in life expectancy, mortality and other measures of population health status. Compared with the previous edition, this chapter includes new measures of inequality in health status by education and income level for key indicators such as life expectancy and perceived health status.

Chapter 2 on Non-medical Determinants of Health focuses on health-related lifestyles and behaviours among children and adults, including tobacco smoking, alcohol drinking, physical activity, nutrition, and overweight and obesity problems. Most of these factors can be modified by public health and prevention policies.

Figure 0.1. **Conceptual framework for health system performance assessment**

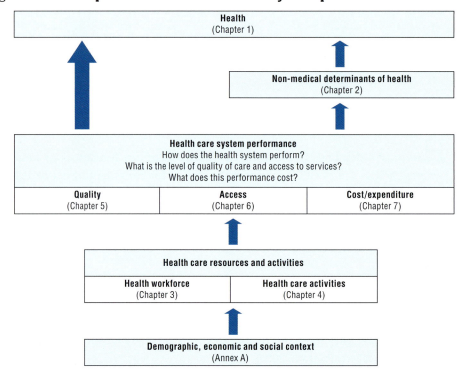

Source: Adapted from Kelley, E. and J. Hurst (2006), "Health Care Quality Indicators Project: Conceptual Framework", *OECD Health Working Paper*, No. 23, OECD Publishing, http://dx.doi.org/10.1787/440134737301.

Chapter 3 looks at the *Health Workforce*, providing data on the supply and remuneration of doctors and nurses in OECD countries. It also presents trends on the number of new graduates from medical and nursing education programmes, a key determinant of future supply.

Chapter 4 on *Health Care Activities* describes some of the main characteristics of health service delivery in different OECD countries. It begins by looking at consultations with doctors, and the supply and use of diagnostic technologies such as medical resonance imaging and computed tomography scanners. The hospital sector continues to absorb the largest share of health spending in OECD countries, hence a focus on the availability of hospital beds, their utilisation rate, the number of hospital discharges and average length of stay. The chapter also looks at variations in the use of high-volume and high-cost procedures, such as caesarean sections, cardiac procedures, and hip and knee replacement. It concludes by looking at the pharmaceutical market, comparing the use of certain pharmaceutical drugs and the share of the generic market in different countries.

Chapter 5 examines *Quality of Care* or the degree to which care is delivered in accordance with established standards and improves health outcomes. It provides comparisons on quality of care for chronic conditions and pharmaceutical prescriptions, acute care for life-threatening diseases, patient safety, care for mental disorders, cancer care, the prevention of communicable diseases and, for the first time, some important aspects of patient experiences.

Chapter 6 on *Access to Care* presents a set of indicators that can be used to assess to what extent OECD countries are meeting their policy goal of ensuring adequate access to essential health services on the basis of individual need. It begins by describing the proportion of population covered by public or private health insurance and the share of out-of-pocket spending in household consumption. The chapter then discusses issues around geographic access to care, focusing in particular on the "density" of doctors in different regions in each country. Another approach to measuring access to care is to look at inequalities among different socioeconomic groups in the use of health services. Three indicators look at the use of doctors, dentists and screening rates for cancer, either by income group or education level. The last indicator relates to timely access to care, comparing waiting times for certain elective surgery in a group of OECD countries where this is considered to be an important issue.

Chapter 7 on *Health Expenditure and Financing* compares how much OECD countries spend on health, both on a per capita basis and in relation to GDP. The chapter also provides an analysis of the different types of health services and goods consumed across OECD countries, including a separate focus on pharmaceuticals. It also looks at how these health services and goods are paid for in different countries (i.e. the mix between public funding, private health insurance where it exists, and direct out-of-pocket payments). Lastly, in the context of the growth in medical tourism and international trade in health services, current levels and trends are examined.

Chapter 8 focuses on *Ageing and Long-term Care*, starting by a review of demographic trends and the rising share of the population aged over 65 and 80 in all OECD countries. The chapter presents the most recent data on life expectancy and life expectancy in good health at age 65, self-reported health and disability status, as important factors affecting the current and future demand for long-term care. This is followed by a set of indicators on older persons currently receiving long-term care at home or in institutions, on care providers (including both formal and informal caregivers), and on the capacity to provide long-term care in institutions in different countries. The final indicator reviews levels and trends in long-term care expenditure over the past decade.

A *Statistical Annex* provides additional information on the demographic and economic context within which health and long-term care systems operate.

Presentation of indicators

Each of the topics covered in the different chapters of this publication is presented over two pages. The first provides a brief commentary highlighting the key findings conveyed by the data, defines the indicator and signals any significant national variation from the definition which might affect data comparability. On the facing page is a set of figures. These typically show current levels of the indicator and, where possible, trends over time. Where an OECD average is included in a figure, it is the unweighted average of the OECD countries presented, unless otherwise specified.

Data limitations

Limitations in data comparability are indicated both in the text (in the box related to "Definition and comparability") as well as in footnotes to figures.

Data sources

Readers interested in using the data presented in this publication for further analysis and research are encouraged to consult the full documentation of definitions, sources and methods presented in *OECD Health Statistics* on OECD.Stat (*http://stats.oecd.org/index.aspx*, then choose "Health"). More information on *OECD Health Statistics* is available at *www.oecd.org/health/healthdata*. Information about data sources used for non-OECD countries is available at *www.oecd.org/health/healthataglance*.

Population figures

The population figures presented in Annex A and used to calculate rates per capita throughout this publication come from the OECD Historical Population Data and Projections (as of end of May 2013), and refer to mid-year estimates. Population estimates are subject to revision, so they may differ from the latest population figures released by the national statistical offices of OECD member countries.

Note that some countries such as France, the United Kingdom and the United States have overseas colonies, protectorates or territories. These populations are generally excluded. The calculation of GDP per capita and other economic measures may, however, be based on a different population in these countries, depending on the data coverage.

OECD country ISO codes

Australia	AUS	Japan	JPN
Austria	AUT	Korea	KOR
Belgium	BEL	Luxembourg	LUX
Canada	CAN	Mexico	MEX
Chile	CHL	Netherlands	NLD
Czech Republic	CZE	New Zealand	NZL
Denmark	DNK	Norway	NOR
Estonia	EST	Poland	POL
Finland	FIN	Portugal	PRT
France	FRA	Slovak Republic	SVK
Germany	DEU	Slovenia	SVN
Greece	GRC	Spain	ESP
Hungary	HUN	Sweden	SWE
Iceland	ISL	Switzerland	CHE
Ireland	IRL	Turkey	TUR
Israel	ISR	United Kingdom	GBR
Italy	ITA	United States	USA

Emerging country ISO codes

Brazil	BRA	Indonesia	IDN
China	CHN	Russian Federation	RUS
India	IND	South Africa	ZAF

1. HEALTH STATUS

The statistical data for Israel are supplied by and under the responsibility of the relevant Israeli authorities. The use of such data by the OECD is without prejudice to the status of the Golan Heights, East Jerusalem and Israeli settlements in the West Bank under the terms of international law.

1.1. Life expectancy at birth

Life expectancy has increased greatly over the past few decades in all OECD countries and many emerging economies. Improvement in living conditions, a reduction of certain risk factors (e.g., smoking rates) and progress in health care are the main factors explaining increased longevity.

For the first time in history, in 2011, life expectancy on average across OECD countries exceeded 80 years, an increase of ten years since 1970 (Figure 1.1.1). Switzerland, Japan and Italy lead a large group of over two-thirds of OECD countries in which life expectancy at birth now exceeds 80 years. A second group, including the United States, Chile and a number of central and eastern European countries, have a life expectancy between 75 and 80 years. Among OECD countries life expectancy was lowest in Mexico and Turkey. While life expectancy in Turkey has increased rapidly and steadily over the past four decades, the increase in Mexico has slowed down markedly since 2000.

Emerging countries such as Brazil, China, Indonesia and India have also achieved large gains in longevity over the past decades, with life expectancy in these countries converging rapidly towards the OECD average. There has been much less progress in South Africa (due mainly to the epidemic of HIV/AIDS) and the Russian Federation (due mainly to the impact of the economic transition in the 1990s and the rise in risky behaviors among men).

In the United States, the gains in life expectancy since 1970 have also been much more modest than in most other OECD countries. While life expectancy in the United States used to be one year *above* the OECD average in 1970, it is now more than one year *below* the average. Many possible explanations have been suggested for these lower gains in life expectancy, including: 1) the highly fragmented nature of the US health system, with relatively few resources devoted to public health and primary care, and a large share of the population uninsured; 2) health-related behaviours, including higher calorie consumption per capita and obesity rates, higher consumption of prescription and illegal drugs, higher deaths from road traffic accidents and higher homicide rates; and 3) adverse socio-economic conditions affecting a large segment of the US population, with higher rates of poverty and income inequality than in most other OECD countries (National Research Council and Institute of Medicine, 2013).

Higher national income (as measured by GDP per capita) is generally associated with higher life expectancy at birth, although the relationship is less pronounced at the highest levels of national income (Figure 1.1.2). There are also notable differences in life expectancy between countries with similar income per capita. For example, Japan and Italy have higher, and the United States and the Russian Federation have lower life expectancies than would be predicted by their GDP per capita alone.

Figure 1.1.3 shows the relationship between life expectancy at birth and health expenditure per capita across OECD countries and emerging countries. Higher health spending per capita is generally associated with higher life expectancy at birth, although this relationship tends to be less pronounced in countries with the highest health spending per capita. Japan, Italy and Spain stand out as having relatively high life expectancies, and the United States and the Russian Federation relatively low life expectancies, given their levels of health spending.

Many other factors, beyond national income and total health spending, affect life expectancy and explain variations across countries.

Definition and comparability

Life expectancy at birth measures how long, on average, people would live based on a given set of age-specific death rates. However, the actual age-specific death rates of any particular birth cohort cannot be known in advance. If age-specific death rates are falling (as has been the case over the past decades), actual life spans will be higher than life expectancy calculated with current death rates.

The methodology used to calculate life expectancy can vary slightly between countries. This can change a country's estimates by a fraction of a year.

Life expectancy at birth for the total population is calculated by the OECD Secretariat for all OECD countries, using the unweighted average of life expectancy of men and women.

1.1.1. Life expectancy at birth, 1970 and 2011 (or nearest year)

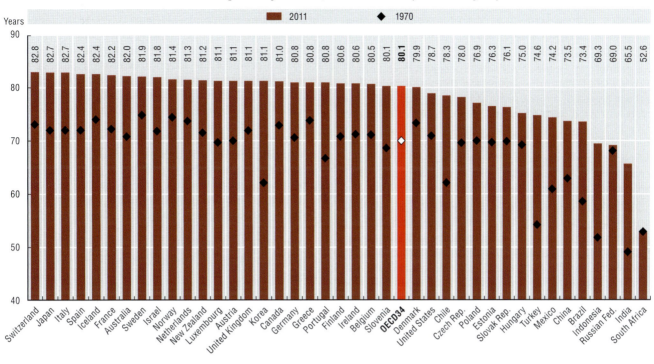

Source: OECD Health Statistics 2013, *http://dx.doi.org/10.1787/health-data-en*; World Bank for non-OECD countries.

StatLink ⬛ *http://dx.doi.org/10.1787/888932916002*

1.1.2. Life expectancy at birth and GDP per capita, 2011 (or nearest year)

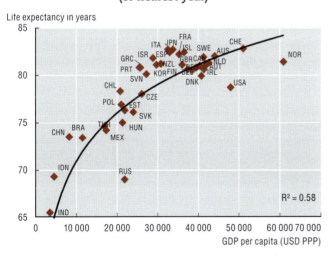

Source: OECD Health Statistics 2013, *http://dx.doi.org/10.1787/health-data-en*.

StatLink ⬛ *http://dx.doi.org/10.1787/888932916021*

1.1.3. Life expectancy at birth and health spending per capita, 2011 (or nearest year)

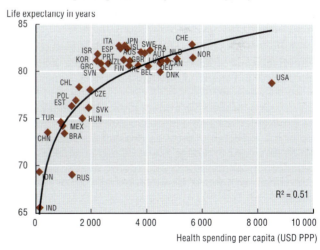

Source: OECD Health Statistics 2013, *http://dx.doi.org/10.1787/health-data-en*; World Bank for non-OECD countries.

StatLink ⬛ *http://dx.doi.org/10.1787/888932916040*

1.2. Life expectancy by sex and education level

There remain large gaps in life expectancy between women and men in all OECD countries. On average across OECD countries, life expectancy at birth for women reached 82.8 years in 2011, compared with 77.3 years for men, a gap of 5.5 years (Figure 1.2.1).

The gender gap in life expectancy increased substantially in many OECD countries during the 1970s and early 1980s to reach a peak of almost seven years in the mid-1980s, but it has narrowed during the past 25 years, reflecting higher gains in life expectancy among men than among women. This can be attributed at least partly to the narrowing of differences in risk-increasing behaviours, such as smoking, accompanied by sharp reductions in mortality rates from cardiovascular diseases among men.

In 2011, the life expectancy for women in OECD countries varied from a low of 77 years in Turkey and Mexico to a high of nearly 86 years in Japan and France. Life expectancy for men ranged from 71 years in Estonia, Hungary and Mexico, to over 80 years in Iceland, Switzerland and Italy. The life expectancy for both women and men is much shorter in South Africa (at only 53 and 52 years respectively in 2011), due largely to the HIV/AIDS epidemic.

In the United States, the life expectancy for both women and men is now slightly shorter than the OECD average, and the gap with leading countries has been widening. The life expectancy for US men in 2011 was 4.2 years shorter than in Switzerland (up from less than three years in 1970); for US women, it was 4.8 years shorter than in Japan in 2011 (there was no gap in 1970). Possible explanations for this slower progress are provided in Indicator 1.1.

Among OECD countries, the gender gap in life expectancy is relatively narrow in Iceland, Israel, New Zealand, the Netherlands and Sweden (a gap of less than four years), but much larger in Estonia (more than ten years), Hungary, the Slovak Republic and Poland (7.5 years or more), and France (seven years). In the Russian Federation, the gender gap in life expectancy reached almost 12 years in 2011. This large gap in life expectancy between Russian men and women can be explained to a large extent by higher smoking rates and alcohol consumption, and higher death rates from road traffic accidents, homicides and suicides (OECD, 2012c).

Life expectancy in OECD countries varies not only by gender, but also by socio-economic status as measured for instance by education level (Figure 1.2.2). Higher education level not only provides the means to improve the socio-economic conditions in which people live and work, but may also promote the adoption of more healthy lifestyles and facilitate access to appropriate health care. On average among 14 OECD countries for which data are available, people with the highest level of education can expect to live six years more than people with the lowest level of education at age 30 (53 years versus 47 years). These differences in life expectancy by education level are particularly pronounced for men, with a gap of almost eight years on average. They are particularly large in central and eastern European countries (Czech Republic, Estonia, Hungary, Poland and Slovenia), where the life expectancy gap between higher and lower educated men reaches more than ten years. Differences in Portugal, Sweden, Switzerland and Italy are less pronounced, although not negligible.

Definition and comparability

Life expectancy at birth measures how long, on average, people would live based on a given set of age-specific death rates. However, the actual age-specific death rates of any particular birth cohort cannot be known in advance. If age-specific death rates are falling (as has been the case over the past decades), actual life spans will be higher than life expectancy calculated with current death rates.

The methodology used to calculate life expectancy can vary slightly between countries. This can change a country's estimates by a fraction of a year.

To calculate life expectancies by education level, detailed data on deaths by sex, age and education level are needed. However, not all countries have information on education as part of their deaths data. Data linkage to another source (e.g. a census) which does have information on education may be required (Corsini, 2010).

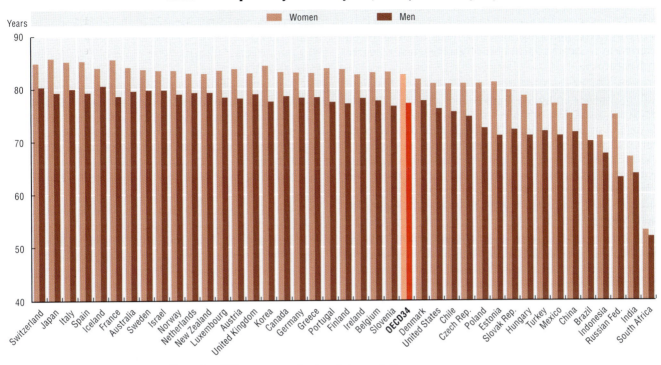

1.2.1. **Life expectancy at birth by sex, 2011 (or nearest year)**

Note: Countries are ranked in descending order of life expectancy for the whole population.
Source: OECD Health Statistics 2013, http://dx.doi.org/10.1787/health-data-en; World Bank for non-OECD countries.

StatLink http://dx.doi.org/10.1787/888932916059

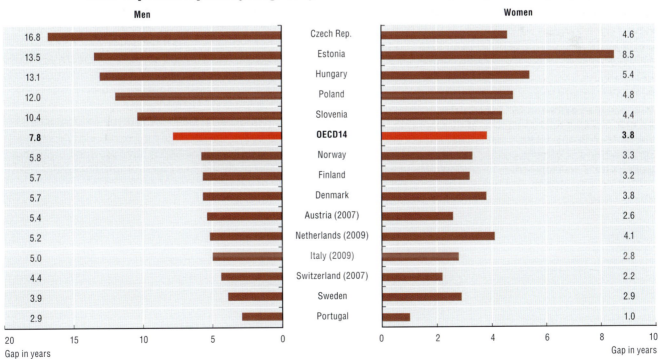

1.2.2. **Gap in life expectancy at age 30 by sex and education level, 2010 (or nearest year)**

Note: The figures show the gap in the expected years of life remaining at age 30 between adults with the highest level ("tertiary education") and the lowest level ("below upper secondary education") of education.
Source: Eurostat database complemented with national data for Austria, Netherlands and Switzerland.

StatLink http://dx.doi.org/10.1787/888932916078

1.3. Mortality from cardiovascular diseases

Cardiovascular diseases are the main cause of mortality in most OECD countries, and accounted for 33% of all deaths in 2011. They cover a range of diseases related to the circulatory system, including ischemic heart disease (often referred to as heart attack) and cerebrovascular diseases such as stroke.

Ischemic heart disease (IHD) is caused by the accumulation of fatty deposits lining the inner wall of a coronary artery, restricting blood flow to the heart. IHD alone was responsible for 12% of all deaths in OECD countries in 2011. Mortality from IHD varies considerably, however, across countries (Figure 1.3.1). Central and eastern European countries report the highest IHD mortality rates; Japan, Korea and France are the countries with the lowest rates. Across OECD countries, IHD mortality rates in 2011 were 90% higher for men than women.

IHD mortality rates have declined in nearly all OECD countries, with an average fall of 40% since 1990. The decline has been most remarkable in Denmark, the Netherlands, and Norway, where rates fell by two-thirds or more. Declining tobacco consumption contributed significantly to reducing the incidence of IHD, and consequently to reducing mortality rates. Improvements in medical care have also contributed to reduced mortality rates (see Indicator 4.6 "Cardiac procedures" and 5.3 "Mortality following acute myocardial infarction").

The Slovak Republic and Mexico as well as Korea have witnessed a rise in IHD mortality rates. The increase was particularly large in Korea; however IHD mortality remains low in Korea and has started to fall after peaking in 2006. The initial rise has been attributed to changes in lifestyle and dietary patterns as well as environmental factors at the time of birth, with people born between 1940 and 1950 facing higher relative risks (OECD, 2012b; Juhn et al., 2011; Lee et al., 2012).

Cerebrovascular disease was the underlying cause for about 8% of all deaths in OECD countries in 2011. Cerebrovascular diseases refer to a group of diseases that relate to problems with the blood vessels that supply the brain. Common types of cerebrovascular disease include ischemic stroke, which develops when the brain's blood supply is blocked or interrupted, and haemorrhagic stroke which occurs when blood leaks from blood vessels onto the surface of the brain. In addition to being an important cause of mortality, the disability burden from stroke and other cerebrovascular diseases is also substantial (Murray et al., 2013).

There are large variations in cerebrovascular disease mortality rates across countries (Figure 1.3.2). Hungary and the Slovak Republic report a cerebrovascular mortality that is more than three times higher than that of Switzerland and France. Many of the central and eastern European countries including the Czech Republic and Estonia have high mortality rates for both IHD and cerebrovascular disease. The high prevalence of risk factors common to both diseases (e.g. smoking and high blood pressure) helps explain this link.

Since 1990, cerebrovascular disease mortality has decreased in all OECD countries, although only marginally in Poland and the Slovak Republic. On average, the mortality burden from cerebrovascular disease has been halved across OECD countries. In Estonia, Luxembourg, Portugal and Spain, the rates have been cut by at least two-thirds. As with IHD, the reduction in mortality from cerebrovascular disease can be attributed at least partly to a reduction in risk factors as well as improvements in medical treatments (see Indicator 5.4 "Mortality following stroke").

Definition and comparability

Mortality rates are based on numbers of deaths registered in a country in a year divided by the size of the corresponding population. The rates have been directly age-standardised to the 2010 OECD population to remove variations arising from differences in age structures across countries and over time. The source is the *WHO Mortality Database*.

Deaths from ischemic heart disease are classified to ICD-10 codes I20-I25, and cerebrovascular disease to I60-I69. Mathers et al. (2005) have provided a general assessment of the coverage, completeness and reliability of data on causes of death.

1.3.1. Ischemic heart disease mortality, 2011 and change between 1990 and 2011 (or nearest year)

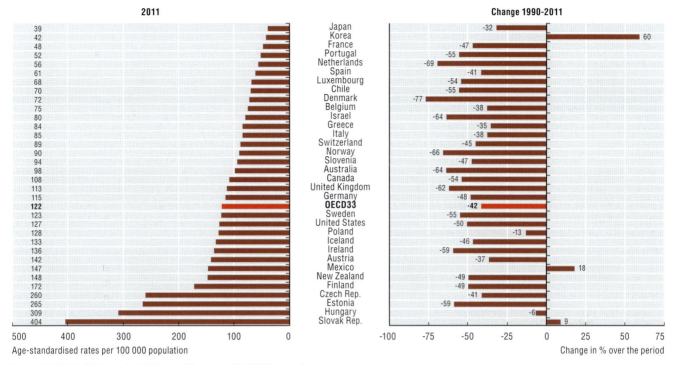

Source: OECD Health Statistics 2013, http://dx.doi.org/10.1787/health-data-en.

StatLink http://dx.doi.org/10.1787/888932916097

1.3.2. Cerebrovascular disease mortality, 2011 and change between 1990 and 2011 (or nearest year)

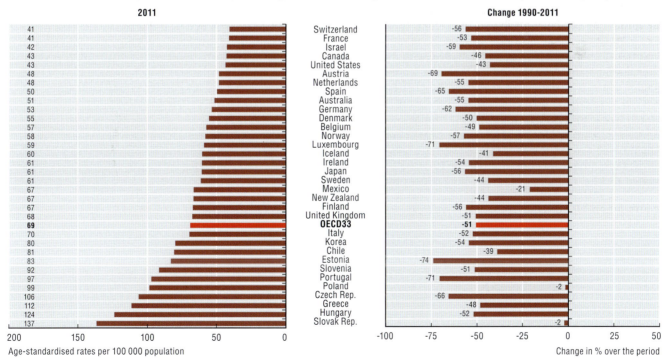

Source: OECD Health Statistics 2013, http://dx.doi.org/10.1787/health-data-en.

StatLink http://dx.doi.org/10.1787/888932916116

1.4. Mortality from cancer

Cancer accounts for over one-fourth of all deaths in OECD countries and, after diseases of the circulatory system, it is the second leading cause of death. The proportion of deaths that are due to cancer has increased over time, and in countries such as Canada, Denmark, France, Japan and the Netherlands it has become the number one cause of death. This rise reflects the fact that mortality from other causes, particularly circulatory diseases, has been declining at a faster pace than the mortality rate for cancer.

There are more than 100 different types of cancers, with most named for the organ in which they start. Cancer occurs when abnormal cells divide without control and are able to invade other tissues. For a large number of cancer types, the risk of developing the disease rises with age. While genetics is a risk factor, only about 5% to 10% of all cancers are inherited. Modifiable risk factors such as smoking, obesity, exercise, and excess sun exposure, as well as environmental exposures, explain as much as 90-95% of all cancer cases (Anand et al., 2008). Prevention, early detection and treatment remain at the forefront in the battle to reduce the burden of cancer.

In 2011, the average cancer mortality rate across OECD countries was 211 per 100 000 population. Mortality was lowest in Mexico, Brazil and Finland, with rates less than 180 per 100 000 population. Central and eastern European countries such as Hungary, Slovenia and the Slovak Republic as well Denmark bear the biggest cancer burden with mortality rates in excess of 240 per 100 000 population (Figure 1.4.1).

Cancer mortality rates are persistently higher for men than for women in all countries (Figure 1.4.1). The gender gap was particularly wide in Korea, Spain and Estonia, along with the Slovak Republic, Japan and France; with mortality rates among men more than twice those for women. This gender gap can be explained partly by the greater prevalence of risk factors among men, notably smoking rates.

Among men, lung cancer imposes the highest mortality burden, accounting for 23% of all cancer-related deaths. In Belgium and Greece, this percentage was in excess of 30%. For women, lung cancer accounted for 16% of all cancer-related deaths. In many countries, lung cancer mortality rates for men have decreased over the last 20 years, whereas the opposite trend can be observed for women. These conflicting trends are, to a large degree, explained by the large number of females who started smoking several decades later than males (Ahmedin et al., 2011). Mortality, survival and screening rates for cervical, breast and colorectal cancer are discussed further in Chapter 5.

In most OECD countries, cancer-related death rates have fallen since 1990. On average, cancer-related mortality rates fell by nearly 15% between 1990 and 2011 (Figure 1.4.2). Substantial declines in mortality from stomach, colorectal, breast and cervical cancer for women, as well as prostate and lung cancer for men contributed to this reduction. However, these gains were partially offset by increases in the number of deaths due to cancer of the pancreas and liver for both sexes as well as lung cancer for women.

In the case of Brazil, Korea, South Africa and Slovenia, however, cancer-related mortality increased over this period (Figure 1.4.2). In all other countries, mortality rates fell, but there is substantial variation between countries in the rate of decline. Mortality rates fell by a modest 2% to 5% in Greece, the Slovak Republic and Estonia, but by more than 25% in Switzerland, Luxembourg and the Czech Republic.

Definition and comparability

Mortality rates are based on numbers of deaths registered in a country in a year divided by the size of the corresponding population. The rates have been directly age-standardised to the 2010 OECD population to remove variations arising from differences in age structures across countries and over time. The source is the *WHO Mortality Database*.

Deaths from all cancers are classified to ICD-10 codes C00-C97. Mathers et al. (2005) have provided a general assessment of the coverage, completeness and reliability of data on causes of death.

1.4.1. All cancer mortality rates, total and by gender, 2011 (or nearest year)

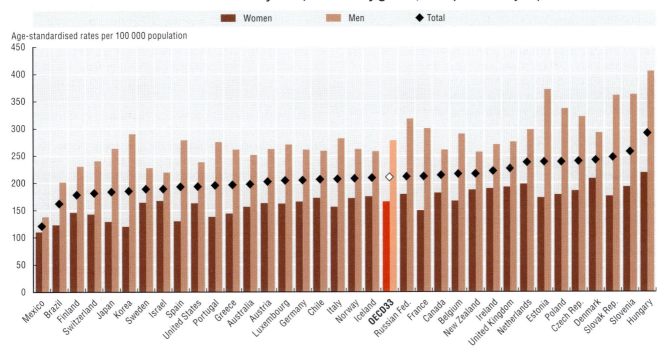

Source: OECD Health Statistics 2013, http://dx.doi.org/10.1787/health-data-en.

StatLink ⁂ http://dx.doi.org/10.1787/888932916135

1.4.2. Change in all cancer mortality rates, 1990-2011 (or nearest year)

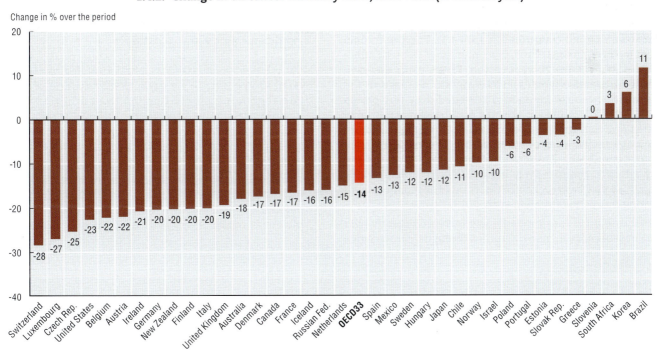

Source: OECD Health Statistics 2013, http://dx.doi.org/10.1787/health-data-en.

StatLink ⁂ http://dx.doi.org/10.1787/888932916154

1. HEALTH STATUS

1.5. Mortality from transport accidents

Worldwide, an estimated 1.3 million people are killed in transport accidents each year, most of which are due to road traffic accidents. Globally, road transport accidents account for 0.5% of deaths among women aged 15-45 but over 10% for men in this age group (Lozano et al., 2012). In OECD countries, 107 000 lives were lost due to transport accidents in 2011. Seventy-four per cent of these fatalities occurred among men. The largest number of road transport accidents occurs among younger age groups with the risk of dying due to a road accident peaking at ages 15-24 (Walls et al., 2012; OECD/ITF, 2013).

The average OECD mortality rate due to transport accidents was 7.7 per 100 000 population in 2011 (Figure 1.5.1). There is great dispersion between countries with transport accidents claiming more than five times as many lives per 100 000 population in Mexico compared to Sweden. Fatalities were in excess of 14 deaths per 100 000 population in Mexico and Chile, and were even higher in other large emerging countries such as Brazil and the Russian Federation. They were lowest in Sweden, the United Kingdom and Denmark with four deaths or less per 100 000 population.

Most fatal traffic injuries occur in passenger vehicles, although other road users also face substantial risks. In Korea, Israel, Japan and Korea, pedestrians account for over one third of all road user fatalities. Motorcyclists account for over 25% of road transport accident deaths in Greece, Italy and France (OECD/ITF, 2013).

Deaths due to transport accidents have decreased in almost all countries over the last few decades. Since 1990, the average OECD mortality rate due to transport accidents has fallen by more than half (Figure 1.5.2). Spain, Estonia and Iceland have slashed their mortality rates by more than 75% over the 20-year period. These gains are even more impressive when considering the increase in the number of vehicle kilometres travelled over this period (OECD/ITF, 2013). Chile is the only country where mortality rates due to transport accidents have increased, and are now at a similar level to countries such as Korea, the United States and Greece. At the start of the 1990s, Chile's mortality rate was comparatively low and its rise in road traffic fatalities may be associated with its rapid economic growth during this period (Nghiem et al., 2013).

Road safety for car occupants has increased greatly over the past decades in many countries through improvements

of road systems, education and prevention campaigns as well as vehicle design. In addition, the adoption of new laws and regulations and the enforcement of these laws to improve compliance with speed limits, seatbelt use and drink-driving rules, have had a major impact on reducing the burden of road transport accidents. More gains can be made if countries can further improve seatbelt use (OECD/ITF, 2013).

Declines in mortality rates for vulnerable road users such as pedestrians, cyclists and motorcyclists were substantially less than those for car occupants. Between 2000 and 2010, fatalities among motorcyclists fell by only 14% across the OECD, with some countries such as the United States, Poland and Finland witnessing significant increases among this class of road users (although there have been reports of recent reductions in deaths from motorcycle accidents in Finland since 2010).

In some countries hard-hit by the economic recession, the downward trend has accelerated after 2008. Preliminary data suggests that the rate of decline between 2009 and 2012 in Greece and Ireland is even greater than the long-term average observed in those countries. One possible explanation for this is that the economic crisis has reduced reliance on motor vehicle use. However, this impact is likely to be short-lived and over the longer term, effective road safety policies will remain the primary contributor to reduced mortality (OECD/ITF, 2011).

Definition and comparability

Mortality rates are based on numbers of deaths registered in a country in a year divided by the size of the corresponding population. The rates have been directly age-standardised to the 2010 OECD population to remove variations arising from differences in age structures across countries and over time. The source is the *WHO Mortality Database*.

Deaths from transport accidents are classified to ICD-10 codes V01-V89. Mathers et al. (2005) have provided a general assessment of the coverage, completeness and reliability of data on causes of death.

1.5.1. Transport accident mortality rates, 2011 (or nearest year)

Age-standardised rates per 100 000 population

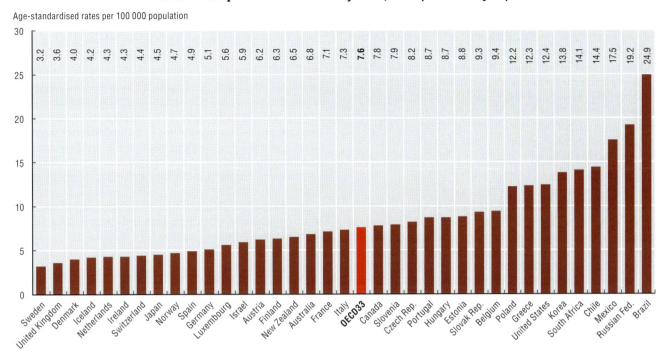

Source: OECD Health Statistics 2013, http://dx.doi.org/10.1787/health-data-en; and Ministry of Health for New Zealand.

StatLink ⫘⫘ http://dx.doi.org/10.1787/888932916173

1.5.2. Trends in transport accident mortality rates, selected OECD countries, 1990-2011

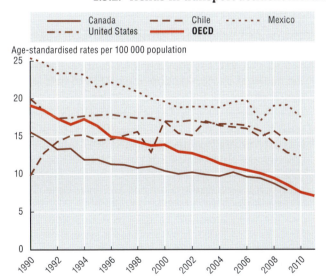

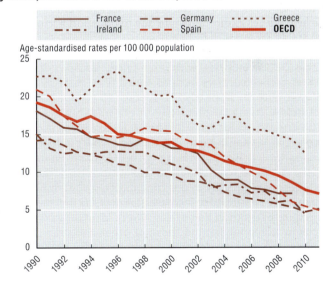

Source: OECD Health Statistics 2013, http://dx.doi.org/10.1787/health-data-en.

StatLink ⫘⫘ http://dx.doi.org/10.1787/888932916192

1.6. Suicide

Suicide is a significant cause of death in many OECD countries, and accounted for over 150 000 deaths in 2011. There is a complex set of reasons why some people choose to attempt or commit suicide, with multiple risk factors that can predispose a person to attempt to take their own life. Over 90% of people who have attempted or committed suicide have been diagnosed with psychiatric disorders such as severe depression, bipolar disorder and schizophrenia (Nock et al., 2008). The social context in which an individual lives is also important. Low income, alcohol and drug abuse, unemployment and unmarried status are all associated with higher rates of suicide (Qin et al., 2003; Crump et al., 2013).

Figure 1.6.1 shows that suicide rates were lowest in Greece, Turkey, Mexico, Brazil and Italy, at six or fewer deaths per 100 000 population. In Korea, Hungary, the Russian Federation and Japan, on the other hand, suicide is responsible for more than 20 deaths per 100 000 population. There is a ten-fold difference between Korea and Greece, the two countries with the highest and lowest suicide rates. However, the number of suicides in certain countries may be under-reported because of the stigma that is associated with the act, or because of data issues associated with reporting criteria (see "Definition and comparability").

Death rates from suicide are four times greater for men than for women across OECD countries. In Greece and Poland, men are at least seven times more likely to commit suicide than women. The gender gap in those two countries has widened in recent years. While in Luxembourg and the Netherlands the gender gap is smaller, male suicide rates are still twice those of females.

Since 1990, suicide rates have decreased by more than 20% across OECD countries, with pronounced declines of over 40% in some countries such as Hungary (Figure 1.6.2). In Estonia, rates fell by nearly 50% over the 20-year period, but not before rising substantially in the mid-1990s. Death rates from suicides have increased in countries such as Korea and Japan. In Japan, there was a sharp rise in the mid-to-late 1990s, coinciding with the Asian Financial Crisis; but rates have remained stable since then. Suicide rates also rose sharply at this time in Korea and, unlike in Japan, have continued to increase. It is now the fourth leading cause of death in Korea (Jeon, 2011). Mental health services in Korea lag behind those of other countries with fragmented support, focused largely around institutions, with insufficient or ineffective support provided to those who remain in the community. Further efforts are also needed to remove the stigma associated with seeking care (OECD, forthcoming).

Previous studies have shown a strong link between adverse economic conditions and higher levels of suicide (Ceccherini-Nelli et al., 2011; Classen and Dunn, 2012; Zivin et al., 2011). Figure 1.6.2 shows suicide rates for a number of countries that have been hard hit by the recent economic crisis. Suicide rates rose slightly at the start of the economic crisis in a number of countries such as Ireland but more recent data suggest that this trend did not persist. In Greece, overall suicide rates were stable in 2009 and 2010, despite worsening economic conditions. There is a need for countries to continue monitoring developments closely in order to be able to respond quickly, including monitoring high-risk populations such as the unemployed and those with psychiatric disorders (see Indicator 5.8 for further information).

Definition and comparability

The World Health Organization defines suicide as an act deliberately initiated and performed by a person in the full knowledge or expectation of its fatal outcome. Comparability of data between countries is affected by a number of reporting criteria, including how a person's intention of killing themselves is ascertained, who is responsible for completing the death certificate, whether a forensic investigation is carried out, and the provisions for confidentiality of the cause of death. Caution is required therefore in interpreting variations across countries.

Mortality rates are based on numbers of deaths registered in a country in a year divided by the size of the corresponding population. The rates have been directly age-standardised to the 2010 OECD population to remove variations arising from differences in age structures across countries and over time. The source is the WHO Mortality Database. Deaths from suicide are classified to ICD-10 codes X60-X84. Mathers et al. (2005) have provided a general assessment of the coverage, completeness and reliability of data on causes of death.

1.6.1. Suicide mortality rates, 2011 (or nearest year)

Age-standardised rates per 100 000 population

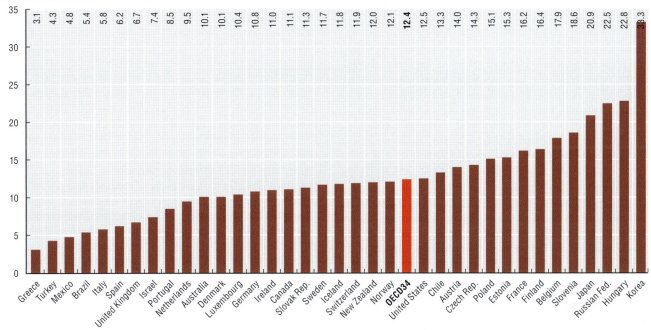

Source: OECD Health Statistics 2013, http://dx.doi.org/10.1787/health-data-en.

StatLink ⌐ℳ⤵ http://dx.doi.org/10.1787/888932916211

1.6.2. Trends in suicide rates, selected OECD countries, 1990-2011

Age-standardised rates per 100 000 population

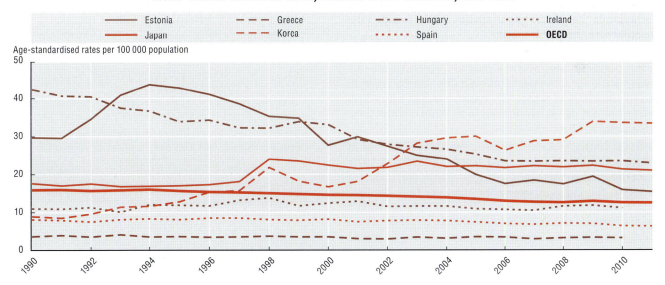

Source: OECD Health Statistics 2013, http://dx.doi.org/10.1787/health-data-en.

StatLink ⌐ℳ⤵ http://dx.doi.org/10.1787/888932916230

1.7. Infant mortality

Infant mortality, the rate at which babies and children of less than one year of age die, reflects the effect of economic and social conditions on the health of mothers and new-borns, the social environment, individual lifestyles as well as the characteristics and effectiveness of health systems.

In most OECD countries, infant mortality is low and there is little difference in rates (Figure 1.7.1). In 2011, the average in OECD countries was just over four deaths per 1 000 live births, with rates being the lowest in Nordic countries (Iceland, Sweden, Finland, Norway), Japan and Estonia. A small group of OECD countries still have relatively high rates of infant mortality (Mexico, Turkey and Chile), although in these three countries infant mortality rates have come down rapidly over the past few decades (Figure 1.7.2).

In some large non-member countries (India, South Africa and Indonesia), infant mortality rates remain above 20 deaths per 1 000 live births. In India, nearly one-in-twenty children die before their first birthday, although the rates have fallen sharply over the past few decades. Infant mortality rates have also been reduced greatly in Indonesia.

In OECD countries, around two-thirds of the deaths that occur during the first year of life are neonatal deaths (i.e., during the first four weeks). Birth defects, prematurity and other conditions arising during pregnancy are the principal factors contributing to neonatal mortality in developed countries. With an increasing number of women deferring childbearing and a rise in multiple births linked with fertility treatments, the number of pre-term births has tended to increase (see Indicator 1.8 "Infant health: Low birth weight"). In a number of higher-income countries, this has contributed to a levelling-off of the downward trend in infant mortality rates over the past few years. For deaths beyond a month (post-neonatal mortality), there tends to be a greater range of causes – the most common being SIDS (sudden infant death syndrome), birth defects, infections and accidents.

All OECD countries have achieved remarkable progress in reducing infant mortality rates from the levels of 1970, when the average was approaching 30 deaths per 1 000 live births, to the current average of just over four. Besides Mexico, Chile and Turkey where the rates have converged rapidly towards the OECD average (Figure 1.7.2), Portugal and Korea have also achieved large reductions in infant mortality rates, moving from countries that were well above the OECD average in 1970 to being well below the OECD average in 2011.

By contrast, in the United States, the reduction in infant mortality has been slower than in most other OECD countries. In 1970, the US rate was well below the OECD average,

but it is now well above (Figure 1.7.1). Part of the explanation for the relatively high infant mortality rates in the United States is due to a more complete registration of very premature or low birth weight babies than in other countries (see box on "Definition and comparability"). However, this cannot explain why the post-neonatal mortality rate (deaths after one month) is also greater in the United States than in most other OECD countries. There are large differences in infant mortality rates among racial groups in the United States, with black (or African-American) women more likely to give birth to low birth weight infants, and with an infant mortality rate more than double that for white women (11.6 vs. 5.2 in 2010) (NCHS, 2013).

Many studies use infant mortality as a health outcome to examine the effect of a variety of medical and non-medical determinants of health (e.g., OECD, 2010a). Although most analyses show that higher health spending tends to be associated with lower infant mortality, the fact that some countries with a high level of health expenditure do not exhibit low levels of infant mortality suggests that more health spending is not necessarily required to obtain better results (Retzlaff-Roberts et al., 2004). A body of research also suggests that many factors beyond the quality and efficiency of the health system, such as income inequality, the socio-economic environment and individual lifestyles, influence infant mortality rates (Kiely et al., 1995).

Definition and comparability

The infant mortality rate is the number of deaths of children under one year of age, expressed per 1 000 live births. Neonatal mortality refers to the death of children during the first four weeks of life. Post-neonatal mortality refers to deaths occurring between the second and the twelfth months of life.

Some of the international variation in infant and neonatal mortality rates is due to variations among countries in registering practices for premature infants. The United States and Canada are two countries which register a much higher proportion of babies weighing less than 500 g, with low odds of survival, resulting in higher reported infant mortality (Joseph et al., 2012). In Europe, several countries apply a minimum gestational age of 22 weeks (or a birth weight threshold of 500g) for babies to be registered as live births (Euro-Peristat, 2013).

1.7.1. Infant mortality rates, 2011 (or nearest year)

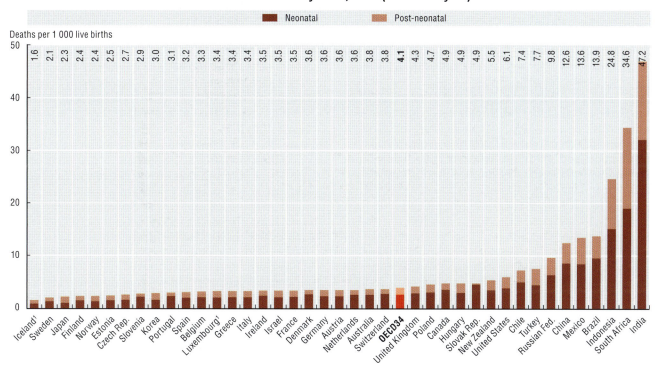

1. Three-year average (2009-11).
Source: OECD Health Statistics 2013, http://dx.doi.org/10.1787/health-data-en; World Bank for non-OECD countries.

StatLink ⟐ᴉᴸᴸ *http://dx.doi.org/10.1787/888932916249*

1.7.2. Infant mortality rates, selected OECD countries, 1970-2011

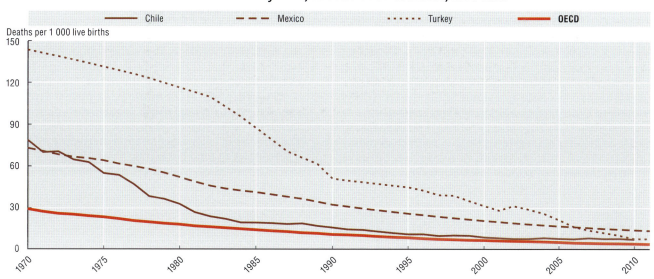

Source: OECD Health Statistics 2013, http://dx.doi.org/10.1787/health-data-en.

StatLink ⟐ᴉᴸᴸ *http://dx.doi.org/10.1787/888932916268*

1.8. Infant health: Low birth weight

Low birth weight – defined as newborns weighing less than 2 500 grams – is an important indicator of infant health because of the close relationship between birth weight and infant morbidity and mortality. There are two categories of low birth weight babies: those occurring as a result of restricted foetal growth and those resulting from pre-term birth. Low birth weight infants have a greater risk of poor health or death, require a longer period of hospitalisation after birth, and are more likely to develop significant disabilities (UNICEF and WHO, 2004). Risk factors for low birth weight include maternal smoking and excessive alcohol consumption, poor nutrition, low body mass index, lower socio-economic status, and having had in-vitro fertilisation treatment and multiple births.

One in 15 babies born in OECD countries in 2011 – or 6.8% of all births – weighed less than 2 500 grams at birth (Figure 1.8.1). The proportions of low-weight births were lowest in Nordic countries (Iceland, Finland, Sweden, Norway, with the exception of Denmark) and Estonia, with less than 5% of live births defined as low birth weight. Alongside a number of key emerging countries (India, South Africa and Indonesia), Turkey, Greece and Japan have the highest proportions among OECD countries, with rates of low birth weight infants above 9%. Some of these variations across countries may be due to physiological differences in size between populations (Euro-Peristat, 2013). In some emerging countries, the high proportion of low birth weight infants is mainly associated with maternal malnutrition before and during pregnancy, poor health and limited access to proper health care during pregnancy.

In almost all OECD countries, the proportion of low birth weight infants has increased over the past two decades (Figure 1.8.1, right panel and Figure 1.8.2). There are several reasons for this rise. The number of multiple births, with the increased risks of pre-term births and low birth weight, has risen steadily, partly as a result of the rise in fertility treatments. Other factors which may explain the rise in low birth weight are older age at childbearing, and increases in the use of delivery management techniques such as induction of labour and caesarean delivery, which have increased the survival rates of low birth weight babies.

Korea, Spain, Greece, Japan and Portugal have seen large increases of low birth weight babies over the past two decades. In Japan, this increase can be explained by changes in obstetric interventions, in particular the greater use of caesarean sections, along with changes in maternal socio-demographic and behavioural factors (Yorifuji et al., 2012). This contrasts with sharp decreases in Poland and Hungary, although most of the reduction in these two countries occurred in the first half of the 1990s, with little change since then.

Comparisons of different population groups within countries indicate that the proportion of low birth weight infants may also be influenced by differences in education level, income and associated living conditions. In the United States, there are marked differences in the proportion of low birth weight infants among racial groups, with black infants having a rate almost double that of white infants (13.2% versus 7.1% in 2010) (NCHS, 2013). Similar differences have also been observed among the indigenous and non-indigenous populations in Australia, Mexico and New Zealand, often reflecting the disadvantaged living conditions of many of these mothers.

The proportion of low birth weight infants is also much higher among women who smoke than for non-smokers. In the United States, the rate reached 12.0% for cigarette smokers compared with 7.4% for non-smokers in 2010 (NCHS, 2013).

Definition and comparability

Low birth weight is defined by the World Health Organization (WHO) as the weight of an infant at birth of less than 2 500 grams (5.5 pounds) irrespective of the gestational age of the infant. This threshold is based on epidemiological observations regarding the increased risk of death to the infant and serves for international comparative health statistics. The number of low weight births is then expressed as a percentage of total live births.

1.8.1. Low birth weight infants, 2011 and change between 1990 and 2011 (or nearest year)

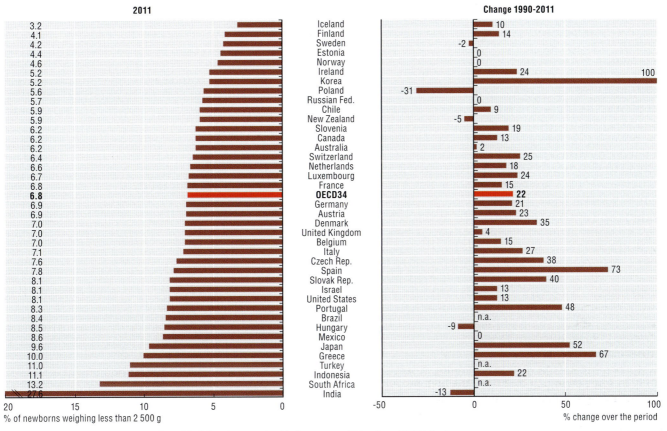

2011

3.2	Iceland	
4.1	Finland	
4.2	Sweden	
4.4	Estonia	
4.6	Norway	
5.2	Ireland	
5.2	Korea	
5.6	Poland	
5.7	Russian Fed.	
5.9	Chile	
5.9	New Zealand	
6.2	Slovenia	
6.2	Canada	
6.2	Australia	
6.4	Switzerland	
6.6	Netherlands	
6.7	Luxembourg	
6.8	France	
6.8	**OECD34**	
6.9	Germany	
6.9	Austria	
7.0	Denmark	
7.0	United Kingdom	
7.0	Belgium	
7.1	Italy	
7.6	Czech Rep.	
7.8	Spain	
8.1	Slovak Rep.	
8.1	Israel	
8.1	United States	
8.3	Portugal	
8.4	Brazil	
8.5	Hungary	
8.6	Mexico	
9.6	Japan	
10.0	Greece	
11.0	Turkey	
11.1	Indonesia	
13.2	South Africa	
27.6	India	

% of newborns weighing less than 2 500 g

Change 1990-2011

Country	% change over the period
Iceland	10
Finland	14
Sweden	-2
Estonia	0
Norway	0
Ireland	24
Korea	100
Poland	-31
Russian Fed.	0
Chile	9
New Zealand	-5
Slovenia	19
Canada	13
Australia	2
Switzerland	25
Netherlands	18
Luxembourg	24
France	15
OECD34	**22**
Germany	21
Austria	23
Denmark	35
United Kingdom	4
Belgium	15
Italy	27
Czech Rep.	38
Spain	73
Slovak Rep.	40
Israel	13
United States	13
Portugal	48
Brazil	n.a.
Hungary	-9
Mexico	0
Japan	52
Greece	67
Turkey	n.a.
Indonesia	22
South Africa	n.a.
India	-13

% change over the period

Source: OECD Health Statistics 2013, http://dx.doi.org/10.1787/health-data-en; World Bank and WHO for key partners.

StatLink ᐧᒥᔑᓚ http://dx.doi.org/10.1787/888932916287

1.8.2. Trends in low birth weight infants, selected OECD countries, 1990-2011

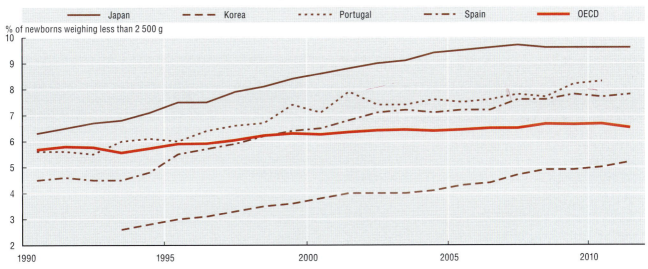

Japan — — Korea ···· Portugal —·· Spain — OECD

% of newborns weighing less than 2 500 g

Source: OECD Health Statistics 2013, http://dx.doi.org/10.1787/health-data-en.

StatLink ᐧᒥᔑᓚ http://dx.doi.org/10.1787/888932916306

1.9. Perceived health status

Most OECD countries conduct regular health surveys which allow respondents to report on different aspects of their health. A commonly asked question relates to self-perceived health status, of the type: "How is your health in general?". Despite the subjective nature of this question, indicators of perceived general health have been found to be a good predictor of people's future health care use and mortality (DeSalvo et al., 2005; Bond et al., 2006).

For the purpose of international comparisons, cross-country variations in perceived health status are difficult to interpret because responses may be affected by the formulation of survey questions and responses, and by social and cultural factors. Since they rely on the subjective views of the respondents, self-reported health status will reflect cultural biases or other influences.

With these limitations in mind, in almost all OECD countries, a majority of the adult population reports their health as good or better (Figure 1.9.1; left panel). The United States, New Zealand and Canada are the three leading countries, with about nine out of ten people reporting to be in good health. However, the response categories offered to survey respondents in these three countries are different from those used in European countries and Asian OECD countries, which introduce an upward bias in the results (see box on "Definition and comparability").

On the other hand, less than half of adults in Japan, Korea and Portugal rate their health as good or very good. The proportion is also relatively low in Estonia, Hungary, Poland, Chile and the Czech Republic, where less than 60% of adults consider themselves to be in good health.

The percentage of adults rating their health as good or very good has remained fairly stable over the past few decades in most countries, although Japan has seen some decline since the mid-1990s.

In all OECD countries, men are more likely than women to report being in good health, except in Australia where the proportion is equal. The gender gap is especially large in Chile, Portugal and Turkey (Figure 1.9.1; right panel).

There are also large disparities in self-reported health across different socio-economic groups, as measured for instance by income level. Figure 1.9.2 shows that, in all countries, people with a lower level of income tend to report poorer health than people with higher income, although the gap varies. On average across OECD countries, nearly 80% of people in the highest income quintile reports being in good health, compared with just over 60% for people in the lowest income group. These disparities may be explained by differences in living and working conditions, as well as differences in health-related lifestyles (e.g., smoking, harmful alcohol drinking, physical inactivity, and obesity problems). In addition, people in low-income households may have more limited access to certain health services, for financial or non-financial reasons (see

Chapter 6 on "Access to care"). It is also possible that the causal link goes the other way around, with poor health status in the first place leading to lower employment and lower income.

Greater emphasis on public health and disease prevention among disadvantaged groups, and improving access to health services may contribute to further improvements in population health status and reducing health inequalities.

Definition and comparability

Perceived health status reflects people's overall perception of their health, including both physical and psychological dimensions. Typically ascertained through health interview surveys, respondents are asked a question such as: "How is your health in general? Is it very good, good, fair, poor, very poor." *OECD Health Statistics* provides figures related to the proportion of people rating their health to be "good/very good" combined.

Caution is required in making cross-country comparisons of perceived health status, for at least two reasons. First, people's assessment of their health is subjective and can be affected by factors such as cultural background and national traits. Second, there are variations in the question and answer categories used to measure perceived health across surveys and countries. In particular, the response scale used in the United States, Canada, New Zealand and Australia is *asymmetric* (skewed on the positive side), including the following response categories: "excellent, very good, good, fair, poor." The data in *OECD Health Statistics* refer to respondents answering one of the three positive responses ("excellent, very good or good"). By contrast, in most other OECD countries, the response scale is *symmetric*, with response categories being: "very good, good, fair, poor, very poor." The data reported from these countries refer only to the first two categories ("very good, good"). Such a difference in response categories biases upward the results from those countries that are using an asymmetric scale by about 5-8%.

Self-reported health by income level is reported for the first quintile (lowest 20% of income group) and the fifth quintile (highest 20%). Depending on the surveys, the income may relate either to the individual or the household (in which case the income is equivalised to take into account the number of persons in the household).

1.9.1. Percentage of adults reporting to be in good health, 2011 (or nearest year)

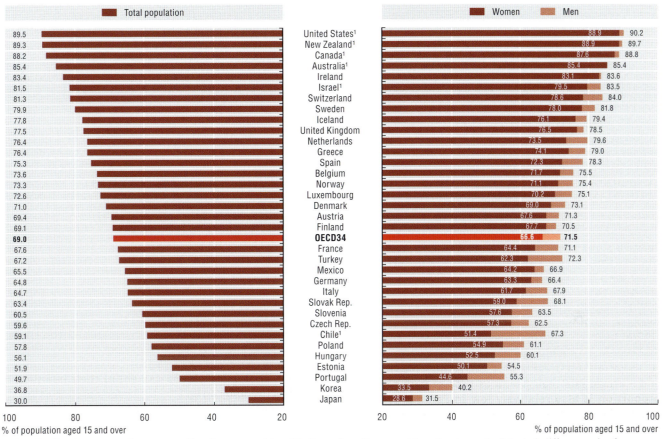

Country	Total population	Women	Men
United States[1]	89.5	88.9	90.2
New Zealand[1]	89.3	88.9	89.7
Canada[1]	88.2	87.6	88.8
Australia[1]	85.4	85.4	85.4
Ireland	83.4	83.1	83.6
Israel[1]	81.5	79.5	83.5
Switzerland	81.3	78.6	84.0
Sweden	79.9	78.0	81.8
Iceland	77.8	76.1	79.4
United Kingdom	77.5	76.5	78.5
Netherlands	76.4	73.5	79.6
Greece	76.4	74.1	79.0
Spain	75.3	72.3	78.3
Belgium	73.6	71.7	75.5
Norway	73.3	71.1	75.4
Luxembourg	72.6	70.2	75.1
Denmark	71.0	69.0	73.1
Austria	69.4	67.6	71.3
Finland	69.1	67.7	70.5
OECD34	**69.0**	**66.6**	**71.5**
France	67.6	64.4	71.1
Turkey	67.2	62.3	72.3
Mexico	65.5	64.2	66.9
Germany	64.8	63.3	66.4
Italy	64.7	61.7	67.9
Slovak Rep.	63.4	59.0	68.1
Slovenia	60.5	57.6	63.5
Czech Rep.	59.6	57.3	62.5
Chile[1]	59.1	51.4	67.3
Poland	57.8	54.9	61.1
Hungary	56.1	52.5	60.1
Estonia	51.9	50.1	54.5
Portugal	49.7	44.6	55.3
Korea	36.8	33.5	40.2
Japan	30.0	28.6	31.5

% of population aged 15 and over

1. Results for these countries are not directly comparable with those for other countries, due to methodological differences in the survey questionnaire resulting in an upward bias.

Source: OECD Health Statistics 2013 (EU-SILC for European countries), http://dx.doi.org/10.1787/health-data-en.

StatLink http://dx.doi.org/10.1787/888932916325

1.9.2. Perceived health status by income level, 2011 (or nearest year)

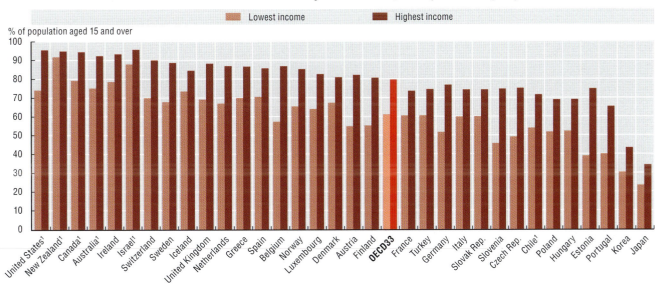

% of population aged 15 and over

Note: Countries are ranked in descending order of perceived health status for the whole population.
1. Results for these countries are not directly comparable with those for other countries, due to methodological differences in the survey questionnaire resulting in an upward bias.

Source: OECD Health Statistics 2013 (EU-SILC for European countries), http://dx.doi.org/10.1787/health-data-en.

StatLink http://dx.doi.org/10.1787/888932916344

1.10. Diabetes prevalence and incidence

Diabetes is a chronic disease, characterised by high levels of glucose in the blood. It occurs either because the pancreas stops producing the hormone insulin (Type-1 diabetes), or through a reduced ability to produce insulin (Type-2 diabetes). People with diabetes are at a greater risk of developing cardiovascular diseases such as heart attack and stroke. They also have elevated risks for sight loss, foot and leg amputation due to damage to nerves and blood vessels, and renal failure requiring dialysis or transplantation.

Over 85 million people living in OECD countries are estimated to have had diabetes in 2011. This represents 6.9% of people aged 20-79 years (Figure 1.10.1). In Mexico, more than 15% of adults have diabetes. By contrast, less than 5% of adults suffer from diabetes in Belgium, Iceland, Luxembourg, Norway and Sweden (IDF, 2011).

Diabetes is slightly more common among men than women and prevalence increases substantially with age. A Spanish study showed that around 1% of those aged less than 45 were diagnosed with diabetes, whereas among those aged 76 and over, the prevalence rate was over 20% (Soriguer et al., 2012). The study also showed that around 50% of patients in the sample did not know that they had diabetes, confirming findings from other countries that a substantial proportion of the population have undiagnosed diabetes (e.g. Gardete-Correia et al., 2011). The International Diabetes Federation estimates that around 31 million people in OECD countries have undiagnosed diabetes.

Diabetes disproportionally affects those in lower socio-economic groups and people from certain cultural backgrounds. Guize et al. (2008) found that elderly people living in lower socio-economic conditions were two to three times more likely to have diabetes than wealthier segments of the population. In Australia, Indigenous people have been found to be three times more likely than other Australians to report having diabetes (AIHW, 2011).

For many people, the onset of Type-2 diabetes can be prevented (or delayed) through regular physical exercise and maintaining a healthy weight. But in most countries, the prevalence of obesity and physical inactivity continues to increase (see Indicator 2.7 "Overweight and obesity among adults"). Alongside the rise in risk factors, diabetes has been increasing rapidly in every part of the world. Based on current trends, the number of people with diabetes in OECD countries is projected to reach almost 108 million by 2030 (IDF, 2011).

On average across OECD countries, over 17 new cases of Type-1 diabetes were identified per 100 000 children aged under 15 in 2011 (Figure 1.10.2). The incidence rate is particularly high in Nordic countries (Finland, Sweden and Norway), with over 25 new cases detected every year per 100 000 children. In Mexico and Korea, the rate is less than five new cases per 100 000 children aged under 15. While Type-1 diabetes currently accounts for only 10-15% of all diabetes cases, there is evidence that incidence rates are rising strongly in some countries. Between 2005 and 2020, new cases of Type-1 diabetes for those under age 5 are expected to double and the prevalence of cases in those younger than 15 years is expected to increase by 70% in Europe (Patterson et al., 2009). There is no clear consensus on why incidence is rising so fast, but a changing environment, infant and maternal diets are all plausible explanations (Myers and Zimmet, 2008).

Both Type-1 and Type-2 diabetes inflict enormous health burdens on the community. In 2011, there were almost 660 000 diabetes-related deaths in OECD countries, and the 2010 Global Burden of Disease study showed that diabetes was the ninth leading cause of death in the world (IDF, 2011; Lozano et al., 2012). Diabetes-related health expenditure was estimated to be USD 176 billion in the United States alone, and USD 390 billion across OECD countries in 2011 (ADA, 2013; IDF, 2011). These burdens underline the need for preventive actions and effective management of diabetes and its complications (also see Indicator 5.1 "Avoidable hospital admissions").

Definition and comparability

The sources and methods used by the International Diabetes Federation for publishing national prevalence and incidence estimates of diabetes are outlined in their *Diabetes Atlas, 5th edition* (IDF, 2011). Country data were derived from studies published between 1980 and April 2011, and were only included if they met several criteria for reliability. Prevalence rates were adjusted to the age-standardised rates using the world population, based on the distribution provided by the World Health Organization. See Guariguata et al. (2011) for more details on the methodology used.

1.10.1. Prevalence estimates of diabetes, adults aged 20-79 years, 2011

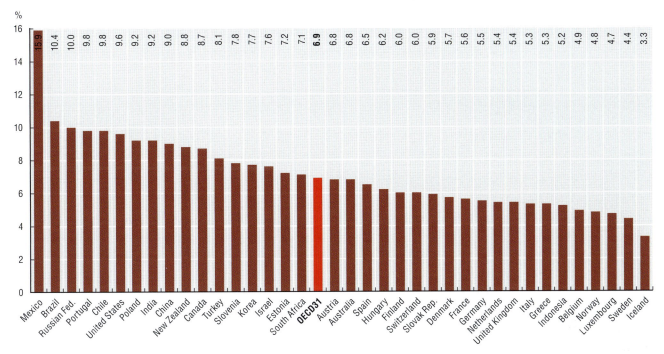

%

Mexico 15.9, Brazil 10.4, Russian Fed. 10.0, Portugal 9.8, Chile 9.8, United States 9.6, Poland 9.2, India 9.2, China 9.0, New Zealand 8.8, Canada 8.7, Turkey 8.1, Slovenia 7.8, Korea 7.7, Israel 7.6, Estonia 7.2, South Africa 7.1, **OECD31 6.9**, Austria 6.8, Australia 6.8, Spain 6.5, Hungary 6.2, Finland 6.0, Switzerland 6.0, Slovak Rep. 5.9, Denmark 5.7, France 5.6, Germany 5.5, Netherlands 5.4, United Kingdom 5.4, Italy 5.3, Greece 5.3, Indonesia 5.2, Belgium 4.9, Norway 4.8, Luxembourg 4.7, Sweden 4.4, Iceland 3.3

Note: The data cover both Type-1 and Type-2 diabetes. Data are age-standardised to the World Standard Population.
Source: International Diabetes Federation (2011).

StatLink ᴍᴸ *http://dx.doi.org/10.1787/888932916363*

1.10.2. Incidence estimates of Type-1 diabetes, children aged 0-14 years, 2011

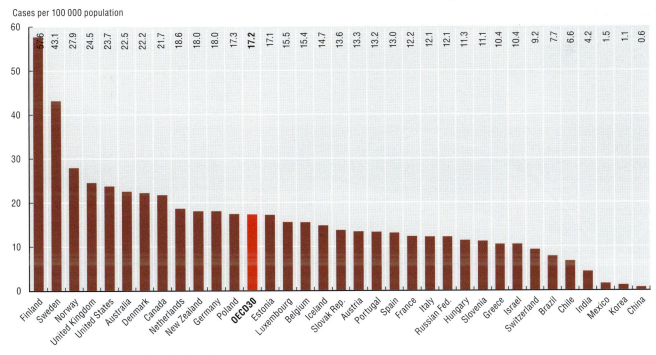

Cases per 100 000 population

Finland 57.6, Sweden 43.1, Norway 27.9, United Kingdom 24.5, United States 23.7, Australia 22.5, Denmark 22.2, Canada 21.7, Netherlands 18.6, New Zealand 18.0, Germany 18.0, Poland 17.3, **OECD30 17.2**, Estonia 17.1, Luxembourg 15.5, Belgium 15.4, Iceland 14.7, Slovak Rep. 13.6, Austria 13.3, Portugal 13.2, Spain 13.0, France 12.2, Italy 12.1, Russian Fed. 12.1, Hungary 11.3, Slovenia 11.1, Greece 10.4, Israel 10.4, Switzerland 9.2, Brazil 7.7, Chile 6.6, India 4.2, Mexico 1.5, Korea 1.1, China 0.6

Source: International Diabetes Federation (2011).

StatLink ᴍᴸ *http://dx.doi.org/10.1787/888932916382*

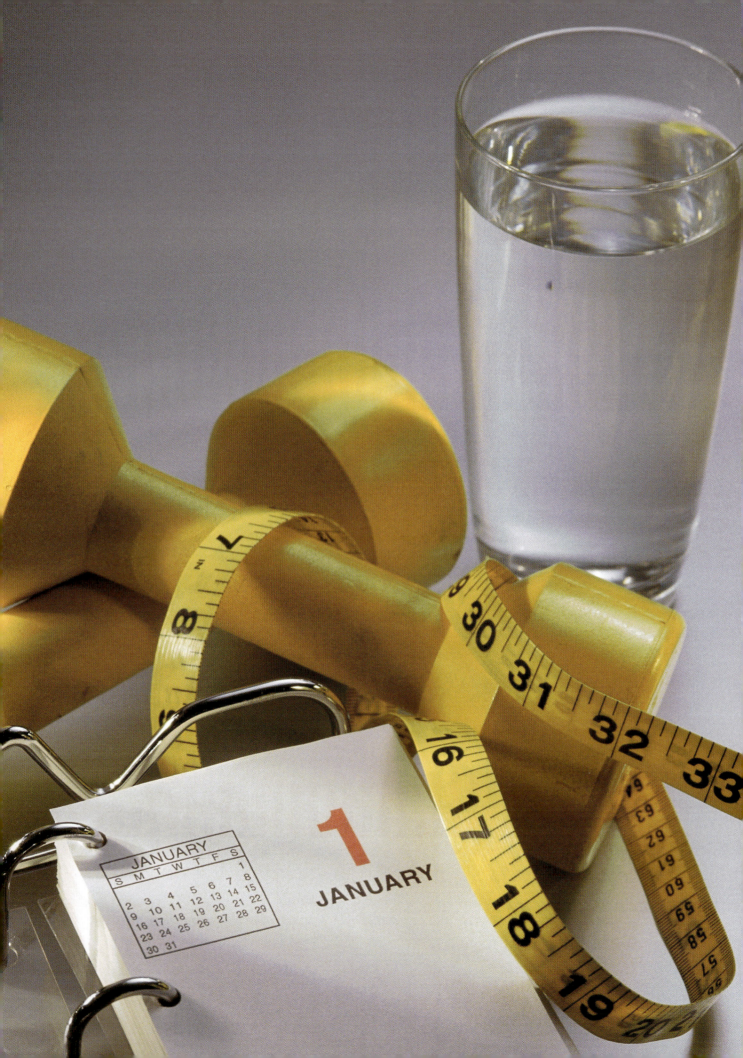

2. NON-MEDICAL DETERMINANTS OF HEALTH

2.1.   Smoking and alcohol consumption among children

2.2.   Overweight and obesity among children

2.3.   Fruit and vegetable consumption among children

2.4.   Physical activity among children

2.5.   Tobacco consumption among adults

2.6.   Alcohol consumption among adults

2.7.   Overweight and obesity among adults

2.8.   Fruit and vegetable consumption among adults

The statistical data for Israel are supplied by and under the responsibility of the relevant Israeli authorities. The use of such data by the OECD is without prejudice to the status of the Golan Heights, East Jerusalem and Israeli settlements in the West Bank under the terms of international law.

HEALTH AT A GLANCE 2013: OECD INDICATORS © OECD 2013

45

2.1. Smoking and alcohol consumption among children

Regular smoking and excessive drinking in adolescence have both immediate and long-term health consequences. Children who establish smoking habits in early adolescence increase their risk of cardiovascular diseases, respiratory illnesses and cancer. They are also more likely to experiment with alcohol and other drugs. Alcohol misuse is itself associated with a range of social, physical and mental health problems, including depressive and anxiety disorders, obesity and accidental injury (Currie et al., 2012).

Results from the Health Behaviour in School-aged Children (HBSC) surveys, a series of collaborative cross-national studies conducted in a number of countries worldwide, allow for monitoring of smoking and drinking behaviours among adolescents.

Fifteen-year-old children in Austria, the Czech Republic, and Hungary smoke the most, with more than 25% reporting that they smoke at least once a week (Figure 2.1.1). In contrast, less than 10% of 15-year-olds smoke weekly in Canada, Iceland, Norway, and the United States. On average, the same proportion of boys and girls (16%) smoke at least once a week. However, there are gender disparities in some countries. Smoking is much more prevalent among boys in Estonia and Greece, while a much higher proportion of girls report smoking at least once a week in the Czech Republic and Spain.

Drunkenness is reported to have been experienced at least twice by more than 40% of 15-year-olds in the Czech Republic, Denmark, Estonia, Finland, Hungary, Slovenia and the United Kingdom (Figure 2.1.2). Much lower rates (less than 20%) are reported in Iceland, Italy, Luxembourg, the Netherlands, and the United States. Across all surveyed OECD countries, boys are more likely than girls to report repeated drunkenness (32% vs. 28%). France, Hungary, and Slovenia have the biggest differences, with rates of alcohol abuse among boys at least 9% points higher than those of girls. In four countries, Finland, Spain, Sweden and the United Kingdom, more girls than boys report repeated drunkenness (around 5-7% points).

Risk-taking behaviours among adolescents have fallen in many countries, with regular smoking for both boys and girls and drunkenness rates for boys showing some decline from the levels of the late 1990s on average (Figures 2.1.3 and 2.1.4). Levels of smoking for both sexes are at their lowest for a decade, with, on average, fewer than one in five children of either sex smoking regularly. However, increasing rates of smoking and/or drunkenness among adolescents in the Czech Republic, Estonia, Hungary, Poland, the Slovak Republic and Spain are cause for concern.

Definition and comparability

Estimates for smoking refer to the proportion of 15-year-old children who self-report smoking at least once a week. Estimates for drunkenness record the proportions of 15-year-old children saying they have been drunk twice or more in their lives.

The Health Behaviour in School-aged Children (HBSC) surveys were undertaken every four years between 1993-94 and 2009-10 and include up to 26 OECD countries and the Russian Federation. Data are drawn from school-based samples of 1 500 in each age group (11-, 13- and 15-year-olds) in most countries. Turkey was included in the 2009-10 HBSC survey, but children were not asked about their alcohol drinking and smoking.

2.1.1. Smoking among 15-year-olds, 2009-10

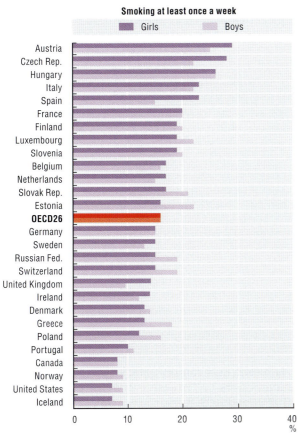

2.1.2. Drunkenness among 15-year-olds, 2009-10

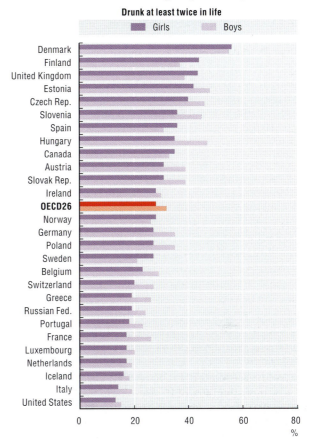

Source: Currie et al. (2012).

StatLink ᴍSᴸ http://dx.doi.org/10.1787/888932916401

Source: Currie et al. (2012).

StatLink ᴍSᴸ http://dx.doi.org/10.1787/888932916420

2.1.3. Trends in regular smoking among 15-year-olds, 19 OECD countries

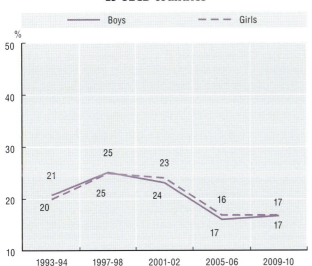

2.1.4. Trends in repeated drunkenness among 15-year-olds, 19 OECD countries

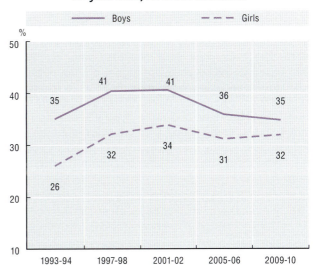

Source: Currie et al. (2000); Currie et al. (2004); Currie et al. (2008); Currie et al. (2012); WHO (1996).

StatLink ᴍSᴸ http://dx.doi.org/10.1787/888932916439

Source: Currie et al. (2000); Currie et al. (2004); Currie et al. (2008); Currie et al. (2012); WHO (1996).

StatLink ᴍSᴸ http://dx.doi.org/10.1787/888932916458

2.2. Overweight and obesity among children

Children who are overweight or obese are at greater risk of poor health in adolescence, as well as in adulthood. Among young people, orthopaedic problems and psychosocial problems such as low self-image, depression and impaired quality of life can result from being overweight. Excess weight problems in childhood are associated with an increased risk of being an obese adult, at which point cardiovascular disease, diabetes, certain forms of cancer, osteoarthritis, a reduced quality of life and premature death become health concerns (Lobstein, 2010; Currie et al., 2012).

Obesity and overweight rates rely on individual height and weight data which can either be measured by examination or self-reported. The latter type of data is collected consistently among 15-year-olds through the Health Behaviour in School-aged Children (HBSC) surveys every four years in a number of countries (Currie et al., 2004, 2008, 2012). However, self-reported data tend to under-estimate obesity and overweight.

Overweight (including obesity) rates based on measured height and weight are about 23% for boys and 21% for girls, on average, in OECD countries, although rates are measured in different age groups in different countries (Figure 2.2.1, left panel). Boys tend to carry excess weight more often than girls, with the largest gender differences observed in Slovenia, China and Iceland. In contrast, Turkey and South Africa show larger overweight rates among girls. More than 30% of boys and girls are overweight in Greece, Italy, New Zealand and the United States, and this is also the case for boys in Slovenia.

Self-reported overweight (including obesity) rates are about 18% for boys and 11% for girls on average in OECD countries among the 15-year-olds (Figure 2.2.1, right panel), although this average relates to a different set of countries compared with the average based on measured data. Rates based on self-reports are lower than those based on measured data, except for overweight boys in the United States, Austria, Sweden, Czech Republic, Norway and Turkey, due to age differences. Consistent with measured data, overweight rates based on self-reports are higher among boys than girls. More than 20% of boys are defined as overweight in Greece, Italy, Slovenia, the United States and Canada based on self-reported data, and more than 20% of girls in the United States. Young people who are overweight are more likely to miss eating breakfast, are less physically active, and spend more time watching television (Currie et al., 2012).

Rates of excess weight based on self-reports have increased slightly over the past decade in most OECD countries (Figure 2.2.2). Average of overweight rates (including obesity) across OECD countries increased between 2001-02 and 2009-10 from 13% to 15% in 15-year-olds. The largest increases during this eight-year period were in the Czech Republic, Estonia, Poland and Slovenia, all greater than 5%. Significant reductions in the proportion of overweight or obese children at age 15 were only observed in Denmark and the United Kingdom between 2001-02 and 2009-10, although non-response rates to questions about self-reported height and weight demand cautious in interpretation.

Childhood is an important period for forming healthy behaviours, and the increased focus on obesity at both a national and international level has stimulated the implementation of many community-based initiatives in OECD countries in recent years. Studies show that locally focussed interventions, targeting children up to 12 years of age can be effective in changing behaviours. Schools provide opportunities to ensure that children understand the importance of good nutrition and physical activity, and can benefit from both. Teachers and health professionals are often involved as providers of health and nutrition education, and the most frequent community-based initiatives target professional training, the social or physical environment, and actions for parents (Bemelmans et al., 2011).

Definition and comparability

Estimates of overweight and obesity are based on body mass index (BMI) calculations using either measured or child self-reported height and weight. Overweight and obese children are those whose BMI is above a set of age- and sex-specific cut-off points (Cole et al., 2000). Data presented here use the International Obesity Task Force (IOTF) BMI cut-off points.

Measured data are gathered by the International Association for the Study of Obesity (IASO) from different national studies. The estimates are based on national surveys of measured height and weight among children at various ages. Caution is therefore needed in comparing rates across countries. Definitions of overweight and obesity among children may sometimes vary among countries, although whenever possible the IOTF BMI cut-off points are used.

Self-reported data are from the Health Behaviour in School-aged Children (HBSC) surveys undertaken between 2001-02 and 2009-10. Data are drawn from school-based samples of 1 500 in each age group (11-, 13-and 15-year-olds) in most countries. Self-reported height and weight are subject to under-reporting, missing data and error, and require cautious interpretation.

2.2.1. Overweight (including obesity) among children, 2010 (or latest year)

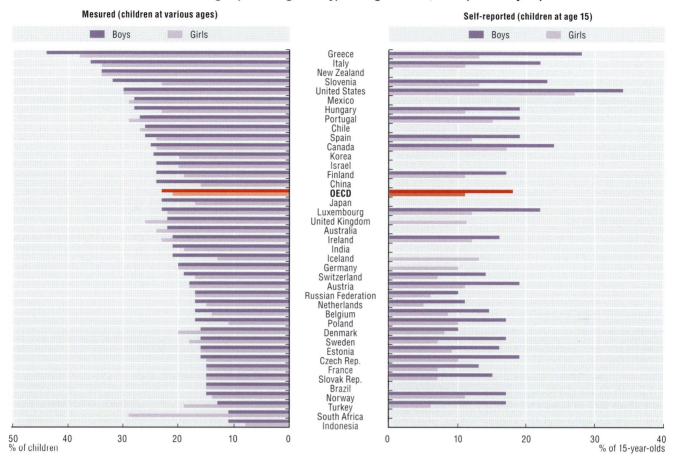

Mesured (children at various ages)

Self-reported (children at age 15)

% of children

% of 15-year-olds

Note: Measured data for United Kingdom refer to England.
Source: International Association for the Study of Obesity, 2013; Bös et al. (2004) for Luxembourg; and KNHANES for Korea (measured data). Currie et al. (2012) (self-reported data).

StatLink ᓇᗒ http://dx.doi.org/10.1787/888932916477

2.2.2. Change in self-reported overweight among 15-year-olds, 2001-02, 2005-06 and 2009-10

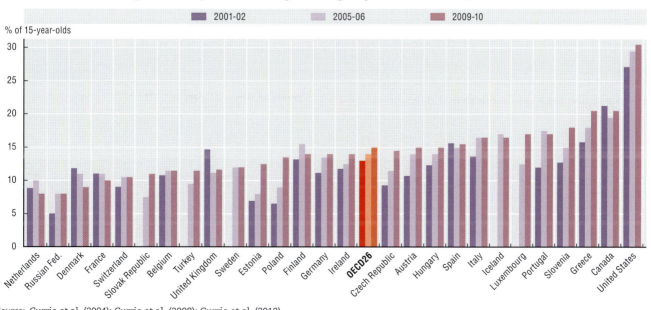

% of 15-year-olds

Source: Currie et al. (2004); Currie et al. (2008); Currie et al. (2012).

StatLink ᓇᗒ http://dx.doi.org/10.1787/888932916496

Nutrition is important for children's development and long-term health. Eating fruit during adolescence, for example in place of foods high in fat, sugar and salt, can protect against health problems such as obesity, diabetes, and cardiovascular diseases. Moreover, eating fruit and vegetables when young can be habit forming, promoting healthy eating in adult life.

A number of factors influence the amount of fruit consumed by adolescents, including family income, the cost of alternatives, preparation time, whether parents eat fruit, and the availability of fresh fruit which can be linked to the country or local climate (Rasmussen et al., 2006). Fruit consumption and vegetable consumption have a high priority as indicators of healthy eating in most OECD countries.

Overall, boys in Canada, Denmark and Portugal, and girls in Denmark, Norway and Canada had the highest rates of daily fruit consumption, while consumption was relatively low in Poland, Sweden, Estonia, and Finland, with rates of around one in four for girls and one in five, or even less, for boys (Figure 2.3.1). In all countries, girls were more likely than boys to eat fruit daily. The gap between the fruit consumption of boys and girls was especially large in Denmark, where 56% of girls, but only 34% of boys reported eating fruit each day. Norway and Germany also had large differences.

Daily vegetable eating was reported by around one in three girls and one in four boys on average across OECD member states in 2009-10 (Figure 2.3.2). Girls in Belgium most commonly ate vegetables daily (60%), followed by Denmark, France, Canada and Switzerland (45-50%). Belgium also led the way for boys (46%), with close to 40% in France, Canada and Ireland. Eating vegetables daily was less common in Austria, Estonia and Spain, as well as in Hungary (girls), and Finland (boys).

Average reported rates of daily vegetable consumption across OECD countries showed some increase between 2001-02 and 2009-10, for both girls and boys (Figure 2.3.3). The largest increases (above 10%) are observed in Denmark and Greece (in both genders), and in Norway and Spain (in girls only). For fruit consumption, trends show on average a small increase over the past decade among boys and girls. Rates have grown by 10% or more in Canada, Denmark, Norway, the United Kingdom, and the United States, whereas they have fallen in Poland and in Germany (in boys only).

Effective and targeted strategies are required to ensure that children are eating enough fruit and vegetables to conform to recommended national dietary guidelines. A European study found that schoolchildren generally hold a positive attitude toward fruit intake, and report good availability of fruit at home, but a lesser availability at school and during leisure time. Improved access to fruit and vegetables, combined with educational and motivational activities may help to increase consumption (Sandvik et al., 2005).

Definition and comparability

Dietary habits are measured here in terms of the proportions of children who report eating fruit and vegetables at least every day or more than once a day. In addition to fruit and vegetables, healthy nutrition also involves other types of foods.

Data are from the Health Behaviour in School-aged Children (HBSC) surveys. They are drawn from school-based samples of 1 500 in each age group (11-, 13- and 15-year-olds) in most countries.

2.3.1. Daily fruit eating among 15-year-olds, 2009-10

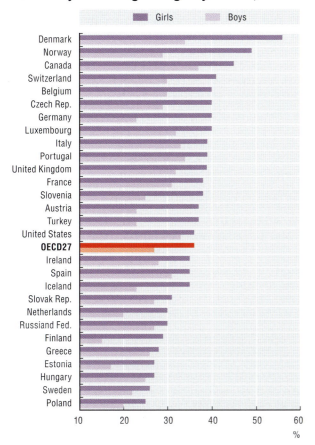

Source: Currie, C. et al. (2012).

StatLink http://dx.doi.org/10.1787/888932916515

2.3.2. Daily vegetable eating among 15-year-olds, 2009-10

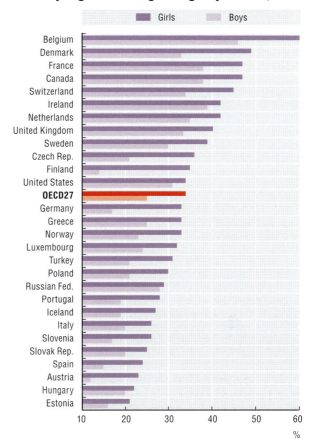

Source: Currie, C. et al. (2012).

StatLink http://dx.doi.org/10.1787/888932916534

2.3.3. Trends in daily fruit and vegetable eating among 15-year-olds, 27 OECD countries, 2001-02 to 2009-10

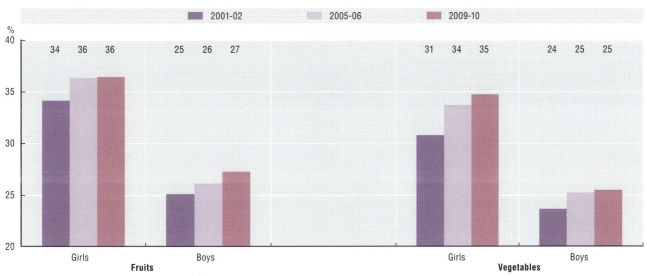

Source: Currie et al. (2004); Currie et al. (2008); Currie et al. (2012).

StatLink http://dx.doi.org/10.1787/888932916553

2.4. Physical activity among children

Undertaking physical activity in adolescence is beneficial for health, and can set standards for adult physical activity levels, thereby influencing health outcomes later in life. Research suggests that physical activity has a role in child and adolescent development, learning and well-being, and in the prevention and treatment of a range of youth health issues including asthma, mental health, and bone health. More direct links to adult health are found between physical activity in adolescence and its effect on overweight and obesity and related diseases, breast cancer rates and bone health in later life. The health effects of adolescent physical activity are sometimes dependent on the activity type, e.g. water physical activities in adolescence are effective in the treatment of asthma, and exercise is recommended in the treatment of cystic fibrosis (Hallal et al., 2006; Currie et al., 2012).

A large study recommends that children participate in at least 60 minutes of moderate-to-vigorous physical activity daily, although evidence suggests that many children do not meet these guidelines (Strong et al., 2005; Borraccino et al., 2009; Hallal et al., 2012). Some of the factors influencing the levels of physical activity undertaken by adolescents include the availability of space and equipment, children's present health conditions, their school curricula and other competing pastimes.

In OECD countries, fewer than one in four children report that they undertake moderate-to-vigorous exercise regularly, according to results from the 2009-10 HBSC survey (Figure 2.4.1). At age 11, Austria, Ireland, Spain, and Finland stand out as strong performers with over 30% of children reporting exercising for at least 60 minutes per day over the past week. At age 15, children in the United States are the most active, followed by Ireland, Czech Republic, the Slovak Republic and Canada. Children in Denmark, France, Italy, and Switzerland were least likely to report exercising regularly. Italy ranks at the bottom end of the spectrum for both boys and girls, and at both ages. A consistently higher proportion of boys than girls reported undertaking physical activity, whether moderate or vigorous, across all countries and all age groups (Figure 2.4.1).

It is of concern that physical activity tends to fall between ages 11 to 15 in almost all OECD countries, with boys in Italy and in the United States the only exceptions. In Austria, Finland, Norway and Germany, the rate of boys exercising at recommended levels is reduced by half between age 11 and age 15. This is also the case for girls in many countries. In Austria, Ireland, Spain and Finland, rates of physical activity among girls fall by over 60%.

The change in activity levels between age 11 and age 15 may reflect a move to different types of activity, since free play is more common among younger children, and structured activities at school or in sports clubs become more common later. Boys tend to be more physically active than girls in all countries, also suggesting that the opportunities to undertake physical activity may be gender-biased (Currie et al., 2012).

On average across OECD countries, daily moderate-to-vigorous physical activity fell slightly for both boys and girls, and in all age groups between 2005-06 and 2009-10 as shown in Figure 2.4.2.

Definition and comparability

Data for physical activity consider the regularity of moderate-to-vigorous physical activity as reported by 11-, 13- and 15-year-olds in 2005-06 and 2009-10. Moderate-to-vigorous physical activity refers to exercise undertaken for at least an hour each day which increases the heart rate, and leaves the child out of breath sometimes.

Data for OECD countries are from the Health Behaviour in School-aged Children (HBSC) surveys. They are drawn from school-based samples of 1 500 in each age group in most countries.

2.4.1. Daily moderate-to-vigorous physical activity, 11- and 15-year-olds, 2009-10

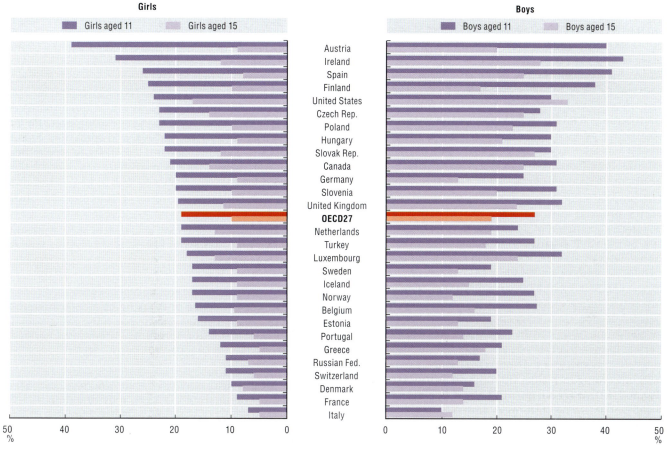

Source: Currie et al. (2012).

StatLink ᴍ🖷➡ http://dx.doi.org/10.1787/888932916572

2.4.2. Trends in daily moderate-to-vigorous physical activity, 27 OECD countries, 2005-06 to 2009-10

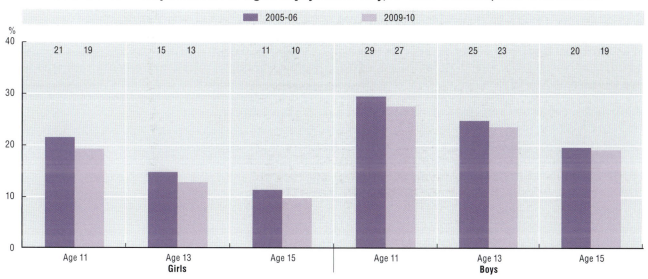

Source: Currie et al. (2008); Currie et al. (2012).

StatLink ᴍ🖷➡ http://dx.doi.org/10.1787/888932916591

2.5. Tobacco consumption among adults

Tobacco kills nearly 6 million people each year, of whom more than 5 million are from direct tobacco use and more than 600 000 are non-smokers exposed to second-hand smoke (WHO, 2013). It is a major risk factor for at least two of the leading causes of premature mortality – circulatory disease and cancer, increasing the risk of heart attack, stroke, lung cancer, cancers of the larynx and mouth, and pancreatic cancer. Smoking also causes peripheral vascular disease and hypertension. In addition, it is an important contributing factor for respiratory diseases such as chronic obstructive pulmonary disease (COPD). Smoking in pregnancy can lead to low birth weight and illness among infants. It remains the largest avoidable risk factor for health in OECD countries.

The proportion of daily smokers in the adult population varies greatly, even between neighboring countries (Figure 2.5.1). Fifteen of 34 OECD countries had less than 20% of the adult population smoking daily in 2011. Rates were lowest in Sweden, Iceland and the United States (less than 15%). Rates were also less than 15% in India, South Africa, and Brazil. Although large disparities remain, smoking rates across most OECD countries have shown a marked decline. On average, smoking rates have decreased by about one fifth over the past ten years, with a steeper decline in men than in women. Large reductions occurred since 2000 in Norway (32% to 17%), Iceland (22% to 14%), Netherlands (32% to 21%), Denmark (31% to 20%) and New Zealand (25% to 17%). Greece maintains the highest level of daily smoking among OECD countries, at around 32% of the adult population, along with Chile and Ireland, with around 30%, although the latest figure for Ireland dates from 2007. Smoking rates were even higher in the Russian Federation.

In the post-war period, most OECD countries tended to follow a pattern marked by very high smoking rates among men (50% or more) through to the 1960s and 1970s, while the 1980s and the 1990s were characterised by a marked downturn in tobacco consumption. Much of this decline can be attributed to policies aimed at reducing tobacco consumption through public awareness campaigns, advertising bans and increased taxation, in response to rising rates of tobacco-related diseases. In addition to government policies, actions by anti-smoking interest groups were very effective in reducing smoking rates by changing beliefs about the health effects of smoking, particularly in North America (Cutler and Glaeser, 2006).

Smoking prevalence is higher among men compared to women in all OECD countries except Norway, although male and female rates in Denmark, Iceland and the United Kingdom are similar (Figure 2.5.2). Female smoking rates continue to decline in most OECD countries, and in a number of cases (Ireland, Turkey, and New Zealand) at an even faster pace than male rates. However, in three countries, female smoking rates have been increasing over the last ten years (Czech Republic, Portugal and Korea), but even in these countries women are still less likely to smoke than men. In 2011, the gender gap in smoking rates was particularly large in Korea, Japan, Mexico, and Turkey, as well as in the Russian Federation, India, Indonesia and China (Figure 2.5.2).

Several studies provide strong evidence of socio-economic differences in smoking and mortality (Mackenbach et al., 2008). People in less affluent social groups have a greater prevalence and intensity of smoking, a higher all-cause mortality rate and lower rates of cancer survival (Woods et al., 2006). The influence of smoking as a determinant of overall health inequalities is such that, if the entire population was non-smoking, mortality differences between social groups would be halved (Jha et al., 2006).

Definition and comparability

The proportion of daily smokers is defined as the percentage of the population aged 15 years and over who report smoking every day.

International comparability is limited due to the lack of standardisation in the measurement of smoking habits in health interview surveys across OECD countries. Variations remain in the age groups surveyed, the wording of questions, response categories and survey methodologies (e.g. in a number of countries, respondents are asked if they smoke regularly, rather than daily).

2.5.1. Adult population smoking daily, 2011 and change between 2000 and 2011 (or nearest year)

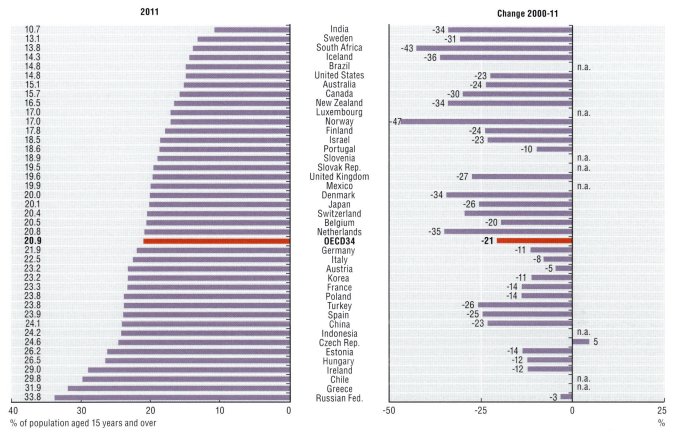

2011

%	Country
10.7	India
13.1	Sweden
13.8	South Africa
14.3	Iceland
14.8	Brazil
14.8	United States
15.1	Australia
15.7	Canada
16.5	New Zealand
17.0	Luxembourg
17.0	Norway
17.8	Finland
18.5	Israel
18.6	Portugal
18.9	Slovenia
19.5	Slovak Rep.
19.6	United Kingdom
19.9	Mexico
20.0	Denmark
20.1	Japan
20.4	Switzerland
20.5	Belgium
20.8	Netherlands
20.9	**OECD34**
21.9	Germany
22.5	Italy
23.2	Austria
23.2	Korea
23.3	France
23.8	Poland
23.8	Turkey
23.9	Spain
24.1	China
24.2	Indonesia
24.6	Czech Rep.
26.2	Estonia
26.5	Hungary
29.0	Ireland
29.8	Chile
31.9	Greece
33.8	Russian Fed.

% of population aged 15 years and over

Change 2000-11

India -34; Sweden -31; South Africa -43; Iceland -36; Brazil n.a.; United States -23; Australia -24; Canada -30; New Zealand -34; Luxembourg n.a.; Norway -47; Finland -24; Israel -23; Portugal -10; Slovenia n.a.; Slovak Rep. n.a.; United Kingdom -27; Mexico n.a.; Denmark -34; Japan -26; Switzerland -20; Belgium -35; Netherlands -21 (OECD34); Germany -11; Italy -8; Austria -5; Korea -11; France -14; Poland -14; Turkey -26; Spain -25; China -23; Indonesia n.a.; Czech Rep. 5; Estonia -14; Hungary -12; Ireland -12; Chile n.a.; Greece n.a.; Russian Fed. -3

%

Source: OECD Health Statistics 2013, http://dx.doi.org/10.1787/health-data-en; national sources for non-OECD countries.

StatLink http://dx.doi.org/10.1787/888932916610

2.5.2. Gender gap in adults smoking daily, 2011 (or nearest year)

■ Men   ■ Women

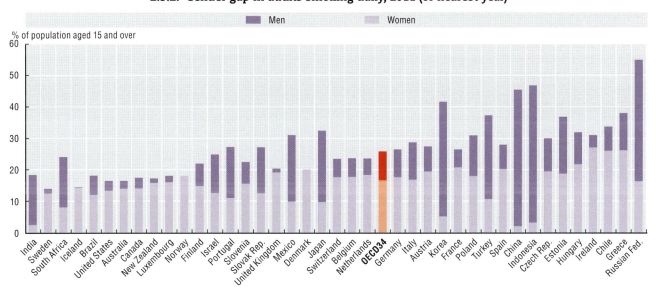

% of population aged 15 and over

Note: Countries are ranked in increasing order of smoking rates for the whole population.

Source: OECD Health Statistics 2013, http://dx.doi.org/10.1787/health-data-en; national sources for non-OECD countries.

StatLink http://dx.doi.org/10.1787/888932916629

2.6. Alcohol consumption among adults

The health burden related to harmful alcohol consumption, both in terms of morbidity and mortality, is considerable in most parts of the world (Rehm et al., 2009; WHO, 2011d). Alcohol use is associated with numerous harmful health and social consequences, including an increased risk of a range of cancers, stroke, and liver cirrhosis, among others. Foetal exposure to alcohol increases the risk of birth defects and intellectual impairment. Alcohol also contributes to death and disability through accidents and injuries, assault, violence, homicide and suicide, and is estimated to cause more than 2.5 million deaths worldwide per year (WHO, 2011d). WHO estimates that 4% of the global burden of disease is attributable to alcohol, which accounts for about as much mortality and disability as tobacco and hypertension (Rehm et al., 2009). In the United States, excessive alcohol consumption is the third leading cause of death, accounting for 80,000 deaths per year and 2.3 million potential years of life lost (CDC, 2012). Health care costs associated with excessive drinking in the United States are estimated at USD 25.6 billion (Bouchery et al., 2006). In the Russian Federation, alcohol misuse was a major contributing factor to the sharp rise in premature mortality and decline in life expectancy during the 1990s (OECD, 2012c).

Alcohol consumption, as measured by annual sales, stands at 9.4 litres per adult, on average, across OECD countries, based on the most recent data available (Figure 2.6.1). Leaving aside Luxembourg – given the high volume of purchases by non-residents in that country – France, Austria, Estonia reported the highest consumption of alcohol, with 12.0 litres or more per adult per year in 2011. Low alcohol consumption was recorded in Turkey and Israel, as well as in Indonesia and India, where religious and cultural traditions restrict the use of alcohol in some population groups.

Although average alcohol consumption has gradually fallen in many OECD countries over the past two decades, it has risen in several Northern European countries (Iceland, Sweden, Norway and Finland) as well as in Poland and Israel. There has been a degree of convergence in drinking habits across the OECD, with wine consumption increasing in many traditional beer-drinking countries and vice versa. The traditional wine-producing countries of Italy, Greece, Spain, Portugal and France, as well as the Slovak Republic, Switzerland and Hungary have seen per capita consumption fall by one fifth or more since 1990 (Figure 2.6.1).

Alcohol consumption in the Russian Federation, as well as in Brazil, India, and China has risen substantially, although in the latter two countries per capita consumption is still low.

Variations in alcohol consumption across countries and over time reflect not only changing drinking habits but also the policy responses to control alcohol use. Curbs on advertising, sales restrictions and taxation have all proven to be effective measures to reduce alcohol consumption (Babor et al., 2010).

Although adult alcohol consumption per capita gives useful evidence of long-term trends, it does not identify subpopulations at risk from harmful drinking patterns. The consumption of large quantities of alcohol in a single session (heavy episodic drinking, or binge drinking), is an especially dangerous pattern of consumption (Institute of Alcohol Studies, 2007), which is on the rise in some countries and social groups, especially among young people (Devaux and Sassi, forthcoming).

In 2010, the World Health Organization endorsed a global strategy to combat the harmful use of alcohol, through direct measures such as medical services for alcohol-related health problems, and indirect measures such as the dissemination of information on alcohol-related harm (WHO, 2010a).

> ### *Definition and comparability*
>
> Alcohol consumption is defined as annual sales of pure alcohol in litres per person aged 15 years and over. The methodology to convert alcoholic drinks to pure alcohol may differ across countries. Official statistics do not include unrecorded alcohol consumption, such as home production.
>
> Italy reports consumption for the population 14 years and over, Sweden for 16 years and over, and Japan 20 years and over. In some countries (e.g. Luxembourg), national sales do not accurately reflect actual consumption by residents, since purchases by non-residents create a significant gap between sales and consumption.

2.6.1. Alcohol consumption among adults, 2011 and change between 1990 and 2011 (or nearest year)

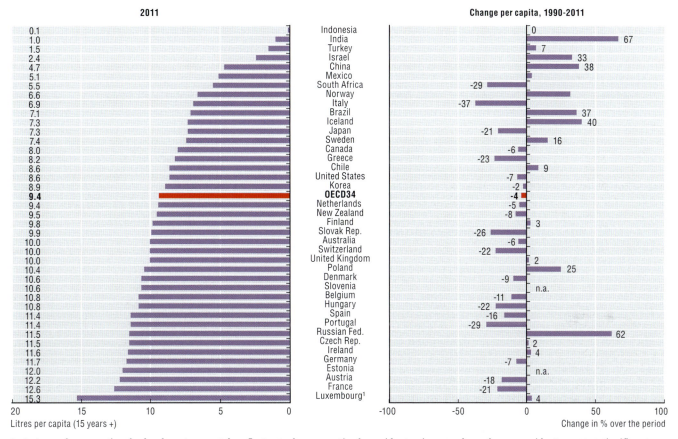

1. In Luxembourg, national sales do not accurately reflect actual consumption by residents, since purchases by non-residents create a significant gap.
Source: OECD Health Statistics 2013, http://dx.doi.org/10.1787/health-data-en; WHO for non-OECD countries.

StatLink ᴍₛₚ http://dx.doi.org/10.1787/888932916648

2.6.2. Trends in alcohol consumption, selected OECD countries, 1990-2011

Source: OECD Health Statistics 2013, http://dx.doi.org/10.1787/health-data-en.

StatLink ᴍₛₚ http://dx.doi.org/10.1787/888932916667

2.7. Overweight and obesity among adults

The rise in overweight and obesity is a major public health concern. Obesity is a known risk factor for numerous health problems, including hypertension, high cholesterol, diabetes, cardiovascular diseases, respiratory problems (asthma), musculoskeletal diseases (arthritis) and some forms of cancer. Mortality also increases progressively once the overweight threshold is crossed (Sassi, 2010).

Based on the latest available surveys, more than half (52.6%) of the adult population in the OECD report that they are overweight or obese. In countries where height and weight were measured (as opposed to self-reported), the proportion was even greater, at 55.6%. The prevalence of overweight and obesity among adults exceeds 50% in no less than 20 of 34 OECD countries. In contrast, overweight and obesity rates are much lower in Japan and Korea and in some European countries (France and Switzerland), although even in these countries rates have been increasing.

The prevalence of obesity, which presents even greater health risks than overweight, varies nearly tenfold in OECD countries, from a low of 4% in Japan and Korea, to over 32% in Mexico and the United States (Figure 2.7.1). Across OECD countries, 18% of the adult population are obese. Average obesity rates in men and women are similar in most countries. However, in South Africa, the Russian Federation, Turkey, Chile, and Mexico, a greater proportion of women are obese, while the reverse is true in Iceland and Norway.

The prevalence of obesity has increased over the past decade in all OECD countries (Figure 2.7.2). In 2011, at least one in five adults was obese in ten OECD countries, compared to five a decade ago. Since 2000, obesity rates have increased by a third or more in 16 countries. The rapid rise occurred regardless of where levels stood a decade ago. Obesity increased by almost half in both Iceland and Norway, even though the current rate in Norway is around half that of Iceland.

The rise in obesity has affected all population groups, regardless of sex, age, race, income or education level, but to varying degrees. Evidence from Australia, Austria, Canada, England, France, Italy, Korea, Spain and the United States shows that obesity tends to be more common in disadvantaged socio-economic groups, especially in women (Sassi et al., 2009). There is also a relationship between the number of years spent in full-time education and obesity, with the more educated displaying lower rates. Again, the gradient in obesity is stronger in women than in men (Devaux et al., 2011).

A number of behavioural and environmental factors have contributed to the global spread of overweight and obesity, including falling real prices of food and more time spent in sedentary activities. Overweight and obesity have risen rapidly in children in recent decades, reaching double-figure rates in most OECD countries (see Indicator 2.2 "Overweight and obesity among children").

Because obesity is associated with higher risks of chronic illnesses, it is linked to significant additional health care costs. There is a time lag between the onset of obesity and related health problems, suggesting that the rise in obesity over the past decade will mean higher health care costs in the future. A 2007 study estimated that total costs linked with overweight and obesity in England in 2015 could increase by as much as 70% relative to 2007 and could be 2.4 times higher in 2025 (Foresight, 2007).

Definition and comparability

Overweight and obesity are defined as excessive weight presenting health risks because of the high proportion of body fat. The most frequently used measure is based on the body mass index (BMI), which is a single number that evaluates an individual's weight in relation to height (weight/height^2, with weight in kilograms and height in metres). Based on the WHO classification (WHO, 2000), adults with a BMI from 25 to 30 are defined as overweight, and those with a BMI of 30 or over as obese. This classification may not be suitable for all ethnic groups, who may have equivalent levels of risk at lower or higher BMI. The thresholds for adults are not suitable to measure overweight and obesity among children.

For most countries, overweight and obesity rates are self-reported through estimates of height and weight from population-based health interview surveys. However, around one-third of OECD countries derive their estimates from health examinations. These differences limit data comparability. Estimates from health examinations are generally higher, and more reliable than estimates from health interviews. Note that the OECD average is based on both types of estimates (self-reported and measured) and, thus, may be underestimated.

2.7.1. Obesity among adults, 2011 (or nearest year)

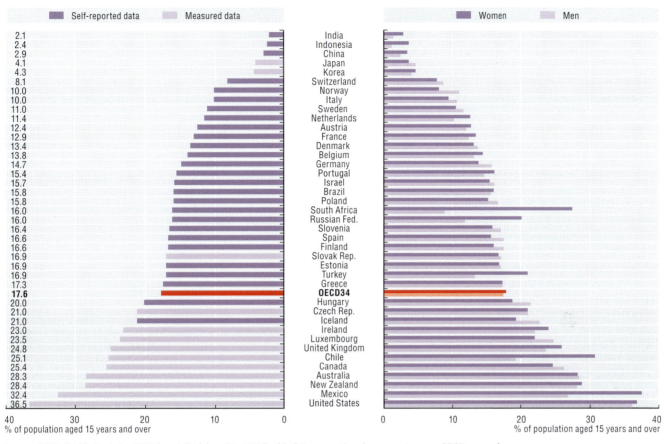

Source: OECD Health Statistics 2013, http://dx.doi.org/10.1787//health-data-en; national sources for non-OECD countries.

StatLink http://dx.doi.org/10.1787/888932916686

2.7.2. Increasing obesity among adults in OECD countries, 2000 and 2011 (or nearest year)

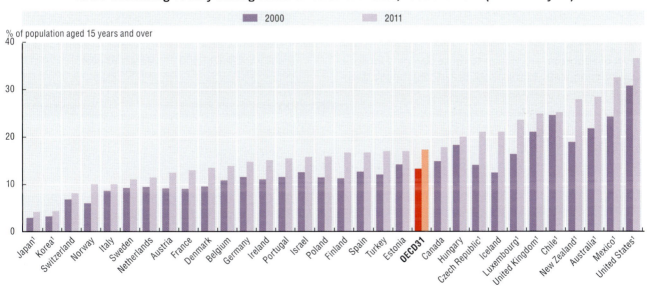

1. Data are based on measurements rather than self-reported height and weight.
Source: OECD Health Statistics 2013, http://dx.doi.org/10.1787/health-data-en.

StatLink http://dx.doi.org/10.1787/888932916705

2.8. Fruit and vegetable consumption among adults

Nutrition is an important determinant of health. Inadequate consumption of fruit and vegetables is one factor that can play a role in increased morbidity. Proper nutrition assists in preventing a number of chronic conditions, including cardiovascular disease, hypertension, Type-2 diabetes, stroke, certain cancers, musculoskeletal disorders and a range of mental health conditions.

In response to a health survey question asking "How often do you eat fruit?", the percentage of adults consuming fruit daily varied from 20% in men in Finland, to more than 90% in Australia (Figure 2.8.1). Across the 24 countries providing data, an average 57% of men and 69% of women reported to eat fruit daily. Women reported eating fruit more often than men in all countries, with the largest gender differences in Denmark, the Slovak Republic, Germany, and Iceland (20 percentage points or more). In Australia, Greece, Turkey and Mexico, gender differences were much smaller, under 5%.

Persons aged 65 and over were more likely to eat fruit than those in younger age group, with the lowest consumption in people aged 15-24 years (see also Indicator 2.3, "Fruit and vegetable consumption among children"). Fruit consumption also varies by socio-economic status, generally being highest among persons with higher educational levels (Figure 2.8.3). However, this was not the case in Spain and Greece, where less educated persons reported eating fruit more often.

Daily vegetable consumption ranged from around 30% in men in Germany to nearly 100% in Korea, with Australia and New Zealand at about the same levels, but counting potatoes as vegetables (Figure 2.8.2). The average across 28 OECD countries was 64% for men and 73% for women. Again, more women than men reported eating vegetables daily in all countries, except in Korea and Australia where rates were similar. In Norway, Denmark, Finland and Germany, gender differences exceeded 15%.

Patterns of vegetable consumption across age groups and by level of education are similar to those observed for fruit. Older persons were more likely to eat vegetables daily.

Highly educated persons ate vegetables more often, although the difference between educational groups was small in Belgium, Italy, Greece, Slovenia and the Slovak Republic (Figure 2.8.4).

The availability of fruit and vegetables is the most important determinant of consumption. Despite large variations between countries, vegetable, and especially fruit, availability is higher in Southern European countries, with cereals and potatoes more available in central and eastern European countries. Fruit and vegetable availability also tends to be higher in families where household heads have a higher level of education (Elmadfa, 2009).

The promotion of fruit and vegetable consumption, especially in schools and at the workplace, features in the EU platform for action on diet, physical activity and health (European Commission, 2011a).

Definition and comparability

Estimates of daily fruit and vegetable consumption are derived from national and European Health Interview Survey questions. Typically, respondents were asked "How often do you eat fruit (excluding juice)?" and "How often do you eat vegetables or salad (excluding juice and potatoes)?"

Data for Greece and Switzerland include juices as a portion of fruit, and juices and soups as a portion of vegetable. Data for Australia, Greece, New Zealand, and the United Kingdom include potatoes as vegetables. Data rely on self-reporting, and are subject to errors in recall. The same surveys also ask for information on age, sex and educational level. Data are not age standardised, with aggregate country estimates representing crude rates among respondents aged 15 years and over in all countries, except Germany and Australia which is 18 years and over.

2.8.1. Daily fruit eating among adults, 2011 (or nearest year)

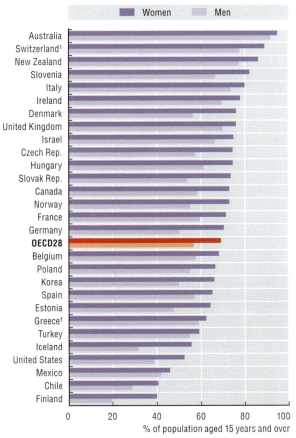

1. Include juices.

StatLink 𝗺𝗦▸ http://dx.doi.org/10.1787/888932916724

2.8.2. Daily vegetable eating among adults, 2011 (or nearest year)

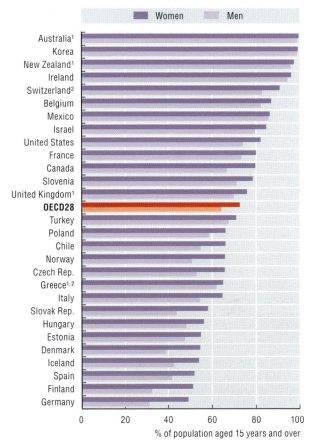

1. Include potatoes.
2. Include juices and soups.

Source: OECD Health Statistics 2013, http://dx.doi.org/10.1787/health-data-en.

StatLink 𝗺𝗦▸ http://dx.doi.org/10.1787/888932916743

2.8.3. Daily fruit eating among adults, by educational level, European countries, 2008 (or nearest year)

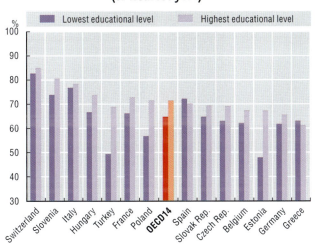

Source: Eurostat Statistics Database 2013 (EHIS collection round 2008).

StatLink 𝗺𝗦▸ http://dx.doi.org/10.1787/888932916762

2.8.4. Daily vegetable eating among adults, by educational level, European countries, 2008 (or nearest year)

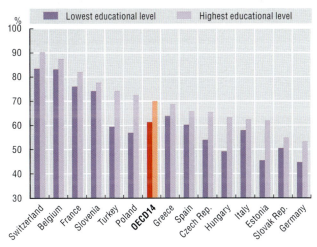

Source: Eurostat Statistics Database 2013 (EHIS collection round 2008).

StatLink 𝗺𝗦▸ http://dx.doi.org/10.1787/888932916781

3. HEALTH WORKFORCE

The statistical data for Israel are supplied by and under the responsibility of the relevant Israeli authorities. The use of such data by the OECD is without prejudice to the status of the Golan Heights, East Jerusalem and Israeli settlements in the West Bank under the terms of international law.

3.1. Doctors (overall number)

The number of doctors per capita varies widely across OECD and emerging countries. In 2011, Greece had by far the highest number of doctors per capita (6.1 per 1 000 population), followed by the Russian Federation and Austria. Chile, Turkey and Korea had the lowest number of doctors per capita among OECD countries, with around two doctors per 1 000 population. This compares with an OECD average of just over three doctors per 1 000 population. The number of doctors per capita is much lower in some emerging countries, with less than one doctor per 1 000 population in Indonesia, India and South Africa (Figure 3.1.1).

Between 2000 and 2011, the number of physicians has grown in most OECD countries, both in absolute number and on a per capita basis. The growth rate was particularly rapid in countries which started with lower levels in 2000 (Turkey, Korea and Mexico), as well as in Australia, the United Kingdom and Greece. In Australia and the United Kingdom, the increasing number of doctors has been driven mainly by a strong rise in graduation rates from domestic medical education programmes (see Indicator 3.5). In Greece, the number of doctors per capita increased strongly between 2000 and 2008, but has stabilised since then. On the other hand, there was almost no growth in the number of physicians per capita in Estonia and France between 2000 and 2011, and there was a decline in Israel.

The absolute number of doctors has continued to grow in most OECD countries during the 2008-09 recession and afterwards, although it has slowed down in some countries that have been hard hit by the recession such as Greece. In Portugal, the absolute number of doctors licensed to practice increased by 12% between 2008 and 2011, although this does not mean that the number of doctors engaged in regular practice has grown at the same pace. In the United Kingdom, there were 15% more employed doctors in 2012 compared with 2008 (Figure 3.1.2).

In France, there has been a slight increase in the absolute number of doctors since 2008, which has grown at the same pace as the population size. The increase over the past few years has been driven mainly by a large number of doctors beyond age 65 remaining in activity (DREES, 2013).

Projecting the future supply and demand of doctors is difficult, because of high levels of uncertainties concerning their working hours and retirement patterns on the supply side, and changing health needs of ageing populations and future trends in economic growth and health expenditure growth on the demand side (Ono et al., 2013). In Australia, the baseline (or comparison) scenario in a recent projection

exercise estimated a possible small shortage of physicians by 2025. The projection explored different scenarios that may either mitigate or exacerbate these baseline results. If the demand for doctor services is growing at a slightly slower pace than projected, the projected shortage would disappear. However, if there is a sharp reduction in the number of immigrant doctors or if a maximum limit is set to the number of working hours of doctors per week, then a growing number of medical graduates would be required to close the projected gap (Health Workforce Australia, 2012).

In the United Kingdom, a recent projection exercise identified a potential surplus of specialist doctors (consultants), based on a set of assumptions about future health expenditure, as well as developments concerning pay rates and inflation. While the supply of GPs is projected to increase by 29% between 2010-11 and 2039-40, the supply of hospital doctors is projected to increase by 64% (based on current levels of student intakes and graduation rates), exceeding by a wide margin the additional staff that the NHS may be able to recruit over that period. One of the conclusions from this projection exercise was that it may be advisable to reduce slightly medical intakes and to reduce the training of hospital doctors more specifically (CfWI, 2012).

Definition and comparability

The data for most countries refer to practising medical doctors, defined as the number of doctors who are providing care directly to patients. In many countries, the numbers include interns and residents (doctors in training). The numbers are based on head counts. The data for Ireland are based on estimations. Several countries also include doctors who are active in the health sector even though they may not provide direct care to patients. Portugal reports the number of physicians entitled to practice (resulting in a large over-estimation of the number of practising doctors). Data for Spain (up to 2010) include dentists, while data for Belgium include stomatologists (also resulting in some over-estimation).

Data for India are also likely over-estimated as they are based on medical registers which are not updated to account for migration, retirement or death, nor do they take into account doctors registered in multiple states.

3.1.1. Practising doctors per 1 000 population, 2000 and 2011 (or nearest year)

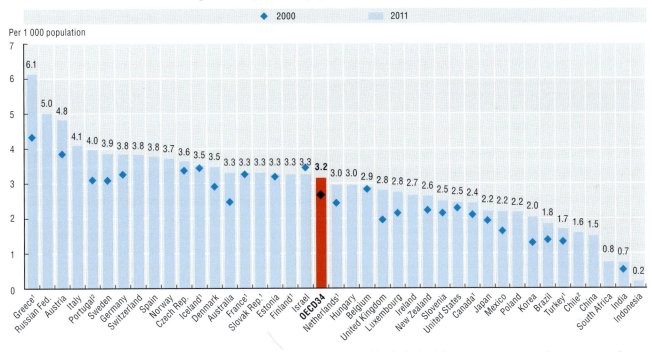

1. Data include not only doctors providing direct care to patients, but also those working in the health sector as managers, educators, researchers, etc. (adding another 5-10% of doctors).
2. Data refer to all doctors licensed to practice (resulting in a large over-estimation of the number of practising doctors in Portugal).
Source: OECD Health Statistics 2013, http://dx.doi.org/10.1787/health-data-en.

StatLink ᵒᵐˢ˥ *http://dx.doi.org/10.1787/888932916800*

3.1.2. Evolution in the number of doctors, selected OECD countries, 2000 to 2012 (or nearest year)

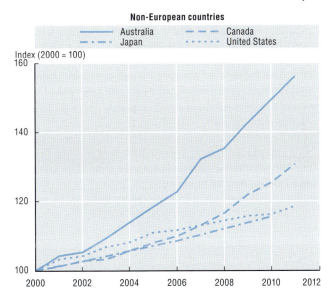

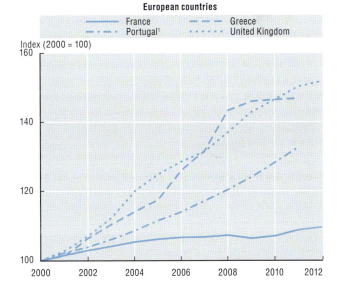

1. Data refer to all doctors who are licensed to practice.
Source: OECD Health Statistics 2013, http://dx.doi.org/10.1787/health-data-en.

StatLink ᵒᵐˢ˥ *http://dx.doi.org/10.1787/888932916819*

3.2. Doctors by age, sex and category

Beyond the overall number of doctors, the age and gender composition of the medical workforce and the mix between different categories of doctors also have important implications on the current and future supply of medical services. The ageing of doctors in OECD countries has, for many years, raised concerns that there may not be sufficient new recruits to replace them, although there is evidence in several countries that the retirement of doctors often only occurs gradually and that their retirement age is increasing (Pong, 2011). The rising share of female doctors (the "feminisation" of medical professions) affects the overall supply of services, as women tend to work fewer hours than men, although it appears that working time preferences are becoming more similar among new generations of men and women doctors (Maiorova, 2007). The growing imbalance in favour of greater specialism over generalist medicine raises concerns in many countries about ensuring adequate access to primary care for all the population.

In 2011, on average across OECD countries, nearly one-third of all doctors were over 55 years of age, up from one-in-five in 2000 (Figure 3.2.1). These doctors might be expected to retire over the next ten years although a significant number of doctors continue to practice after 65 years. In Israel, almost half (49%) of all doctors were over 55 years of age in 2011, but this may be due partly to the fact that these numbers relate to all doctors licensed to practice. This proportion reached over 40% in Belgium, France and Italy. By contrast, less than 15% of doctors in the United Kingdom and Korea were aged over 55, due to large numbers of new graduates entering medical practice over the past decade (Indicator 3.5).

In 2011, 44% of doctors on average across OECD countries were women, up from 38% in 2000 (and 29% in 1990) (Figure 3.2.2). More than half of doctors now are women in nine countries (Estonia, Slovenia, Poland, the Slovak Republic, Finland, Hungary, Czech Republic, Portugal and Spain). By contrast, only one in five doctors in Japan and Korea were women in 2011. Since 2000, the share of female physicians increased in all OECD countries for which data are available, with particularly large increases in the Netherlands and Spain.

The balance in the physician workforce between generalists and specialists has changed over the past few decades, with the number of specialists increasing much more rapidly. Although health service research emphasises the importance and cost-effectiveness of generalist primary care (Starfield et al., 2005), on average across OECD countries, generalists made up only 30% of all physicians. There were more than two specialists for every generalist in 2011 (Figure 3.2.3). Specialists greatly outnumber generalists in central and eastern European countries and in Greece. However, some countries have maintained a more equal balance between specialists and generalists, such as Australia, Canada and France. In Ireland, most generalists are not really general practitioners, but rather non-specialist doctors working in hospitals or other settings. In some countries such as the United States, general internal medicine doctors are categorised as specialists although their practice can be very similar to that of general practitioners, resulting in some underestimation of the capacity of these countries to provide generalist care.

In many OECD countries, specialists earn more and have seen their earnings grow faster than general practitioners (see Indicator 3.6). This creates a financial incentive for doctors to specialise, although other factors such as working conditions and professional prestige also influence choices. In response to concerns about shortages of general practitioners, many countries have taken steps to improve the number of training places and attractiveness of general medicine. For example, in France, about 50% of all graduate medical training places are reserved for general medicine (DREES, 2013). In the Netherlands, the number of graduate training places in different areas of medical training is regularly revised to take into account expected changes in staffing requirements (ACMMP, 2010).

Definition and comparability

The definition of doctors is provided under Indicator 3.1. In some countries, the data are based on all doctors licensed to practice, not only those practising (e.g., Ireland and Portugal).

Not all countries are able to report all their physicians in the two broad categories of specialists and generalists. This may be due to the fact that specialty-specific data are not available for doctors in training or for those working in private practice.

3.2.1. Share of doctors aged 55 years and over, 2000 and 2011 (or nearest year)

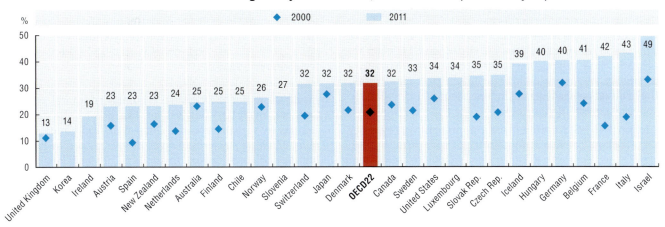

Source: OECD Health Statistics 2013, http://dx.doi.org/10.1787/health-data-en.

StatLink ᗑ᎒᠍ᔆᒪᏜ http://dx.doi.org/10.1787/888932916838

3.2.2. Share of female doctors, 2000 and 2011 (or nearest year)

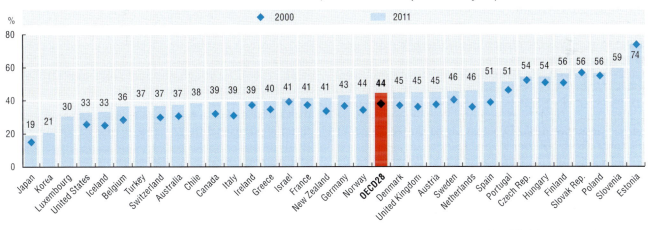

Source: OECD Health Statistics 2013, http://dx.doi.org/10.1787/health-data-en.

StatLink ᗑ᎒᠍ᔆᒪᏜ http://dx.doi.org/10.1787/888932916857

3.2.3. Generalists and specialists as a share of all doctors, 2011 (or nearest year)

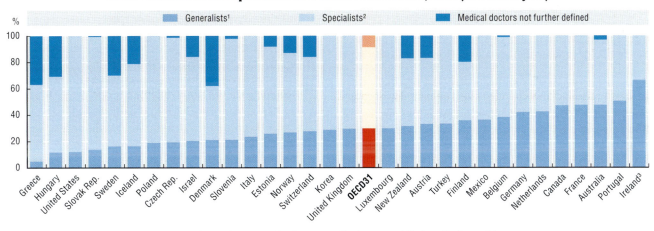

1. Generalists include general practitioners/family doctors and other generalist (non-specialist) medical practitioners.
2. Specialists include paediatricians, obstetricians/gynaecologists, psychiatrists, medical, surgical and other specialists.
3. In Ireland, most generalists are not GPs ("family doctors"), but rather non-specialist doctors working in hospitals or other settings.

Source: OECD Health Statistics 2013, http://dx.doi.org/10.1787/health-data-en.

StatLink ᗑ᎒᠍ᔆᒪᏜ http://dx.doi.org/10.1787/888932916876

3.3. Gynaecologists and obstetricians, and midwives

Gynaecologists are concerned with the functions and diseases affecting the female reproductive system, while obstetricians specialise in pregnancy and childbirth. A doctor will often specialise in both these areas, and the data reported in this section does not distinguish between the two. Midwives provide care and advice to women during pregnancy, labour and childbirth and the post-natal period. They deliver babies working independently or in collaboration with doctors and nurses.

In countries with a medicalised approach to pregnancy, obstetricians provide the majority of care. Where a less medicalised approach exists, trained midwives are the lead professional, often working in collaboration with general practitioners, although obstetricians may be called upon if complications arise. Regardless of the different mix of providers across countries, the progress achieved over the past few decades in the provision of pre-natal advice and pregnancy surveillance, together with progress in obstetrics to deal with complicated births, has resulted in major reductions in perinatal mortality in all OECD countries.

In 2011, the number of gynaecologists and obstetricians per 100 000 women was the highest in the Czech Republic and Greece, followed by Italy and the Slovak Republic (Figure 3.3.1). These are all countries where obstetricians are given a primary role in providing pre-natal and childbirth care. The number of gynaecologists and obstetricians per 100 000 women was the lowest in New Zealand, Canada, Ireland, Chile and the Netherlands.

Since 2000, the number of gynaecologists and obstetricians per 100 000 women has increased in most countries, although the growth rate varied (Figure 3.3.1). It was highest in Mexico, Australia, Switzerland and the United Kingdom. On the other hand, the number of gynaecologists and obstetricians per 100 000 women declined slightly in Japan and the United States. In the United States, this was because the growth in the population number exceeded the growth in the number of gynaecologists and obstetricians.

The number of midwives per 100 000 women was highest in Iceland, Sweden, Turkey and Australia in 2011 (Figure 3.3.2). It was the lowest in Korea, Canada and Slovenia. While the number of midwives has increased significantly in Canada and Slovenia over the past decade, it has fallen in Korea. This decline has coincided with a continued reduction in fertility rates in Korea. The number of midwives per capita also decreased slightly in Estonia, Hungary and Israel between 2000 and 2011. In Hungary, most of the reduction occurred between 2006 and 2007, as the number of beds in maternity wards was cut by more

than one-third in the context of a health reform. In the Netherlands, the number of midwives has increased faster than the number of gynaecologists and obstetricians, and the number of births in hospitals attended by midwives rose from 8% in 1998 to 26% in 2007 (Wiegers and Hukkelhoven, 2010).

The relative mix of providers has both direct and indirect implications for the costs of pre-natal and natal services. Services involving midwives are likely to be cheaper. This reflects in part the lower training time and hence a lower compensating pay for midwives in comparison to gynaecologists and obstetricians. In addition, obstetricians may be inclined to provide more medicalised services. A study of nine European countries found that the cost of delivery is lower in those countries and hospitals that employ more midwives and nurses than obstetricians (Bellanger and Or, 2008).

There is little evidence that systems that rely more on midwives are less effective. A review of a number of studies finds that midwife-led models of care resulted in fewer complications (Hatem et al., 2008). Another review found that midwives are equally effective in providing pre-natal care and advice in the case of normal pregnancies (Di Mario et al., 2005), although support from obstetricians is required for complications.

Definition and comparability

The number of gynaecologists and obstetricians combines these two specialities.

The figures for gynaecologists and obstetricians, and for midwives, are presented as head counts, not taking into account full-time or part-time status (except in Ireland where the data on midwives are based on full-time equivalents). In Spain, the number of gynaecologists and obstetricians only includes those working in hospital.

The number of midwives in Canada may be underestimated, as they may undercount the number of midwives in provinces/territories where there is no regulation requiring licensure as a condition of practice. In Austria, the number of midwives only includes those employed in hospital (resulting in an underestimation of 40 to 50%).

3.3.1. Gynaecologists and obstetricians per 100 000 women, 2011 and change between 2000 and 2011

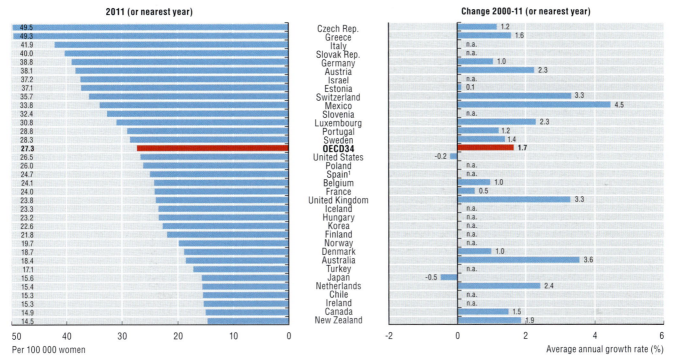

1. In Spain, the number of gynaecologists and obstetricians only includes those working in hospital.
Source: OECD Health Statistics 2013, http://dx.doi.org/10.1787/health-data-en.

StatLink ᵃᵐˢᴾ *http://dx.doi.org/10.1787/888932916895*

3.3.2. Midwives per 100 000 women, 2011 and change between 2000 and 2011

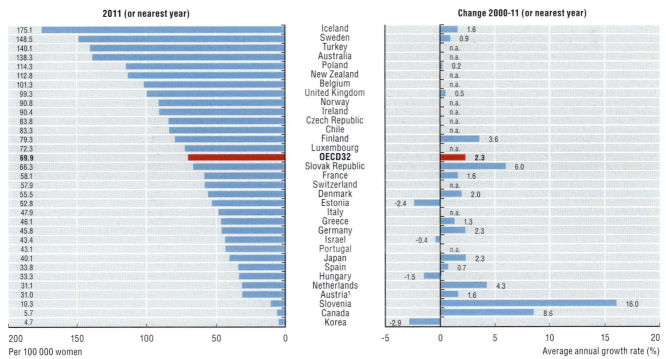

1. In Austria, the number of midwives only includes those working in hospital.
Source: OECD Health Statistics 2013, http://dx.doi.org/10.1787/health-data-en.

StatLink ᵃᵐˢᴾ *http://dx.doi.org/10.1787/888932916914*

3.4. Psychiatrists and mental health nurses

At any point in time, about 10% of the adult population will report having some type of mental or behavioural disorder (WHO, 2001). People with mental health problems may receive help from a variety of professionals, including general practitioners, psychiatrists, psychologists, psychotherapists, social workers, specialist nurses and others. This section focuses on two categories of mental health service providers, psychiatrists and mental health nurses, as the availability of comparable data for other providers is more limited. Psychiatrists are responsible for diagnosing and treating a variety of serious mental health problems, including depression, learning disabilities, alcoholism and drug addiction, eating disorders, and personality disorders such as schizophrenia. A mental health nurse has usually completed a formal training in nursing at a university level and work in mental health care services (WHO, 2011e).

In 2011, there were 15.6 psychiatrists per 100 000 population on average across OECD countries (Figure 3.4.1). The number was by far the highest in Switzerland, with 45 psychiatrists per 100 000 population. Following Switzerland were Iceland, France and Sweden, with 22 psychiatrists per 100 000 population. In most OECD countries, the number was between 10 and 20 per 100 000 population. There were fewer than ten psychiatrists per 100 000 population in Mexico, Turkey, Chile, Korea and Poland.

The number of psychiatrists per capita has increased since 2000 in most OECD countries for which data are available (Figure 3.4.1). The rise has been particularly rapid in Switzerland, Austria, Poland, the Netherlands and the United Kingdom. There was a slight decrease in the number of psychiatrists per capita in the United States, as the increase in the number of psychiatrists did not fully keep up with the increase in the population.

As is the case for many other medical specialties, psychiatrists may be unevenly distributed across regions within each country. For example, in Australia, the number of psychiatrists per capita was two times greater in certain states and territories compared with others in 2009 (AIHW, 2012b).

The role of psychiatrists varies across countries. For example, in Spain, psychiatrists work in close co-operation with general practitioners (GPs). Hence, although the number of psychiatrists is relatively low, consultation rates of psychiatrists by people with mental disorders are higher than in many other countries that have more psychiatrists, because of higher referral rates from their GPs (Kovess-Masfety, 2007).

In many countries, mental health nurses play an important and increasing role in the delivery of mental health services in hospital or outside hospital. In 2011, the Netherlands, Ireland and Japan had the highest rates (with over 100 mental health nurses per 100 000 population), and Turkey, Mexico and Hungary the lowest rates (under ten per 100 000 population). The number of mental health nurses is also relatively low in Portugal and Korea, with between ten and 15 nurses per 100 000 population. The OECD average was 50 mental health nurses per 100 000 population (Figure 3.4.2).

Some countries such as Australia have introduced new programmes to improve access to mental health care by extending the role of mental health nurses in primary care. Under the Mental Health Nurse Incentive Program launched in 2007, mental health nurses in Australia work with general practitioners, psychiatrists and other mental health professionals to treat people suffering from different mental health conditions. A recent evaluation of this programme found that mental health nurses have the potential to make a significant contribution to enhance access and quality of mental care through flexible and innovative approaches (Happell et al., 2010).

Definition and comparability

Psychiatrists are medical doctors who specialise in the prevention, diagnosis and treatment of mental illness. They have post-graduate training in psychiatry, and may also have additional training in a psychiatric specialty, such as neuropsychiatry or child psychiatry. Psychiatrists can prescribe medication, which psychologists cannot do in most countries.

The figures normally include psychiatrists, neuropsychiatrists and child psychiatrists. Psychologists are excluded. The numbers are presented as head counts, regardless of whether psychiatrists work full time or part time. In Spain, the number of psychiatrists only includes those working in hospital.

A mental health nurse is usually defined as a nurse who has completed a formal training in nursing at a university level and work in mental health care services in hospital, in primary care or other settings (WHO, 2011e).

3.4.1. Psychiatrists per 100 000 population, 2011 and change between 2000 and 2011

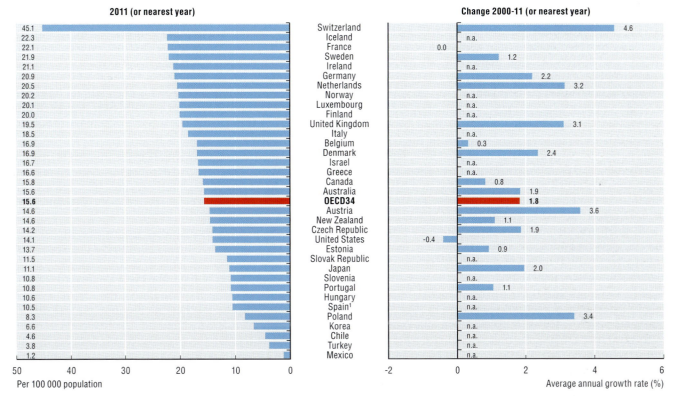

1. In Spain, the number of psychiatrists only includes those working in hospital.
Source: OECD Health Statistics 2013, http://dx.doi.org/10.1787/health-data-en.

StatLink ⬛⬛ *http://dx.doi.org/10.1787/888932916933*

3.4.2. Mental health nurses per 100 000 population, 2011 (or nearest year)

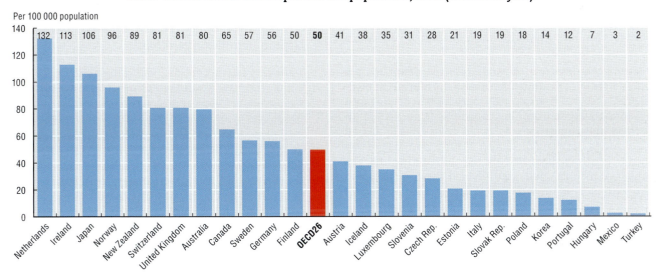

Source: OECD Mental Health Questionnaire 2012, WHO Mental Health Atlas 2011.

StatLink ⬛⬛ *http://dx.doi.org/10.1787/888932916952*

3.5. Medical graduates

Maintaining or increasing the number of doctors requires either investment in training new doctors or recruiting trained physicians from abroad. As it takes about ten years to train a doctor, any current shortages can be met only by recruiting qualified doctors from abroad, unless there are unemployed doctors at home. Conversely, any surpluses or sudden fall in demand may mean that new graduates struggle to find vacant posts at home.

Virtually all OECD countries exercise some form of control over medical school intakes, often by limiting the number of available training places, for example in the form of a *numerus clausus*. Such control is motivated by different factors including: 1) confining medical entry to the most able applicants; 2) the desire to control the total number of doctors for cost-containment reasons (because greater supply induces greater demand); and 3) the cost of training itself (in all countries, including the United States, a significant part of medical education costs are publicly funded, so expansion of the number of medical students involves significant public expenditure).

Austria, Denmark and Ireland had the highest number of medical graduates per 100 000 population in 2011. Graduation rates were the lowest in Israel, Japan and France. The average across OECD countries was slightly more than ten new medical graduates per 100 000 population (Figure 3.5.1). Measured in proportion to the stock of physicians (i.e., a measure of the replacement rate), the number of new medical graduates in 2011 was highest in Mexico, Ireland, the Netherlands, and Denmark, and the lowest in Israel and France. The average across OECD countries was 34 medical graduates per 1 000 currently employed doctors (Figure 3.5.2). The persistently low number of medical graduates in Israel and France over the past two decades has led to a gradual ageing of the physician workforce, with these two countries having amongst the highest share of doctors above age 55 (Indicator 3.2).

In several countries (e.g., Australia, Canada, Denmark, the Netherlands and the United Kingdom), the number of medical graduates has risen strongly since 2000, reflecting past decisions to expand training capacities (Figure 3.5.3). In Australia, the number of medical graduates has increased by 2½ times between 1990 and 2010, with most of the growth occurring since 2000. In the United Kingdom, the number of medical graduates doubled between 1990 and 2011, with most of the growth also taking place in the past ten years. These increases reflect a deliberate policy in Australia and the United Kingdom to reduce their reliance on foreign-trained doctors to meet their own needs. In Canada also, following a reduction in the number of medical graduates in the 1990s, there has been a strong rise of over 50% over the past decade.

In the Netherlands, the number of medical graduates increased steadily over the past decade, following fluctuations in the 1990s. Since 1999, the Dutch Medical Manpower Planning Committee (ACMMP) makes recommendations every two to three years to the different stakeholders and the government concerning the *numerus clausus* (the quantitative limits to enrolments in medical education and training programmes). The recommendations from this Planning Committee have generally been accepted and have led to this steady growth over the past few years (ACMMP, 2010).

In the United States, the increase in the number of medical graduates over the past two decades has been more modest than in several other countries, although it has accelerated slightly in recent years (+6% between 1990 and 2000, and +14% between 2000 and 2011).

By contrast, in Japan, the number of medical graduates was slightly lower in 2011 compared with 1990, following reductions in the 1990s which were only partly offset by small increases since 2000. In Italy, there was a marked decline in the number of medical graduates in the first half of the 1990s (pursuing a trend that had begun in the mid-1980s), after which the number stabilised. The reduction in medical graduate numbers over the past two decades in Italy has led to a growing proportion of doctors aged 55 and over, as in France and Israel (Indicator 3.2). Even with an increase in the number of medical school admissions in recent years in these three countries, the number of doctors who may be leaving the profession is likely to exceed the number of new entrants in the coming years.

Definition and comparability

Medical graduates are defined as the number of students who have graduated from medical schools or similar institutions in a given year. Dental, public health and epidemiology graduates are excluded.

The data for Austria and the United Kingdom exclude foreign graduates, while other countries include them (in the Czech Republic, foreign graduates account for about 30% of all medical graduates). In Denmark, the data refer to the number of new doctors receiving an authorisation to practice.

In Luxembourg, the university does not provide medical training, so all doctors are foreign-trained, mostly in Belgium, France and Germany.

3.5.1. Medical graduates per 100 000 population, 2011 (or nearest year)

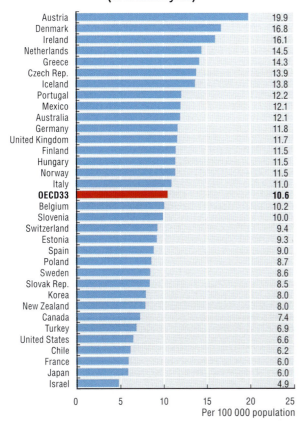

	Per 100 000 population
Austria	19.9
Denmark	16.8
Ireland	16.1
Netherlands	14.5
Greece	14.3
Czech Rep.	13.9
Iceland	13.8
Portugal	12.2
Mexico	12.1
Australia	12.1
Germany	11.8
United Kingdom	11.7
Finland	11.5
Hungary	11.5
Norway	11.5
Italy	11.0
OECD33	**10.6**
Belgium	10.2
Slovenia	10.0
Switzerland	9.4
Estonia	9.3
Spain	9.0
Poland	8.7
Sweden	8.6
Slovak Rep.	8.5
Korea	8.0
New Zealand	8.0
Canada	7.4
Turkey	6.9
United States	6.6
Chile	6.2
France	6.0
Japan	6.0
Israel	4.9

Source: OECD Health Statistics 2013, http://dx.doi.org/10.1787/health-data-en.
StatLink ⧉ http://dx.doi.org/10.1787/888932916971

3.5.2. Medical graduates per 1 000 doctors, 2011 (or nearest year)

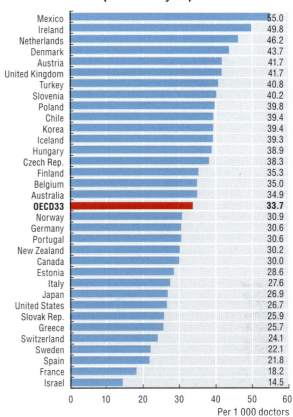

	Per 1 000 doctors
Mexico	55.0
Ireland	49.8
Netherlands	46.2
Denmark	43.7
Austria	41.7
United Kingdom	41.7
Turkey	40.8
Slovenia	40.2
Poland	39.8
Chile	39.4
Korea	39.4
Iceland	39.3
Hungary	38.9
Czech Rep.	38.3
Finland	35.3
Belgium	35.0
Australia	34.9
OECD33	**33.7**
Norway	30.9
Germany	30.6
Portugal	30.6
New Zealand	30.2
Canada	30.0
Estonia	28.6
Italy	27.6
Japan	26.9
United States	26.7
Slovak Rep.	25.9
Greece	25.7
Switzerland	24.1
Sweden	22.1
Spain	21.8
France	18.2
Israel	14.5

Source. OECD Health Statistics 2013, http://dx.doi.org/10.1/8//health-data-en.
StatLink ⧉ http://dx.doi.org/10.1787/888932916990

3.5.3. Evolution in the number of medical graduates, selected OECD countries, 2000 to 2012 (or nearest year)

Non-European countries

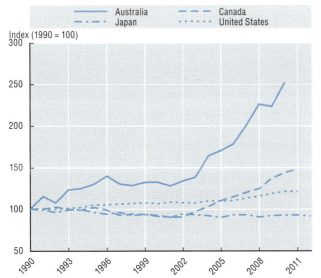

European countries

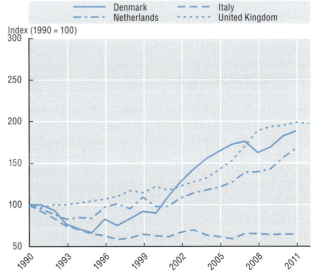

Source: OECD Health Statistics 2013, http://dx.doi.org/10.1787/health-data-en.

StatLink ⧉ http://dx.doi.org/10.1787/888932917009

3.6. Remuneration of doctors (general practitioners and specialists)

The remuneration of doctors is to a certain extent related to the overall level of economic development of a given country, but there are nevertheless significant variations in their remuneration compared with the average wage in each country. The structure of remuneration for different categories of doctors also has an impact on the relative financial attractiveness of different medical specialties. In many countries, governments influence the level and structure of physician remuneration directly as a key employer of physicians or as a purchaser of services, or through regulating their fees.

OECD data on physician remuneration distinguishes between salaried and self-employed physicians, although in some countries this distinction is increasingly blurred, as some salaried physicians are allowed to have a separate private practice and some self-employed doctors may receive part of their remuneration through salaries. A distinction is also made between general practitioners and all other medical specialists combined, though there may be wide differences in the income of different medical specialties.

As expected for highly skilled professionals, the remuneration of doctors (both generalists and specialists) is much higher than that of the average worker in all OECD countries (Figure 3.6.1). Self-employed general practitioners in Australia earned 1.7 times the average wage in 2011, whereas in Ireland, Canada and the Netherlands (2010), self-employed GPs earned three times the average wage. In the United Kingdom, self-employed GPs earned 3.4 times the average wage in 2011. The income of self-employed GPs in the United Kingdom rose strongly following the implementation of a new contract for generalists in 2004 that was designed to increase their income as well as quality of primary care (Fujisawa and Lafortune, 2008).

The income of specialists varied from 1.6 times the average wage for salaried specialists in Hungary and Poland to over five times for self-employed specialists in Belgium and the Netherlands.

In all countries except Denmark, Poland and the United Kingdom, GPs earn less than the average for medical specialists. In Canada, self-employed specialists earned 4.7 times the average wage in 2010, compared with three times for GPs. In France, self-employed specialists earned 3.6 times the average wage, compared with 2.1 times for GPs (the income of both specialists and GPs is underestimated in France – see box on "Definition and comparability"). The income gap between GPs and specialists is particularly large in Belgium, although it has narrowed slightly in recent years.

In many OECD countries, the income gap between general practitioners and specialists has widened over the past decade, reducing the financial attractiveness of general practice. The remuneration of specialists has risen faster than that of general practitioners in countries such as Canada, Finland, France and Hungary. On the other hand, in Austria and Belgium, the gap has narrowed slightly, as the income of GPs grew faster than that of specialists (Figure 3.6.2).

Definition and comparability

The remuneration of doctors refers to average *gross* annual income, including social security contributions and income taxes payable by the employee. It should normally include all extra formal payments, such as bonuses and payments for night shifts, on-call and overtime, and exclude practice expenses for self-employed doctors.

A number of data limitations contribute to an under-estimation of remuneration levels in some countries: 1) payments for overtime work, bonuses, other supplementary income or social security contributions are excluded in some countries (Austria for GPs, Ireland and New Zealand for salaried specialists, France, Italy and the Slovak Republic); 2) incomes from private practices for salaried doctors are not included in some countries (e.g. Czech Republic, Hungary, Slovenia, Spain, Iceland and Ireland); 3) informal payments, which may be common in certain countries (e.g. Greece and Hungary), are not included; 4) data relate only to public sector employees who tend to earn less than those working in the private sector in Chile, Denmark, Hungary, Norway and the Slovak Republic; 5) data relate to net income rather than gross income in France; and 6) physicians in training are included in Australia, the Czech Republic, Germany and the United Kingdom for specialists.

The data for some countries (Australia, Austria, Belgium, the Netherlands and the United Kingdom for GPs) include part-time workers, while in other countries the data refer only to doctors working full time.

In Belgium, the data for self-employed doctors include practice expenses, resulting in an over-estimation.

The income of doctors is compared to the average wage of full-time employees in all sectors in the country. The source for the average wage of workers in the economy is the OECD *Labour Force Statistics Database*.

3.6.1. Remuneration of doctors, ratio to average wage, 2011 (or nearest year)

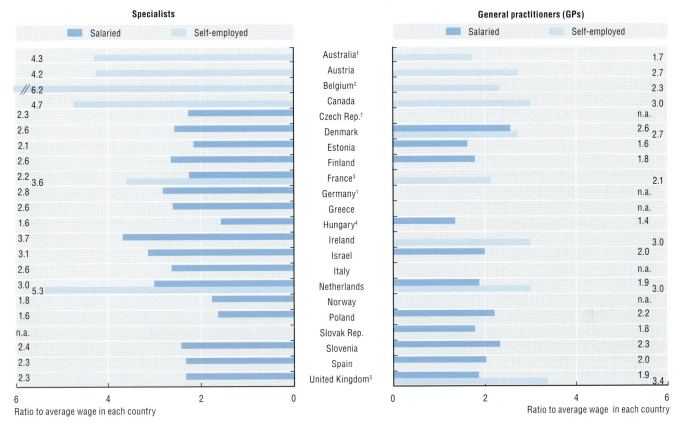

1. Physicians in training included (resulting in an underestimation).
2. Practice expenses included (resulting in an over-estimation).
3. Remuneration of self-employed physicians is net income, rather than gross income (resulting in an underestimation).
4. Public sector employees only (resulting in an underestimation).
5. Specialists in training included (resulting in an underestimation).

Source: OECD Health Statistics 2013, http://dx.doi.org/10.1787/health-data-en.

StatLink ⇒ http://dx.doi.org/10.1787/888932917028

3.6.2. Growth in the remuneration of GPs and specialists, 2005-11 (or nearest year)

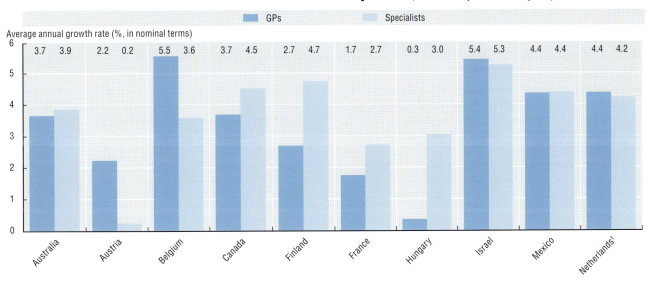

1. The growth rate for the Netherlands is for self-employed GPs and specialists.
Source: OECD Health Statistics 2013, http://dx.doi.org/10.1787/health-data-en.

StatLink ⇒ http://dx.doi.org/10.1787/888932917047

3.7. Nurses

Nurses greatly outnumber physicians in most OECD countries. Nurses play a critical role in providing health care not only in traditional settings such as hospitals and long-term care institutions but increasingly in primary care (especially in offering care to the chronically ill) and in home care settings.

However, there are concerns in many countries about shortages of nurses, and these concerns may well intensify in the future as the demand for nurses continues to increase and the ageing of the "baby-boom" generation precipitates a wave of retirements among nurses. These concerns have prompted actions in many countries to increase the training of new nurses combined with efforts to increase the retention of nurses in the profession, even as the economic crisis has squeezed health budgets.

On average across OECD countries, there were 8.8 nurses per 1 000 population in 2011 (Figure 3.7.1). The number of nurses per capita was highest in Switzerland, Denmark, Belgium and Iceland, with more than 14 nurses per 1 000 population (although the number in Belgium is over-estimated because it refers to all nurses who are licensed to practice). The number of nurses per capita in OECD countries was lowest in Turkey, Mexico and Greece. The number of nurses per capita was also low compared with the OECD average in key emerging countries, such as Indonesia, India, South Africa, Brazil and China where there were fewer than two nurses per 1 000 population in 2011, although numbers have been growing quite rapidly in some of these countries in recent years (Figure 3.7.1).

The number of nurses per capita increased in almost all OECD countries over the past decade. Portugal, Korea, Turkey and Spain saw the largest increase since 2000, although the number of nurses per capita in these four countries remains well below the OECD average. The number of nurses per capita declined between 2000 and 2011 in Israel, as the size of the population grew more rapidly than the number of nurses. It also declined in the Slovak Republic (in both absolute numbers and on a per capita basis), although the recent increase in the number of admissions and graduates from nursing education programmes may lead to an increase in the coming years.

In 2011, the nurse-to-doctor ratio ranged from 4.5 nurses per doctor in Japan to half a nurse per doctor in Greece and one nurse per doctor in Turkey (Figure 3.7.2). The number of nurses per doctor was also relatively low in Mexico, Spain, Israel and Portugal, with 1.5 nurses per doctor or less. The average across OECD countries was just below three nurses per doctor, with most countries reporting between two to four nurses per doctor.

In response to shortages of doctors and to ensure proper access to care, some countries have developed more advanced roles for nurses. Evaluations of nurse practitioners from the United States, Canada, and the United Kingdom show that advanced practice nurses can improve access to services and reduce waiting times, while delivering the same quality of care as doctors for a range of patients, including those with minor illnesses and those requiring routine follow-up. Most evaluations find a high patient satisfaction rate, while the impact on cost is either cost-reducing or cost-neutral. The implementation of new advanced practice nursing roles may require changes to legislation and regulation to remove any barrier to extensions in their scope of practice (Delamaire and Lafortune, 2010).

Definition and comparability

The number of nurses includes those employed in public and private settings providing services directly to patients ("practising") and in some cases also those working as managers, educators or researchers. Belgium reports all nurses licensed to practice (resulting in a large over-estimation).

In those countries where there are different levels of nurses, the data include both "professional nurses" who have a higher level of education and perform higher level tasks and "associate professional nurses" who have a lower level of education but are nonetheless recognised and registered as nurses. Midwives, as well as nursing aids who are not recognised as nurses, should normally be excluded. However, about half of OECD countries include midwives because they are considered as specialist nurses.

Austria reports only nurses working in hospitals, resulting in an under-estimation. Data for Germany does not include about 277 500 nurses (representing an additional 30% of nurses) who have three years of education and are providing services for the elderly.

3.7.1. Practising nurses per 1 000 population, 2011 and change between 2000 and 2011

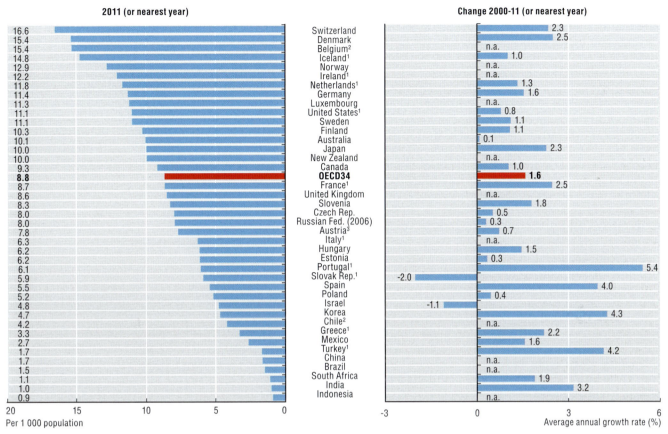

2011 (or nearest year) — Per 1 000 population

Country	2011	Change 2000-11
Switzerland	16.6	2.3
Denmark	15.4	2.5
Belgium[2]	15.4	n.a.
Iceland[1]	14.8	1.0
Norway	12.9	n.a.
Ireland[1]	12.2	n.a.
Netherlands[1]	11.8	1.3
Germany	11.4	1.6
Luxembourg	11.3	n.a.
United States[1]	11.1	0.8
Sweden	11.1	1.1
Finland	10.3	1.1
Australia	10.1	0.1
Japan	10.0	2.3
New Zealand	10.0	n.a.
Canada	9.3	1.0
OECD34	**8.8**	**1.6**
France[1]	8.7	2.5
United Kingdom	8.6	n.a.
Slovenia	8.3	1.8
Czech Rep.	8.0	0.5
Russian Fed. (2006)	8.0	0.3
Austria[3]	7.8	0.7
Italy[1]	6.3	n.a.
Hungary	6.2	1.5
Estonia	6.2	0.3
Portugal[1]	6.1	5.4
Slovak Rep.[1]	5.9	-2.0
Spain	5.5	4.0
Poland	5.2	0.4
Israel	4.8	-1.1
Korea	4.7	4.3
Chile[2]	4.2	n.a.
Greece[1]	3.3	2.2
Mexico	2.7	1.6
Turkey[1]	1.7	4.2
China	1.7	n.a.
Brazil	1.5	n.a.
South Africa	1.1	1.9
India	1.0	3.2
Indonesia	0.9	n.a.

Change 2000-11 (or nearest year) — Average annual growth rate (%)

1. Data include not only nurses providing direct care to patients, but also those working in the health sector as managers, educators, researchers, etc.
2. Data refer to all nurses who are licensed to practice.
3. Austria reports only nurses employed in hospital.
Source: OECD Health Statistics 2013, *http://dx.doi.org/10.1787/health-data-en.*

StatLink ᵐˢᵖ *http://dx.doi.org/10.1787/888932917066*

3.7.2. Ratio of nurses to physicians, 2011 (or nearest year)

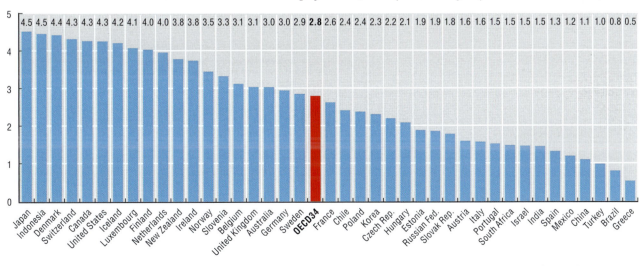

Japan	Indonesia	Denmark	Switzerland	Canada	United States	Iceland	Luxembourg	Finland	Netherlands	New Zealand	Ireland	Norway	Slovenia	Belgium	United Kingdom	Australia	Germany	Sweden	**OECD34**	France	Chile	Poland	Korea	Czech Rep.	Hungary	Estonia	Russian Fed.	Slovak Rep.	Austria	Italy	Portugal	South Africa	Israel	India	Spain	Mexico	China	Turkey	Brazil	Greece
4.5	4.5	4.4	4.3	4.3	4.3	4.2	4.1	4.0	4.0	3.8	3.8	3.5	3.3	3.1	3.1	3.0	3.0	2.9	**2.8**	2.6	2.4	2.4	2.3	2.2	2.1	1.9	1.9	1.8	1.6	1.6	1.5	1.5	1.5	1.5	1.3	1.2	1.1	1.0	0.8	0.5

Note: For those countries which have not provided data for practising nurses and/or practising physicians, the numbers relate to the same concept ("professionally active" or "licensed to practice") for both nurses and physicians, for the sake of consistency.
Source: OECD Health Statistics 2013, *http://dx.doi.org/10.1787/health-data-en.*

StatLink ᵐˢᵖ *http://dx.doi.org/10.1787/888932917085*

3.8. Nursing graduates

Many OECD countries have taken steps in recent years to expand the number of students in nursing education programmes in response to concerns about current or anticipated shortages of nurses. Increasing investment in nursing education is particularly important as the nursing workforce is ageing in many countries and the baby-boom generation of nurses approaches retirement.

In 2011, there were 43 newly graduated nurses per 100 000 population on average across OECD countries (Figure 3.8.1). The number was highest in Korea, Slovenia, Denmark and Switzerland, and lowest in Mexico, Israel, the Czech Republic, Turkey, Italy and Luxembourg, with less than half the OECD average. Nurse graduation rates have traditionally been low in Mexico, Turkey and Israel, three countries which report a relatively low number of nurses per capita (see Indicator 3.7). In Luxembourg, nurse graduation rates are also low, but many nurses are foreign-trained.

The institutional arrangements for nursing education differ across OECD countries. In some countries, the number of students admitted in nursing programmes is not limited. This is the case in Belgium, Chile, the Czech Republic, the Netherlands, New Zealand and the United States, although in this latter case state decisions on public funding for nursing education have a direct impact on the capacity of nursing schools to admit students. In most countries, however, entry into nursing programmes is regulated (OECD, 2008a).

The expansion of nursing education in some countries is also visible in the number of graduates per 1 000 currently employed nurses (Figure 3.8.2). There were 54 nursing graduates per 1 000 employed nurses on average in OECD countries in 2011. The number of new graduates per practising nurse was by far the highest in Korea, with more than 200 nursing graduates per 1 000 currently employed nurses in 2011. This should help to rapidly increase the supply of nurses in Korea, and move it closer to the OECD average. In Luxembourg, the Czech Republic, Israel and Germany, there were fewer than 25 nursing graduates per 1 000 employed nurses.

The number of nursing graduates has increased in many OECD countries over the last decade (Figure 3.8.3). This has been the case in Italy, where concerns about shortages of nurses have led to a large increase in university-level nursing education programmes starting around 2000, with the number of newly graduated nurses more than tripling between 2000 and 2007. This contrasts with a zero growth in the number of medical graduates during the last decade in Italy, following a sharp decline in the 1990s (Indicator 3.5). In Portugal also, there has been a strong growth in the number of nursing graduates between 2003 and 2007, but the number has stabilised since then. In France, the number of nursing graduates increased at a fairly steady pace between 2000 and 2011, with the number rising by two-thirds during this period. In Switzerland, the number increased by 50% between 2000 and 2011.

Definition and comparability

Nursing graduates refer to the number of students who have obtained a recognised qualification required to become a licensed or registered nurse. They include graduates from both higher level and lower level nursing programmes. They exclude graduates from Masters or PhD degrees in nursing to avoid double-counting nurses acquiring further qualifications.

The numbers reported by Sweden do not include graduates from lower level nursing programmes, nor are graduates from three-year education programmes focusing on elderly care included in Germany, resulting in an under-estimation in graduation rates per capita. However, the calculation of graduation rates per practising nurses includes the same categories of nurses in the numerator and the denominator to avoid any under-estimation.

The United Kingdom data are estimates based on the number of nurses newly registered with the Nursing and Midwifery Council. In Denmark, the data refer to the number of new nurses receiving an authorisation to practice.

3.8.1. Nursing graduates per 100 000 population, 2011 (or nearest year)

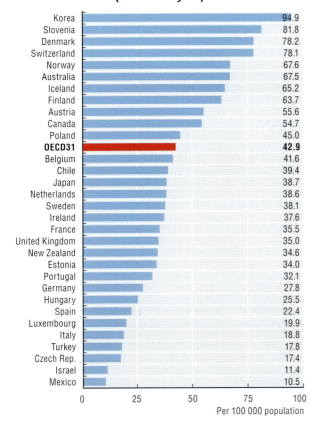

	Per 100 000 population
Korea	94.9
Slovenia	81.8
Denmark	78.2
Switzerland	78.1
Norway	67.6
Australia	67.5
Iceland	65.2
Finland	63.7
Austria	55.6
Canada	54.7
Poland	45.0
OECD31	42.9
Belgium	41.6
Chile	39.4
Japan	38.7
Netherlands	38.6
Sweden	38.1
Ireland	37.6
France	35.5
United Kingdom	35.0
New Zealand	34.6
Estonia	34.0
Portugal	32.1
Germany	27.8
Hungary	25.5
Spain	22.4
Luxembourg	19.9
Italy	18.8
Turkey	17.8
Czech Rep.	17.4
Israel	11.4
Mexico	10.5

Source: OECD Health Statistics 2013, http://dx.doi.org/10.1787/health-data-en.
StatLink ᵐˢᵖ http://dx.doi.org/10.1787/888932917104

3.8.2. Nursing graduates per 1 000 nurses, 2011 (or nearest year)

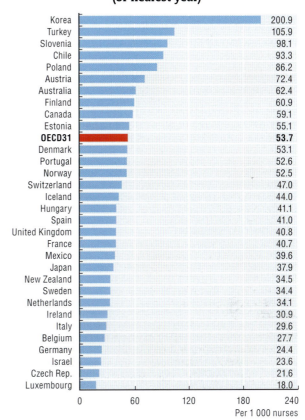

	Per 1 000 nurses
Korea	200.9
Turkey	105.9
Slovenia	98.1
Chile	93.3
Poland	86.2
Austria	72.4
Australia	62.4
Finland	60.9
Canada	59.1
Estonia	55.1
OECD31	53.7
Denmark	53.1
Portugal	52.6
Norway	52.5
Switzerland	47.0
Iceland	44.0
Hungary	41.1
Spain	41.0
United Kingdom	40.8
France	40.7
Mexico	39.6
Japan	37.9
New Zealand	34.5
Sweden	34.4
Netherlands	34.1
Ireland	30.9
Italy	29.6
Belgium	27.7
Germany	24.4
Israel	23.6
Czech Rep.	21.6
Luxembourg	18.0

Source: OECD Health Statistics 2013, http://dx.doi.org/10.1787/health-data-en.
StatLink ᵐˢᵖ http://dx.doi.org/10.1787/888932917123

3.8.3. Evolution in the number of nursing graduates, selected OECD countries, 2000 to 2011 (or nearest year)

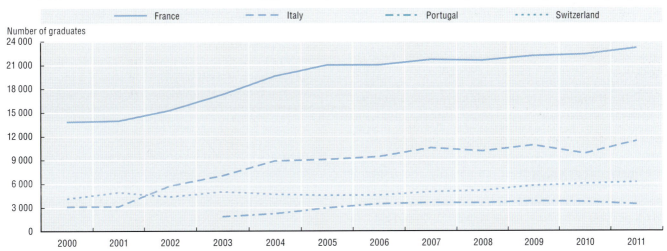

Source: OECD Health Statistics 2013, http://dx.doi.org/10.1787/health-data-en.

StatLink ᵐˢᵖ http://dx.doi.org/10.1787/888932917142

3.9. Remuneration of nurses

The remuneration level of nurses is one of the factors affecting job satisfaction and the attractiveness of the profession. It also has a direct impact on costs, as wages represent one of the main spending items in health systems.

The data presented in this section generally focus on the remuneration of nurses working in hospitals, although the data coverage differs for some countries (see the box below on "Definition and comparability").

The data are presented in two ways. First, it is compared with the average wage of all workers in each country, providing some indication of the relative financial attractiveness of nursing compared to other occupations. Second, the remuneration level in each country is converted into a common currency, the US dollar, and adjusted for purchasing power parity, to provide an indication of the relative economic well-being of nurses compared with their counterparts in other countries.

In most countries, the remuneration of hospital nurses was at least slightly above the average wage of all workers in 2011. In Luxembourg and Israel, the income of nurses was 40% greater than the average wage. In the United States, it was 30% greater than the average wage while in Greece, Spain, Australia and Germany it was 20% higher. However, in other countries, the salary of hospital nurses is roughly equal to the average wage in the economy. In the Slovak Republic and Hungary, it is 20% lower.

When converted to a common currency, the remuneration of nurses was more than four times higher in Luxembourg than in Hungary, the Slovak Republic and Estonia. Nurses in the United States also had relatively high earnings compared with their counterparts in other countries. This partly explains the ability of the United States to attract many nurses from other countries (Aiken and Cheung, 2008).

Prior to the economic crisis, concerns about the competitiveness of nurses' pay, pay equity, and shortages or uneven geographic distribution of nurses motivated pay interventions in some countries. Between 2005 and 2008, a number of countries including the Slovak Republic, the Czech Republic, Hungary, Italy and Iceland implemented pay increases for certain categories of nurses. These pay increases led to increased numbers of applicants in nursing education in some of these countries (Buchan and Black, 2011). Following the economic crisis, some European countries have cut down, at least temporarily, the wages of nurses in response to acute budgetary pressures. In Greece, the annual remuneration of nurses was reduced on average by 6% per year in nominal terms between 2009 and 2011. In

Iceland, the remuneration of nurses was also reduced in 2009 and 2010 (Friðfinnsdóttir and Jónsson, 2010), before returning to their 2008 level in 2011.

Definition and comparability

The remuneration of nurses refers to average *gross* annual income, including social security contributions and income taxes payable by the employee. It should normally include all extra formal payments, such as bonuses and payments for night shifts and overtime. In most countries, the data relate specifically to nurses working in hospitals, although in Canada the data also cover nurses working in other settings. In some federal states, such as Australia, Canada and the United States, the level and structure of nurse remuneration is determined at the subnational level, which may contribute to variations across jurisdictions.

Data refer only to registered ("professional") nurses in Australia, Canada and the United States, resulting in an overestimation compared to other countries where lower-level nurses ("associate professional") are also included.

Data for New Zealand relate to nurses employed by publically funded district health boards.

The data relate to nurses working full time, with the exception of Belgium where part-time nurses are also included (resulting in an under-estimation). The data for some countries do not include additional income such as overtime payments and bonuses (e.g., Italy and Slovenia). Informal payments, which in some countries represent a significant part of total income, are not reported.

The income of nurses is compared to the average wage of full-time employees in all sectors in the country. The source for the average wage of workers in the economy is the *OECD Labour Force Statistics Database*.

In Figure 3.9.3, the growth rate in remuneration levels of nurses covers only the two-year period from 2008 to 2010 in some countries, either because more recent data were not available (Australia, Belgium, Canada, Netherlands) or because there was a break in the time series due to changing sources and methods (Ireland).

3.9.1. Remuneration of hospital nurses, ratio to average wage, 2011 (or nearest year)

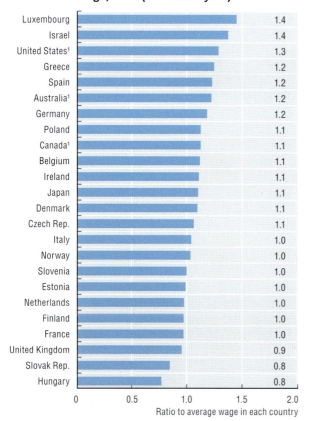

Country	Ratio
Luxembourg	1.4
Israel	1.4
United States[1]	1.3
Greece	1.2
Spain	1.2
Australia[1]	1.2
Germany	1.2
Poland	1.1
Canada[1]	1.1
Belgium	1.1
Ireland	1.1
Japan	1.1
Denmark	1.1
Czech Rep.	1.1
Italy	1.0
Norway	1.0
Slovenia	1.0
Estonia	1.0
Netherlands	1.0
Finland	1.0
France	1.0
United Kingdom	0.9
Slovak Rep.	0.8
Hungary	0.8

Ratio to average wage in each country

1. Data refer to registered ("professional") nurses in the United States, Australia and Canada (resulting in an over-estimation).
Source: OECD Health Statistics 2013, http://dx.doi.org/10.1787/health-data-en.
StatLink ᗤᔐᔝᒪ http://dx.doi.org/10.1787/888932917161

3.9.2. Remuneration of hospital nurses, USD PPP, 2011 (or nearest year)

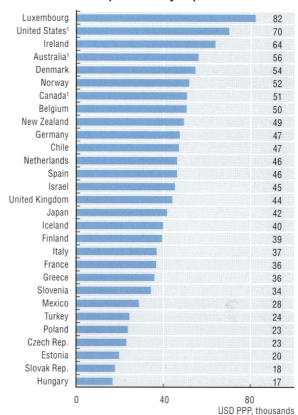

Country	USD PPP, thousands
Luxembourg	82
United States[1]	70
Ireland	64
Australia[1]	56
Denmark	54
Norway	52
Canada[1]	51
Belgium	50
New Zealand	49
Germany	47
Chile	47
Netherlands	46
Spain	46
Israel	45
United Kingdom	44
Japan	42
Iceland	40
Finland	39
Italy	37
France	36
Greece	36
Slovenia	34
Mexico	28
Turkey	24
Poland	23
Czech Rep.	23
Estonia	20
Slovak Rep.	18
Hungary	17

1. Data refer to registered ("professional") nurses in the United States, Australia and Canada (resulting in an over-estimation).
Source: OECD Health Statistics 2013, http://dx.doi.org/10.1787/health-data-en.
StatLink ᗤᔐᔝᒪ http://dx.doi.org/10.1787/888932917180

3.9.3. Growth in the remuneration of hospital nurses, 2005-11 (or nearest year)

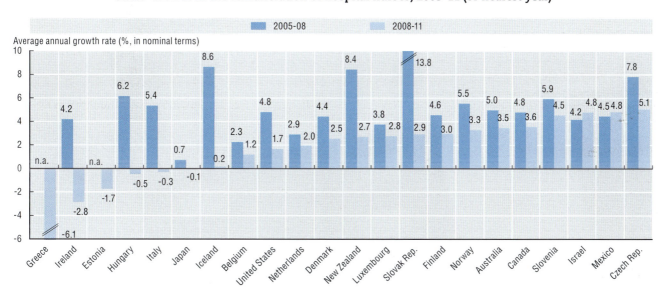

Source: OECD Health Statistics 2013, http://dx.doi.org/10.1787/health-data-en.

StatLink ᗤᔐᔝᒪ http://dx.doi.org/10.1787/888932917199

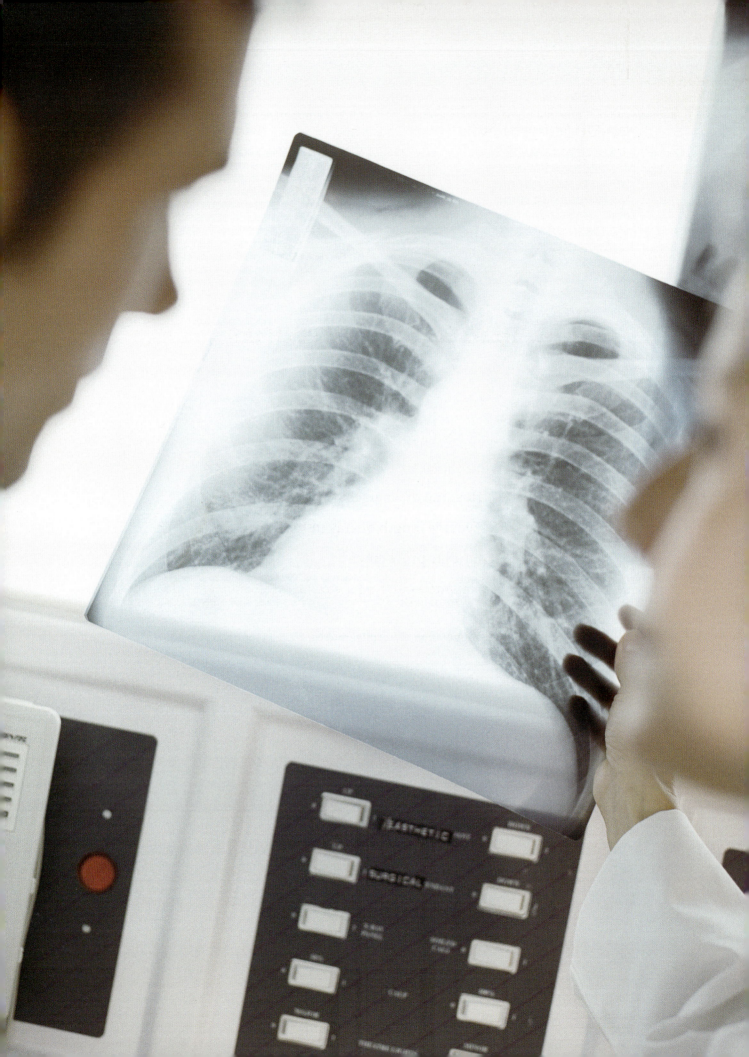

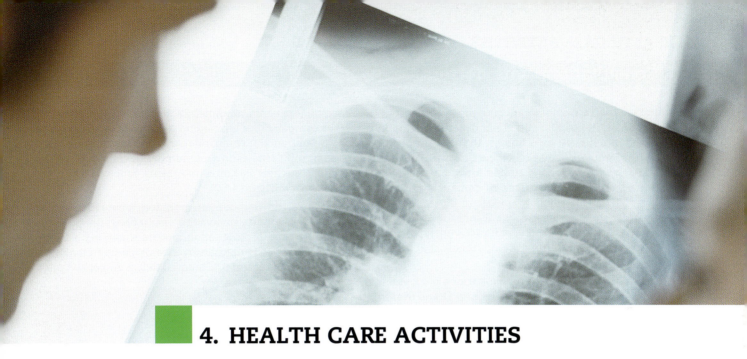

4. HEALTH CARE ACTIVITIES

The statistical data for Israel are supplied by and under the responsibility of the relevant Israeli authorities. The use of such data by the OECD is without prejudice to the status of the Golan Heights, East Jerusalem and Israeli settlements in the West Bank under the terms of international law.

4.1. Consultations with doctors

Consultations with doctors can take place in doctors' offices or clinics, in hospital outpatient departments or, in some cases, in patients' own homes. In many European countries (e.g. Denmark, Italy, Netherlands, Norway, Portugal, the Slovak Republic, Spain and United Kingdom), patients are required or given incentives to consult a general practitioner (GP) about any new episode of illness. The GP may then refer them to a specialist, if indicated. In other countries (e.g. Austria, Czech Republic, Iceland, Japan and Korea), in practice patients may approach specialists directly.

In 2011, the number of doctor consultations per person ranged from over 13 in Korea and Japan, and 11 and over in Hungary, the Czech Republic and the Slovak Republic, to three or fewer in Mexico, Sweden, as well as in South Africa and Brazil (Figure 4.1.1). The OECD average was between six and seven consultations per person per year. Cultural factors play a role in explaining some of the variations across countries, but certain characteristics of health systems also play a role. Countries which pay their doctors mainly by fee-for-service tend to have above-average consultation rates (e.g. Japan and Korea), while countries with mostly salaried doctors tend to have below-average rates (e.g. Mexico and Sweden). However, there are examples of countries, such as Switzerland and the United States, where doctors are paid mainly by fee-for-service and where consultation rates are below average, suggesting that other factors also play a role.

In Sweden, the low number of doctor consultations may be explained partly by the fact that nurses play an important role in primary care (Bourgueil et al., 2006). Similarly, in Finland, nurses and other health professionals play an important role in providing primary care to patients in health centres, lessening the need for consultations with doctors (Delamaire and Lafortune, 2010).

The average number of doctor consultations per person has increased in many OECD countries since 2000. There was a particularly strong rise in Korea, which can be at least partly explained by the rapid increase in the number of physicians during that period (see Indicator 3.1 "Medical doctors"). In some other countries, the number of consultations with doctors fell during that period. This was notably the case in the Slovak Republic, where the number of doctor consultations fell from about 13 to 11 over the past decade, coinciding with a reduction in the number of doctors per capita.

The same information can be used to estimate annual numbers of consultations per doctor in OECD countries. This should not be taken as a measure of doctors' productivity, since consultations can vary in length and effectiveness, and because it excludes the work doctors do on hospital inpatients, administration and research. There are other comparability limitations reported in the box below on "Definition and comparability". Keeping these reservations in mind, the estimated number of consultations per doctor is highest in Korea and Japan, followed by Turkey and Hungary (Figure 4.1.2).

There are significant differences among population groups within each country in doctor consultations. Chapter 6 on "Access to care" provides additional information on disparities in doctor consultations by income group in a number of countries (Indicator 6.4 "Inequalities in doctor consultations").

Definition and comparability

Consultations with doctors refer to the number of contacts with physicians (both generalists and specialists). There are variations across countries in the coverage of different types of consultations, notably in outpatient departments of hospitals.

The data come mainly from administrative sources, although in some countries (Ireland, Israel, Italy, Netherlands, New Zealand, Spain, Switzerland, and the United Kingdom) the data come from health interview surveys. Estimates from administrative sources tend to be higher than those from surveys because of problems with recall and non-response rates.

In Hungary, the figures include consultations for diagnostic exams, such as CT and MRI scans (resulting in an over-estimation). The figures for the Netherlands exclude contacts for maternal and child care. The data for Portugal exclude visits to private practitioners, while those for the United Kingdom exclude consultations with specialists outside hospital outpatient departments (resulting in an under-estimation). In Germany, the data include only the number of cases of physicians' treatment according to reimbursement regulations under the Social Health Insurance Scheme (a case only counts the first contact over a three-month period, even if the patient consults a doctor more often, leading to an under-estimation of consultations with doctors). Telephone contacts are included in some countries (e.g. Ireland, Spain and the United Kingdom). In Turkey, a majority of consultations with doctors occur in outpatient departments in hospitals.

4.1.1. Number of doctor consultations per capita, 2011 (or nearest year)

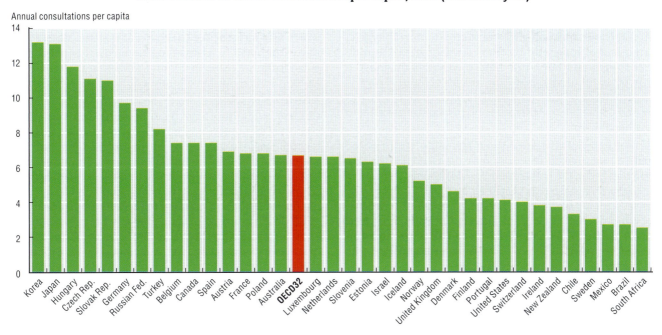

Source: OECD Health Statistics 2013, http://dx.doi.org/10.1787/health-data-en.

StatLink ᵃᵢˢᵇ http://dx.doi.org/10.1787/888932917218

4.1.2. Estimated number of consultations per doctor, 2011 (or nearest year)

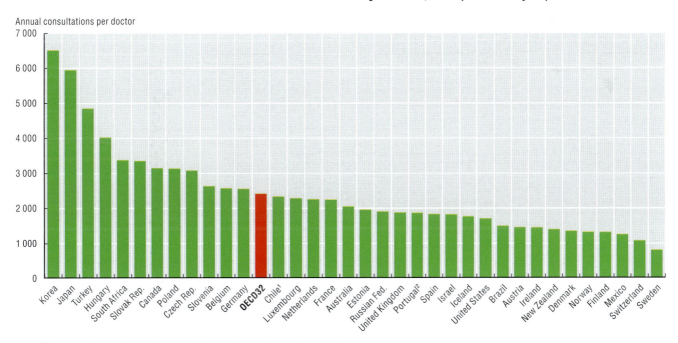

1. In Chile, data for the denominator include all doctors licensed to practice.
2. In Portugal, the number of doctors only includes those working in the public sector to be consistent with the data coverage on consultations.

Source: OECD Health Statistics 2013, http://dx.doi.org/10.1787/health-data-en.

StatLink ᵃᵢˢᵇ http://dx.doi.org/10.1787/888932917237

4.2. Medical technologies

New medical technologies are improving diagnosis and treatment, but they are also increasing health spending. This section presents data on the availability and use of two diagnostic technologies: computed tomography (CT) scanners and magnetic resonance imaging (MRI) units. CT scanners and MRI units help physicians diagnose a range of conditions by producing images of internal organs and structures of the body. Unlike conventional radiography and CT scanning, MRI exams do not expose patients to ionising radiation.

The availability of CT scanners and MRI units has increased rapidly in most OECD countries over the past two decades. Japan has, by far, the highest number of MRI and CT scanners per capita, followed by the United States for MRI units and by Australia for CT scanners (Figures 4.2.1 and 4.2.2). Greece, Iceland, Italy and Korea also had significantly more MRI and CT scanners per capita than the OECD average. The number of MRI units and CT scanners per population was the lowest in Mexico, Hungary and Israel.

There is no general guideline or benchmark regarding the ideal number of CT scanners or MRI units per population. However, if there are too few units, this may lead to access problems in terms of geographic proximity or waiting times. If there are too many, this may result in an overuse of these costly diagnostic procedures, with little if any benefits for patients.

Data on the use of these diagnostic scanners are available for a smaller group of countries, excluding Japan. Based on this more limited country coverage, the number of MRI exams per capita is highest in the United States and Greece, followed by Turkey and Germany (Figure 4.2.3). In the United States, the (absolute) number of MRI exams has doubled between 2000 and 2011. In Turkey, it has grown even more rapidly, doubling over a three-year period only (from 2008 to 2011). The number of CT exams is highest in Greece and the United States (Figure 4.2.4).

In Greece, most CT and MRI scanners are installed in privately-owned diagnostic centres, and only a minority are found in public hospitals. While there are no guidelines regarding the use of CT and MRI scanners in Greece (Paris et al., 2010), since late 2010, a ministerial decree has established certain criteria concerning the purchase of imaging equipment in the private sector (*Official Gazette*, No. 1918/10, December 2010). One of the main criteria is based on a minimum threshold of population density (30 000 population per CT scanner and 40 000 per MRI). These regulations do not apply to the public sector.

In the United States, evidence suggests that there is an overuse of CT and MRI examinations. Between 1997 and 2006, the number of scans in the United States increased rapidly while the occurrence of illnesses remained constant (Smith-Bindman et al., 2008). Furthermore, payment incentives allow doctors to benefit from exam referrals which also increase the likelihood of overuse. Many studies have attempted to assess tangible medical benefits of the substantial increase in CT and MRI examinations in the United States, but have found no conclusive evidence of such benefits (Baker et al., 2008).

Clinical guidelines have been developed in some OECD countries to promote a more rational use of such diagnostic technologies (OECD, 2010b). In the United Kingdom, since the creation of the Diagnostic Advisory Committee by the National Institute for Health and Clinical Excellence (NICE), a number of guidelines have been issued on the appropriate use of MRI and CT exams for different purposes (NICE, 2012). In Australia, clinicians may use Diagnostic Imaging Pathways to guide their choice of the most appropriate diagnostic examinations in the correct sequence for a wide range of clinical scenarios. The objective is to increase the number of appropriate examinations and reduce unnecessary examinations which may expose patients to risk without benefits (Government of Western Australia, 2013).

Definition and comparability

For MRI units and CT scanners, the numbers of equipment per million population are reported. MRI exams and CT exams relate to the number of exams per 1 000 population. In most countries, the data cover equipment installed both in hospitals and the ambulatory sector.

However, there is only partial coverage for some countries. CT scanners and MRI units outside hospitals are not included in some countries (Belgium, Germany and Portugal). For the United Kingdom, the data only include equipment in the public sector. For Australia and Hungary, the number of MRI units and CT scanners includes only those eligible for public reimbursement (in 1999 in Australia, 60% of total MRI units were eligible for reimbursement under Medicare, the universal public health system). Also for Australia, MRI and CT exams only include those for private patients in or out of hospitals. MRI and CT exams for Denmark and Ireland only cover public hospitals, while Korea, the Netherlands and New Zealand only include publicly financed exams.

4.2.1. MRI units, 2011 (or nearest year)

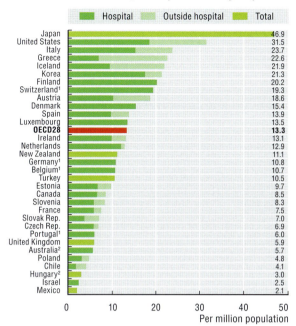

1. Equipement outside hospital not included.
2. Only equipment eligible for public reimbursement.
Source: OECD Health Statistics 2013, http://dx.doi.org/10.1787/health-data-en.
StatLink ᕫᖋᔍᓬ *http://dx.doi.org/10.1787/888932917256*

4.2.2. CT scanners, 2011 (or nearest year)

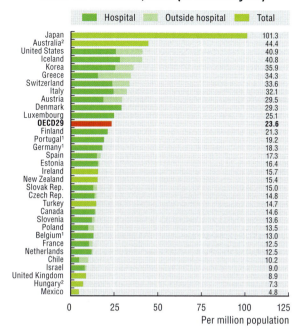

1. Equipement outside hospital not included.
2. Only equipment eligible for public reimbursement.
Source: OECD Health Statistics 2013, http://dx.doi.org/10.1787/health-data-en.
StatLink ᕫᖋᔍᓬ *http://dx.doi.org/10.1787/888932917275*

4.2.3. MRI exams, 2011 (or nearest year)

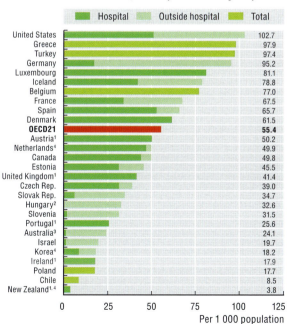

1. Exams outside hospital not included.
2. Exams in hospital not included.
3. Exams on public patients not included.
4. Exams privately-funded not included.
Source: OECD Health Statistics 2013, http://dx.doi.org/10.1787/health-data-en.
StatLink ᕫᖋᔍᓬ *http://dx.doi.org/10.1787/888932917294*

4.2.4. CT exams, 2011 (or nearest year)

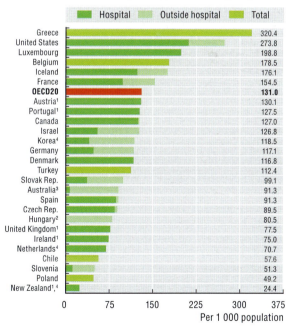

1. Exams outside hospital not included.
2. Exams in hospital not included.
3. Exams on public patients not included.
4. Exams privately-funded not included.
Source: OECD Health Statistics 2013, http://dx.doi.org/10.1787/health-data-en.
StatLink ᕫᖋᔍᓬ *http://dx.doi.org/10.1787/888932917313*

4.3. Hospital beds

The number of hospital beds provides a measure of the resources available for delivering services to inpatients in hospitals. This section presents data on the total number of hospital beds, including those allocated for curative (acute), psychiatric, long-term and other types of care. It also includes an indicator of bed occupancy rates focussing on curative care beds.

Among OECD countries, the number of hospital beds per capita is highest in Japan and Korea, with over nine beds per 1 000 population in 2011 (Figure 4.3.1). Both Japan and Korea have "social admissions", that is, a significant part of hospital beds are devoted to long-term care. The number of hospital beds is also well above the OECD average in the Russian Federation, Germany and Austria. On the other hand, large emerging countries in Asia (India and Indonesia) have relatively few hospital beds compared with the OECD average. This is also the case for OECD and emerging countries in Latin America (Mexico, Chile and Brazil).

The number of hospital beds per capita has decreased at least slightly over the past decade in most OECD countries, falling from 5.6 per 1 000 population in 2000 to 5.0 in 2011. This reduction has been driven partly by progress in medical technology which has enabled a move to day surgery and a reduced need for hospitalisation. The reduction in hospital beds has been accompanied in many countries by a reduction in hospital discharges and the average length of stay (see Indicators 4.4. "Hospital discharges" and 4.5 "Average length of stay in hospitals"). Only in Korea, Turkey and to a lesser extent in Greece has the number of hospital beds per capita grown over the past decade.

More than two-thirds of hospital beds (70%) are allocated for curative care on average across OECD countries. The rest of the beds are allocated for psychiatric care (14%), long-term care (12%) and other types of care (4%). In some countries, the share of beds allocated for psychiatric care and long-term care is much greater than the average. In Finland, 30% of hospital beds are allocated for long-term care, because local governments (municipalities) use beds in health care centres (which are defined as hospitals) for at least some of the needed institution-based long-term care. In Belgium and the Netherlands, close to 30% of hospital beds are devoted to psychiatric care (Figure 4.3.2).

In several countries, the reduction in the number of hospital beds has been accompanied by an increase in their occupancy rates. The occupancy rate of curative (acute) care beds stood at 78% on average across OECD countries in 2011, slightly above the 2000 level (Figure 4.3.3). Israel had the highest rate of hospital bed occupancy at 98%, followed by Norway and Ireland also at over 90%. This is higher than

the 85% level that is considered to be the limit of safe occupancy in countries such as the United Kingdom. These three countries with high occupancy rates have fewer curative care beds than the OECD average.

Definition and comparability

Hospital beds are defined as all beds that are regularly maintained and staffed and are immediately available for use. They include beds in general hospitals, mental health hospitals, and other specialty hospitals. Beds in residential long-term care facilities are excluded.

Curative care beds are accommodating patients where the principal intent is to do one or more of the following: manage labour (obstetric), treat non-mental illness or injury, perform surgery, diagnostic or therapeutic procedures.

Psychiatric care beds are accommodating patients with mental health problems. They include beds in psychiatric departments of general hospitals, and all beds in mental health hospitals.

Long-term care beds are accommodating patients requiring long-term care due to chronic impairments and a reduced degree of independence in activities of daily living. They include beds in long-term care departments of general hospitals, beds for long-term care in specialty hospitals, and beds for palliative care. Data on long-term care beds are not available for several countries (Australia, Germany, Greece, Mexico, New Zealand, Norway, Portugal, Switzerland and the United Kingdom) and may be included with other types of beds (e.g. with curative care beds for Australia and the United Kingdom).

The occupancy rate for curative (acute) care beds is calculated as the number of hospital bed-days related to curative care divided by the number of available curative care beds (multiplied by 365).

In the Netherlands, hospital beds include all beds that are administratively approved rather than only those immediately available for use, resulting in an overestimation (the difference between all administratively approved beds and beds available for immediate use was about 10% in 2007). This also results in an under-estimation of bed occupancy rates.

4.3.1. Hospital beds per 1 000 population, 2000 and 2011 (or nearest year)

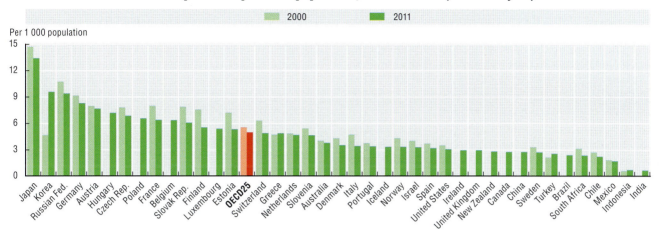

Source: OECD Health Statistics 2013, http://dx.doi.org/10.1787/health-data-en.

StatLink 🔗 http://dx.doi.org/10.1787/888932917332

4.3.2. Hospital beds by function of health care, 2011 (or nearest year)

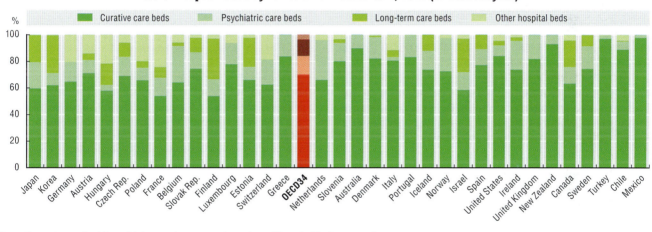

Note: Countries ranked from highest to lowest total number of hospital beds per capita.
Source: OECD Health Statistics 2013, http://dx.doi.org/10.1787/health-data-en.

StatLink 🔗 http://dx.doi.org/10.1787/888932917351

4.3.3. Occupancy rate of curative (acute) care beds, 2000 and 2011 (or nearest year)

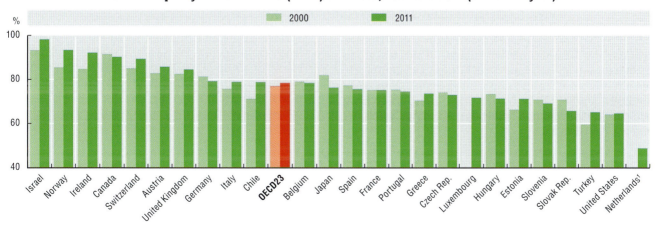

1. In the Netherlands, hospital beds include all beds administratively approved rather than those immediately available for use.
Source: OECD Health Statistics 2013, http://dx.doi.org/10.1787/health-data-en.

StatLink 🔗 http://dx.doi.org/10.1787/888932917370

4.4. Hospital discharges

Hospital discharge rates measure the number of patients who leave a hospital after receiving care. Together with the average length of stay, they are important indicators of hospital activities. Hospital activities are affected by a number of factors, including the demand for hospital services, the capacity of hospitals to treat patients, the ability of the primary care sector to prevent avoidable hospital admissions, and the availability of post-acute care settings to provide rehabilitative and long-term care services.

In 2011, hospital discharge rates were the highest in Austria and Germany, followed by the Russian Federation, Hungary and the Czech Republic (Figure 4.4.1). They were the lowest in Mexico, Brazil, South Africa and China. In general, those countries that have more hospital beds tend to have higher discharge rates. For example, the number of hospital beds per capita in Austria and Germany is more than two-times greater than in Portugal and Spain, and discharge rates are also more than two-times larger (see Indicator 4.3 "Hospital beds").

Across OECD countries, the main conditions leading to hospitalisation in 2011 were circulatory diseases (accounting for 12.3% of all discharges on average in OECD countries), pregnancy and childbirth (10.2%), injuries and other external causes (8.9%), diseases of the digestive system (8.8%), cancers (8.4%), and respiratory diseases (8.2%).

Hungary, Austria and Germany have the highest discharge rates for circulatory diseases, followed by Estonia and the Czech Republic (Figure 4.4.2). The high rates in Hungary, Estonia and the Czech Republic are associated with lots of people having heart and other circulatory diseases (see Indicator 1.3). This is not the case for Germany and Austria.

Austria, Germany and Hungary also have the highest discharge rates for cancers (Figure 4.4.3). While the mortality rate from cancer (a proxy indicator for the incidence of cancers) is the highest in Hungary, it is under the OECD average for Austria and Germany (see Indicator 1.4). In Austria, the high discharge rate is associated with a high rate of hospital readmissions for further investigation and treatment of cancer patients (European Commission, 2008a).

In about one-third of OECD countries, discharge rates have increased over the past ten years. These include countries where discharge rates were low in 2000 (e.g. Korea, Mexico and Turkey) and others where it was already above-average (e.g. Germany, Slovenia and Switzerland). In a second group of countries (e.g. Belgium, Czech Republic, Denmark, Sweden, United Kingdom and United States), they have remained stable, while in the third group (including Canada, Finland, France and Italy), discharge rates fell between 2000 and 2011.

Trends in hospital discharges reflect the interaction of several factors. Demand for hospitalisation may grow as populations age, given that older population groups account for a disproportionately high percentage of hospital discharges. For example, in Austria and Germany, over 40% of all hospital discharges in 2011 were for people aged 65 and over, more than twice their share of the population. However, population ageing alone may be a less important factor in explaining trends in hospitalisation rates than changes in medical technologies and clinical practices. The diffusion of new medical interventions often gradually extends to older population groups, as interventions become safer and more effective for people at older ages (Dormont and Huber, 2006). However, the diffusion of new medical technologies may also involve a reduction in hospitalisation if it involves a shift from procedures requiring overnight stays in hospitals to same-day procedures. In the group of countries where discharge rates have decreased over the past decade, there has been a strong rise in the number of day surgeries (see Indicator 4.9, for example, for evidence on the rise in day surgeries for cataracts).

Definition and comparability

Hospital discharge is defined as the release of a patient who has stayed at least one night in hospital. It includes deaths in hospital following inpatient care. Same-day discharges are usually excluded, with the exceptions of Chile, the Slovak Republic, Turkey and the United States which include some same-day separations.

Healthy babies born in hospitals are excluded from hospital discharge rates in several countries (e.g. Australia, Austria, Canada, Chile, Estonia, Finland, Greece, Ireland, Luxembourg, Mexico, Spain). These comprise some 3-10% of all discharges. The data for Canada also exclude unhealthy babies born in hospitals.

Data for some countries do not cover all hospitals. For instance, data for Denmark, Ireland, Mexico, New Zealand and the United Kingdom are restricted to public or publicly-funded hospitals only. Data for Portugal relate only to public hospitals on the mainland (excluding the Islands of Azores and Madeira). Data for Canada, Ireland, Luxembourg and the Netherlands include only acute care/short-stay hospitals. Data for France and Japan refer to acute care hospitalisations.

4.4.1. Hospital discharges, 2011 (or nearest year)

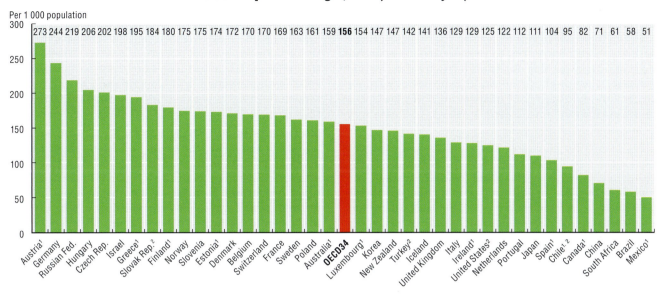

1. Excludes discharges of healthy babies born in hospital (between 3-10% of all discharges).
2. Includes same-day separations.
Source: OECD Health Statistics 2013, http://dx.doi.org/10.1787/health-data-en.

StatLink *http://dx.doi.org/10.1787/888932917389*

4.4.2. Hospital discharges for circulatory diseases, 2011 (or nearest year)

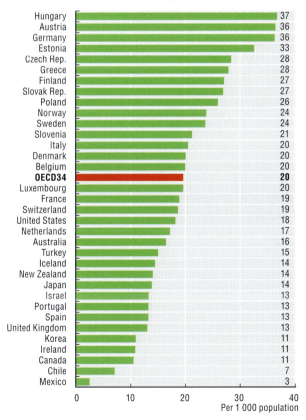

Source: OECD Health Statistics 2013, http://dx.doi.org/10.1787/health-data-en.

StatLink *http://dx.doi.org/10.1787/888932917408*

4.4.3. Hospital discharges for cancers, 2011 (or nearest year)

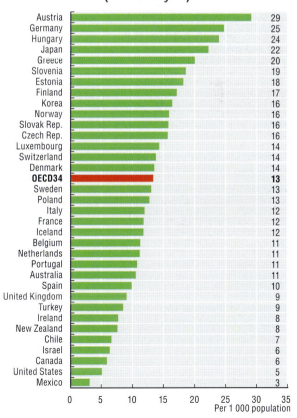

Source: OECD Health Statistics 2013, http://dx.doi.org/10.1787/health-data-en.

StatLink *http://dx.doi.org/10.1787/888932917427*

4.5. Average length of stay in hospitals

The average length of stay in hospitals (ALOS) is often used as an indicator of efficiency. All other things being equal, a shorter stay will reduce the cost per discharge and shift care from inpatient to less expensive post-acute settings. However, shorter stays tend to be more service intensive and more costly per day. Too short a length of stay could also cause adverse effects on health outcomes, or reduce the comfort and recovery of the patient. If this leads to a greater readmission rate, costs per episode of illness may fall only slightly, or even rise.

In 2011, ALOS for all causes across OECD countries was about eight days (Figure 4.5.1). Turkey and Mexico report the shortest stays, at less than half the OECD average, and Japan and Korea the longest stays, at more than double the OECD average. In most countries, ALOS for all causes has fallen over the past decade, from an average of 9.2 days in 2000 to 8.0 days in 2011. It fell particularly quickly in some of the countries that had relatively long stays in 2000 (e.g. Japan, Switzerland and the United Kingdom).

Focusing on ALOS for specific diagnostic groups can remove some of the effect of different case mix and severity. Figure 4.5.2 shows that ALOS following a normal delivery stood at three days on average in 2011, ranging from less than two days in Mexico, Turkey, the United Kingdom, Canada, New Zealand and Iceland, to over five days in Hungary and the Slovak Republic.

ALOS following acute myocardial infarction was around seven days on average in 2011. It was shortest in some of the Nordic countries (Denmark, Norway and Sweden), Turkey and the Slovak Republic, at fewer than five days. It was the highest in Korea and Germany, at more than ten days (Figure 4.5.3). Several factors can explain these cross-country differences. Differences in the clinical need of the patient may obviously play a role. However, clinical need may be subsumed by many other factors. It has been shown, for example, that physicians working in more than one hospital adapt the ALOS associated with their practice to match that of their peers (de Jong et al., 2006).

At the system level, factors such as practice guidelines or payments systems are relevant. The abundant supply of beds and the structure of hospital payments in Japan, for example, provide hospitals with incentives to keep patients longer (see Indicator 4.3 "Hospital beds"). A growing number of countries (France, Germany, Poland) have moved to prospective payment methods often based on diagnosis-related groups (DRGs) to set payments based on the estimated cost of hospital care for different patient groups in advance of service provision. These payment methods have the advantage of encouraging providers to reduce the cost of each episode of care (OECD, 2010b). In Switzerland, the move from per diem payments to diagnosis-related groups (DRG) based payments has contributed to the reduction in length of stay in those cantons that have modified their payment system (OECD and WHO, 2011). In the Netherlands, the introduction of a DRG-based system in 2006 is also credited with contributing to the marked reduction in ALOS between 2000 and 2011 (Westert and Klazinga, 2011).

Most countries are seeking to reduce ALOS whilst maintaining or improving the quality of care. A diverse set of policy options at clinical, service and system level are available to achieve these twin aims (Forde, forthcoming). Strategic reductions in hospital bed numbers alongside development of community care services can be expected to shorten ALOS, such as seen in Denmark's quality-driven reforms of the hospital sector (OECD, 2013d). Other options include promoting the uptake of less invasive surgical procedures, changes in hospital payment methods, the expansion of early discharge programmes which enable patients to return to their home to receive follow-up care, and support for hospitals to improve the co-ordination of care across diagnostic and treatment pathways (Borghans et al., 2012).

Definition and comparability

Average length of stay refers to the average number of days that patients spend in hospital. It is generally measured by dividing the total number of days stayed by all inpatients during a year by the number of admissions or discharges. Day cases are excluded.

Compared with previous editions of *Health at a Glance*, the data cover all inpatient cases (including not only curative/acute care cases) for a greater number of countries, with the exceptions of Canada, Japan and the Netherlands where the data still refer to curative/acute care only (resulting in an under-estimation).

Discharges and average length of stay of healthy babies born in hospitals are excluded in several countries (e.g. Australia, Austria, Canada, Chile, Estonia, Finland, Greece, Ireland, Luxembourg, Mexico, Spain), resulting in a slight over-estimation (e.g., the inclusion of healthy newborns would reduce the ALOS by 0.5 day in Canada).

4.5.1. Average length of stay in hospital, 2000 and 2011 (or nearest year)

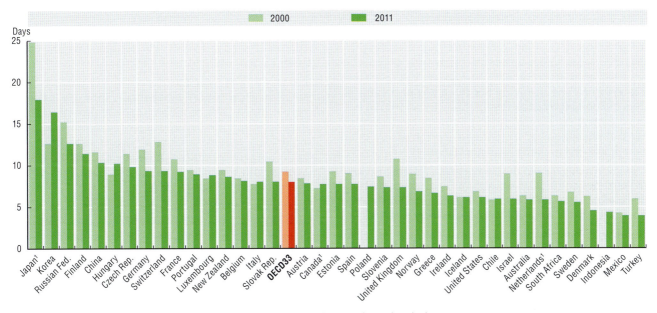

1. Data refer to average length of stay for curative (acute) care (resulting in an under-estimation).
Source: OECD Health Statistics 2013, http://dx.doi.org/10.1787/health-data-en.

StatLink ᕯᔐᐸᔊ *http://dx.doi.org/10.1787/888932917446*

4.5.2. Average length of stay for normal delivery, 2011 (or nearest year)

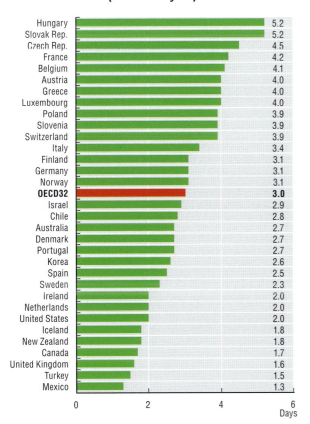

Source: OECD Health Statistics 2013, http://dx.doi.org/10.1787/health-data-en.

StatLink ᕯᔐᐸᔊ *http://dx.doi.org/10.1787/888932917465*

4.5.3. Average length of stay for acute myocardial infarction (AMI), 2011 (or nearest year)

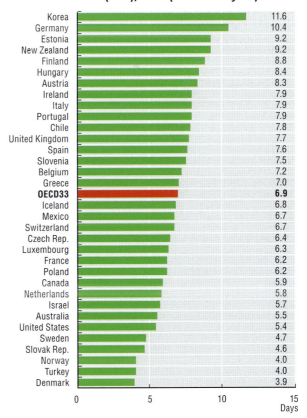

Source: OECD Health Statistics 2013, http://dx.doi.org/10.1787/health-data-en.

StatLink ᕯᔐᐸᔊ *http://dx.doi.org/10.1787/888932917484*

4.6. Cardiac procedures

Heart diseases are a leading cause of hospitalisation and death in OECD countries (see Indicator 1.3). Coronary artery bypass graft and angioplasty have revolutionised the treatment of ischemic heart diseases in the past few decades. A coronary bypass is an open-chest surgery involving the grafting of veins and/or arteries to bypass one or multiple obstructed arteries. A coronary angioplasty is a much less invasive procedure involving the threading of a catheter with a balloon attached to the tip through the arterial system to distend the coronary artery at the point of obstruction; the placement of a stent to keep the artery open accompanies the majority of angioplasties.

In 2011, Germany, Israel, the Netherlands, Austria, Norway and Belgium had the highest rates of coronary angioplasty, while the United States, Denmark, Belgium and Germany had the highest rates of coronary bypass grafts (Figure 4.6.1).

A number of reasons can explain cross-country variations in the rate of coronary bypass and angioplasty, including: 1) differences in the capacity to deliver and pay for these procedures; 2) differences in clinical treatment guidelines and practices; and 3) differences in coding and reporting practices.

However, the large variations in the number of revascularisation procedures across countries do not seem to be closely related to the incidence of ischemic heart disease (IHD), as measured by IHD mortality (see Figure 1.3.1). For example, IHD mortality in Germany is slightly *below* the OECD average, but Germany has the highest rate of revascularisation procedures.

National averages can hide important variations in utilisation rates within countries. For example, in Germany, the rate of coronary bypass surgery is eight times higher in the district with the highest utilisation rate compared with the district with the lowest rate (Nolting et al., 2012; Kumar and Schoenstein, 2013).

The use of angioplasty has increased rapidly over the past 20 years in most OECD countries, overtaking coronary bypass surgery as the preferred method of revascularisation around the mid-1990s – about the same time that the first published trials of the efficacy of coronary stenting began to appear (Moïse et al., 2003). On average across OECD countries, angioplasty now accounts for 78% of all revascularisation procedures (Figure 4.6.2), and exceeds 85% in France, Spain and Israel. In many OECD countries, the growth in angioplasty was more rapid between 2000 and 2005, compared to the 2005-11 period. In Denmark and the United States, the share of angioplasty increased quickly between 2000 and 2005, but has fallen slightly since then. Part of the explanation for this slight reduction may be due to the fact that the data reported by these two countries do not cover the growing number of angioplasties carried out as day cases (without any overnight stay in hospital). In addition, the greater use of drug-eluting stents in the United States and other countries reduces the likelihood that the same patient will need another angioplasty (Epstein et al., 2011).

Coronary angioplasty has expanded surgical treatment options to wider groups of patients. A UK study found that approximately 30% of all angioplasty procedures are a direct substitute for bypass surgery (McGuire et al., 2010). Angioplasty is however not a perfect substitute since bypass surgery is still the preferred method for treating patients with multiple-vessel obstructions, diabetes and other conditions (Taggart, 2009).

Coronary angioplasty is an expensive intervention, but it is much less costly than a coronary bypass surgery because it is less invasive. The estimated price of an angioplasty on average across 24 OECD countries was about USD 7 400 in 2010, compared with 17 400 for a coronary bypass. Hence, for patients who would otherwise have received bypass surgery, the introduction of angioplasty has not only improved outcomes but has also decreased costs. However, because of the expansion of surgical interventions, overall costs have risen.

Definition and comparability

The data for most countries cover both inpatient and day cases, with the exception of Chile, Denmark, Iceland, Norway, Portugal, Switzerland and the United States, where they only include inpatient cases (resulting in some under-estimation in the number of coronary angioplasties; this limitation in data coverage does not affect the number of coronary bypasses since nearly all patients are staying at least one night in hospital after such an operation). Some of the variations across countries may also be due to the use of different classification systems and different codes for reporting these two procedures.

In Ireland, Mexico, New Zealand and the United Kingdom, the data only include activities in publicly-funded hospitals, resulting in an under-estimation (it is estimated that approximately 15% of all hospital activity in Ireland is undertaken in private hospitals). Data for Portugal relate only to public hospitals on the mainland. Data for Spain only partially include activities in private hospitals.

4.6.1. Coronary revascularisation procedures, 2011 (or nearest year)

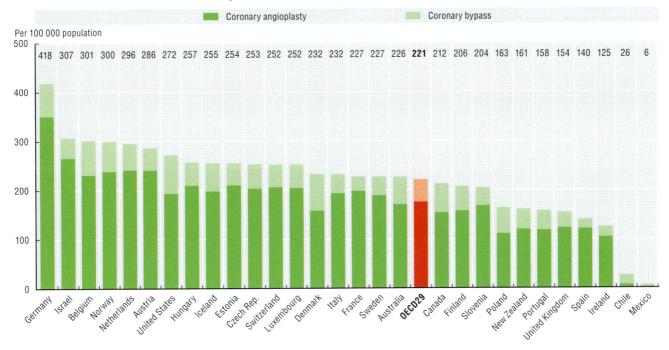

Coronary angioplasty   Coronary bypass

Note: Some of the variations across countries are due to different classification systems and recording practices.
Source: OECD Health Statistics 2013, http://dx.doi.org/10.1787/health-data-en.

StatLink http://dx.doi.org/10.1787/888932917503

4.6.2. Coronary angioplasty as a share of total revascularisation procedures, 2000 to 2011 (or nearest year)

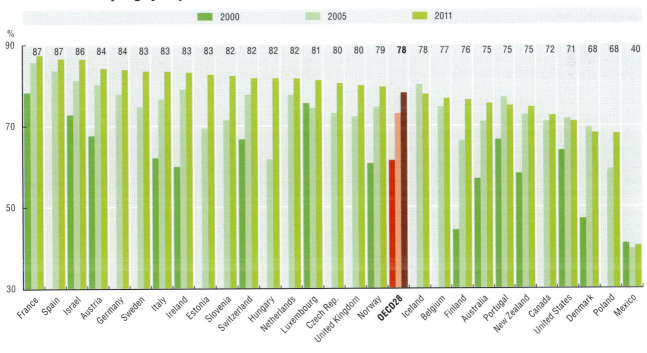

2000   2005   2011

Note: Revascularisation procedures include coronary bypass and angioplasty.
Source: OECD Health Statistics 2013, http://dx.doi.org/10.1787/health-data-en.

StatLink http://dx.doi.org/10.1787/888932917522

4.7. Hip and knee replacement

Significant advances in surgical treatment have provided effective options to reduce the pain and disability associated with certain musculoskeletal conditions. Joint replacement surgery (hip and knee replacement) is considered the most effective intervention for severe osteoarthritis, reducing pain and disability and restoring some patients to near normal function.

Osteoarthritis is one of the ten most disabling diseases in developed countries. Worldwide estimates are that 10% of men and 18% of women aged over 60 years have symptomatic osteoarthritis, including moderate and severe forms (WHO, 2010b). Age is the strongest predictor of the development and progression of osteoarthritis. It is more common in women, increasing after the age of 50 especially in the hand and knee. Other risk factors include obesity, physical inactivity, smoking, excess alcohol and injuries (European Commission, 2008b). While joint replacement surgery is mainly carried out among people aged 60 and over, it can also be performed among people of younger ages.

In 2011, Switzerland, Germany and Austria had the highest rates of hip replacement, while the United States had the highest rate of knee replacement followed by Austria, Germany and Switzerland (Figures 4.7.1 and 4.7.2). Differences in population structure may explain part of these variations across countries, and age standardisation reduces to some extent the cross-country variations. Nonetheless, large differences persist and the country ranking does not change significantly after age standardisation (McPherson et al., 2013).

National averages can mask important variations in hip and knee replacement rates within countries. In Germany, the rate of knee replacement is 3.5 times higher in the district with the highest rate compared with the district with the lowest rate (Nolting et al., 2012; Kumar and Schoenstein, 2013). In the United States, regional variations in hip and knee replacement are substantial, with the rates being four to five times higher in some regional health care markets compared with others in 2005-06 (Dartmouth Atlas, 2010). In Spain also, the age-standardised rate of hip replacement was more than four times higher in some autonomous regions than in others in 2005, and the rate of knee replacement three times higher (Allepuz et al., 2009).

The number of hip and knee replacements has increased rapidly over the past decade in most OECD countries (Figures 4.7.3 and 4.7.4). On average, the rate of hip replacement increased by almost 30% between 2000 and 2011. The growth rate was higher for knee replacement, nearly doubling over the past decade. In the United States, both hip replacement and knee replacement rates doubled since 2000. In Switzerland, the hip replacement rate increased by 27% between 2002 and 2011, while the knee replacement rate nearly doubled. The growth rate for both interventions was more modest in France.

The growing volume of hip and knee replacement is contributing to health expenditure growth as these are expensive interventions. In 2010, the estimated price of a hip replacement on average across 24 OECD countries was about USD 7 800, while the average price of a knee replacement was about USD 7 600.

Definition and comparability

Hip replacement is a surgical procedure in which the hip joint is replaced by a prosthetic implant. It is generally conducted to relieve arthritis pain or treat severe physical joint damage following hip fracture.

Knee replacement is a surgical procedure to replace the weight-bearing surfaces of the knee joint in order to relieve the pain and disability of osteoarthritis. It may also be performed for other knee diseases such as rheumatoid arthritis.

Classification systems and registration practices vary across countries, which may affect the comparability of the data. Some countries only include total hip replacement (e.g. Estonia), while most countries also include partial replacement. In Ireland, Mexico, New Zealand and the United Kingdom, the data only include activities in publicly-funded hospitals (it is estimated that approximately 15% of all hospital activity is undertaken in private hospitals). Data for Portugal relate only to public hospitals on the mainland. Data for Spain only partially include activities in private hospitals.

4.7.1. Hip replacement surgery, 2011 (or nearest year)

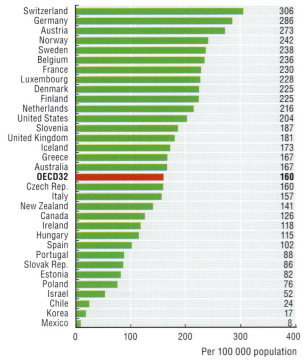

	Per 100 000 population
Switzerland	306
Germany	286
Austria	273
Norway	242
Sweden	238
Belgium	236
France	230
Luxembourg	228
Denmark	225
Finland	225
Netherlands	216
United States	204
Slovenia	187
United Kingdom	181
Iceland	173
Greece	167
Australia	167
OECD32	**160**
Czech Rep.	160
Italy	157
New Zealand	141
Canada	126
Ireland	118
Hungary	115
Spain	102
Portugal	88
Slovak Rep.	86
Estonia	82
Poland	76
Israel	52
Chile	24
Korea	17
Mexico	8

Source: OECD Health Statistics 2013, http://dx.doi.org/10.1787/health-data-en.
StatLink ⟶ http://dx.doi.org/10.1787/888932917541

4.7.2. Knee replacement surgery, 2011 (or nearest year)

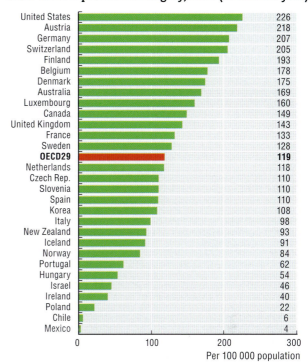

	Per 100 000 population
United States	226
Austria	218
Germany	207
Switzerland	205
Finland	193
Belgium	178
Denmark	175
Australia	169
Luxembourg	160
Canada	149
United Kingdom	143
France	133
Sweden	128
OECD29	**119**
Netherlands	118
Czech Rep.	110
Slovenia	110
Spain	110
Korea	108
Italy	98
New Zealand	93
Iceland	91
Norway	84
Portugal	62
Hungary	54
Israel	46
Ireland	40
Poland	22
Chile	6
Mexico	4

Source: OECD Health Statistics 2013, http://dx.doi.org/10.1787/health-data-en.
StatLink ⟶ http://dx.doi.org/10.1787/888932917560

4.7.3. Trend in hip replacement surgery, selected OECD countries, 2000 to 2011 (or nearest year)

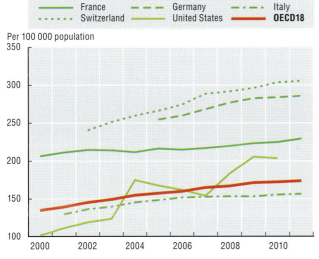

Legend: France — Germany — Italy — Switzerland — United States — OECD18

Per 100 000 population

Source: OECD Health Statistics 2013, http://dx.doi.org/10.1787/health-data-en.
StatLink ⟶ http://dx.doi.org/10.1787/888932917579

4.7.4. Trend in knee replacement surgery, selected OECD countries, 2000 to 2011 (or nearest year)

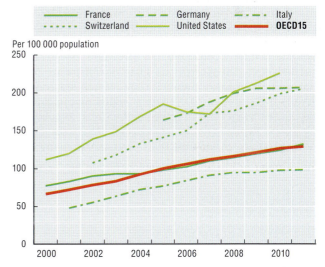

Legend: France — Germany — Italy — Switzerland — United States — OECD15

Per 100 000 population

Source: OECD Health Statistics 2013, http://dx.doi.org/10.1787/health-data-en.
StatLink ⟶ http://dx.doi.org/10.1787/888932917598

4.8. Caesarean sections

Rates of caesarean delivery as a percentage of all live births have increased in all OECD countries in recent decades, although in a few countries this trend has reversed at least slightly in the past few years. Reasons for the increase include reductions in the risk of caesarean delivery, malpractice liability concerns, scheduling convenience for both physicians and patients, and changes in the physician-patient relationship, among others. Nonetheless, caesarean delivery continues to result in increased maternal mortality, maternal and infant morbidity, and increased complications for subsequent deliveries (Minkoff and Chervenak, 2003; Bewley and Cockburn, 2002; Villar et al., 2006). These concerns, combined with the greater financial cost (the average cost associated with a caesarean section is at least two times greater than a normal delivery in many OECD countries; Koechlin et al., 2010), raise questions about the appropriateness of some caesarean delivery that may not be medically required.

In 2011, caesarean section rates were lowest in Nordic countries (Iceland, Finland, Sweden and Norway) and the Netherlands, with rates ranging from 15% to 17% of all live births (Figure 4.8.1). In the Netherlands, 16% of all births occurred at home in 2010 (a much higher proportion than in other countries, although this proportion has come down), while 11% occurred in a birth centre (a homelike setting) under care of the primary midwife (Euro-Peristat, 2013). Among OECD countries, caesarean section rates were highest in Mexico and Turkey (over 45%), followed by Chile, Italy, Portugal and Korea (with rates ranging between 35% and 38%).

Caesarean rates have increased rapidly over the past decade in most OECD countries, with the average rate across countries going up from 20% in 2000 to 27% in 2011 (Figure 4.8.2). Increases in first births among older women and the rise in multiple births resulting from assisted reproduction have contributed to the overall rise in caesarean deliveries. The growth rate since 2000 has been particularly rapid in Mexico and Turkey (which started with already high rates in 2000, thereby widening the gap with the OECD average) and in Slovenia, the Czech Republic and the Slovak Republic (which started with low rates, but are moving rapidly towards the OECD average). In many countries, however, the growth rate has slowed down since 2005.

In some countries such as Finland and Sweden (which had low rates) and Italy and Korea (which had high rates), the trend of rising rates has reversed and the rates have come down at least slightly since the mid-2000s.

There can be substantial variations in caesarean rates across regions and hospitals within the same country. In Switzerland, where caesareans now account for one-third of all births, caesarean rates were less than 20% in certain regions (cantons) while they exceeded 40% in others in 2010. Within the same region (canton), there are also important variations across hospitals. Caesarean sections were substantially higher in private clinics (41%) than in public hospitals (30.5%) (OFSP, 2013). In France, a 2008 study by the French Hospital Federation also found higher caesarean rates in private for-profit facilities than in public facilities, even though the latter are designed to deal with more complicated pregnancies (FHF, 2008).

While caesarean delivery is required in some circumstances, the benefits of caesarean versus vaginal delivery for normal uncomplicated deliveries continue to be debated. Professional associations of obstetricians and gynaecologists in countries such as Canada now encourage the promotion of normal childbirth without interventions such as caesarean sections (Society of Obstetricians and Gynaecologists of Canada et al., 2008).

Definition and comparability

The caesarean section rate is the number of caesarean deliveries performed per 100 live births.

In Mexico, the number of caesarean sections is estimated based on public hospital reports and data obtained from National Health Surveys. Estimation is required to correct for under-reporting of caesarean deliveries in private facilities. The combined number of caesarean deliveries is then divided by the total number of live births as estimated by the National Population Council.

4.8.1. Caesarean section rates, 2011 (or nearest year)

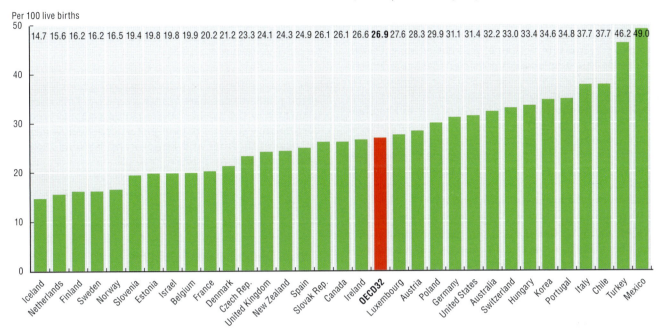

Source: OECD Health Statistics 2013, http://dx.doi.org/10.1787/health-data-en.

StatLink ⌨ http://dx.doi.org/10.1787/888932917617

4.8.2. Increasing caesarean section rates, 2000 to 2011 (or nearest year)

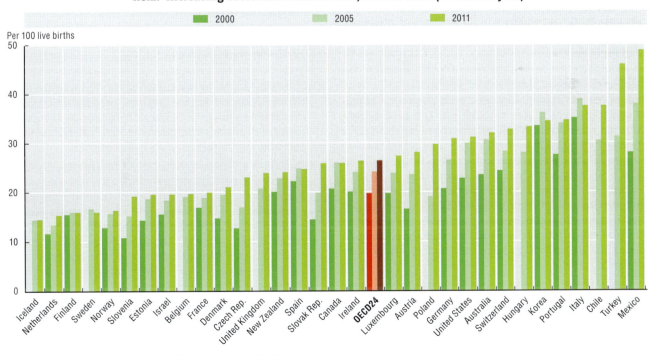

Source: OECD Health Statistics 2013, http://dx.doi.org/10.1787/health-data-en.

StatLink ⌨ http://dx.doi.org/10.1787/888932917636

4.9. Cataract surgeries

In the past few decades, the number of surgical procedures carried out on a same-day basis, without any hospitalisation, has increased markedly in OECD countries. Advances in medical technologies, particularly the diffusion of less invasive surgical interventions, and better anaesthetics have made this development possible. These innovations have also improved patient safety and health outcomes for patients, and have in many cases reduced the unit cost per intervention by shortening the length of stay in hospitals. However, the impact of the rise in same-day surgeries on health spending depends not only on changes in their unit cost, but also on the growth in the volume of procedures performed. There is also a need to take into account any additional cost related to post-acute care and community health services following the intervention.

Cataract surgery provides a good example of a high-volume surgery which is now carried out predominantly on a same-day basis in most OECD countries. From a medical point of view, a cataract surgery using modern techniques should not normally require an hospitalisation, except in some specific cases (e.g., general anesthesia or severe comorbidities) (Lundtstrom et al., 2012). Day surgery now accounts for over 90% of all cataract surgeries in a majority of countries (Figure 4.9.1). In Estonia and Canada, nearly all cataract surgeries are performed as day cases. However, the use of day surgery is still relatively low in some countries, such as Poland, the Slovak Republic and Hungary. This may be explained by more advantageous reimbursement for inpatient stays, national regulations, and obstacles to changing individual practices of surgeons and anaesthetists, and tradition (Castoro et al., 2007). These low rates may also reflect limitations in data coverage of outpatient activities in hospitals or outside hospitals.

The number of cataract surgeries performed on a same-day basis has grown very rapidly over the past decade in many countries, such as Portugal and Austria (Figures 4.9.1 and 4.9.2). Whereas fewer than 10% of cataract surgeries in Portugal were performed on a same-day basis in 2000, this proportion has increased to 92%. In Austria, the share of cataract surgeries performed as day cases increased from 1% only in 2000 to 46% in 2011. The number of cataract surgeries carried out as day cases has also risen rapidly in France, Switzerland and Luxembourg, although it remains below the OECD average, and there is room for further development.

The total number of cataract surgeries has grown substantially over the past decade, so that it has now become the most frequent surgical procedure in many OECD countries. Population ageing is one of the factors behind this rise, but the proven success, safety and cost-effectiveness of cataract surgery as a day procedure has been a more important factor (Fedorowicz et al., 2004).

In Sweden, there is evidence that cataract surgeries are now being performed on patients suffering from less severe vision problems compared to ten years ago. This raises the issue of how the needs of these patients should be prioritised relative to other patient groups (Swedish Association of Local Authorities and Regions and National Board of Health and Welfare, 2010).

Definition and comparability

Cataract surgeries consist of removing the lens of the eye because of the presence of cataracts which are partially or completely clouding the lens, and replacing it with an artificial lens. The surgery may involve in certain cases an overnight stay in hospital (inpatient cases), but in many countries it is now performed mainly as day cases (defined as a patient admitted to the hospital and discharged the same day) or outpatient cases in hospitals or outside hospitals (without any formal admission and discharge). However, the data for many countries do not include such outpatient cases in hospitals or outside hospitals, with the exception of the Czech Republic, Estonia, France, Israel, Luxembourg, Slovenia and the United Kingdom where they are included. Caution is therefore required in making cross-country comparisons of available data, given the incomplete coverage of same-day surgeries in several countries.

In Ireland, Mexico, New Zealand and the United Kingdom, the data only include cataract surgeries carried out in public or publicly-funded hospitals, excluding any procedures performed in private hospitals (in Ireland, it is estimated that approximately 15% of all hospital activity is undertaken in private hospitals). Data for Portugal relate only to public hospitals on the mainland. Data for Spain only partially include activities in private hospitals.

4.9.1. Share of cataract surgeries carried out as day cases, 2000 and 2011 (or nearest year)

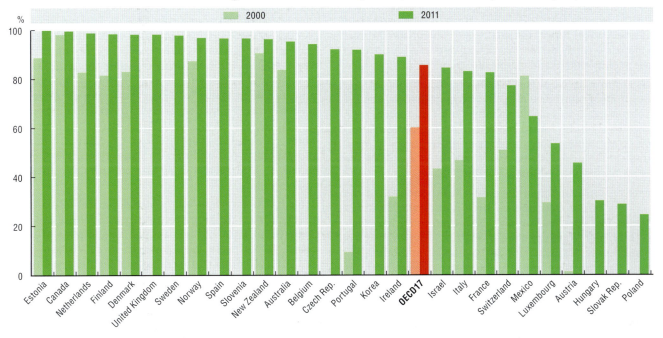

Source: OECD Health Statistics 2013, http://dx.doi.org/10.1787/health-data-en.

StatLink ᵐˢᵖ http://dx.doi.org/10.1787/888932917655

4.9.2. Trends in number of cataract surgeries, inpatient and day cases, 2000 to 2011 (or nearest year)

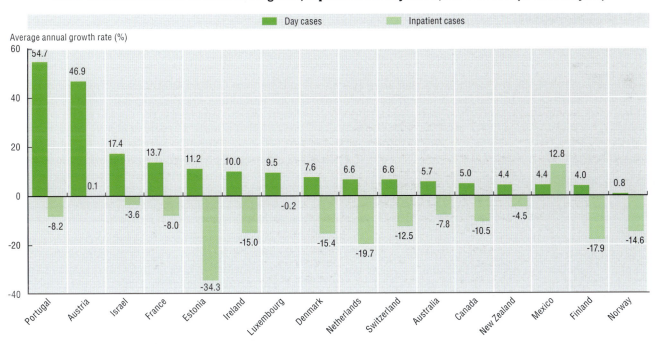

Source: OECD Health Statistics 2013, http://dx.doi.org/10.1787/health-data-en.

StatLink ᵐˢᵖ http://dx.doi.org/10.1787/888932917674

4.10. Pharmaceutical consumption

Growth in pharmaceutical spending slowed down in many OECD countries in recent years (see Indicator 7.4 "Pharmaceutical expenditure"). However, for many categories of pharmaceutical drugs, the quantities consumed continue to increase, partly driven by growing demand for drugs to treat ageing-related and chronic diseases.

This section discusses the volume of consumption of four categories of pharmaceuticals: antihypertensives, cholesterol-lowering drugs, antidiabetics and antidepressants. Indicator 5.2 in Chapter 5 presents data on the consumption of antibiotics. Consumption of these drugs is measured through the defined daily dose (DDD) unit (see the box on "Definition and comparability" below).

Hypertension is an important public health problem. It has been estimated that one in three adults worldwide is affected by hypertension, and 13% of mortality is associated with high blood pressure (WHO, 2012). Hypertension is an important risk factor for cardiovascular and other diseases. The consumption of antihypertensive medications has nearly doubled on average in OECD countries over the past decade, and it has more than tripled in Estonia and Luxembourg (Figure 4.10.1). Consumption is the highest in Germany, Hungary and the Czech Republic, and the lowest in Korea.

The use of cholesterol-lowering drugs has more than tripled across OECD countries from fewer than 30 DDDs per 1 000 people per day in 2000 to over 90 DDDs in 2011 (Figure 4.10.2). Both the epidemiological context – for instance, growing obesity – and increased screening and treatment explain the very rapid growth in the consumption of cholesterol-lowering medications. Australia, the United Kingdom and the Slovak Republic had the highest consumption per capita in 2011, with levels that were over 40% higher than the OECD average. While these cross-country differences may partly reflect differences in the prevalence of cholesterol levels in the population, differences in clinical guidelines for the control of bad cholesterol also play a role.

The use of antidiabetic medications has almost doubled on average across OECD countries between 2000 and 2011 (Figure 4.10.3). This growth can be explained by a rising prevalence of diabetes, largely linked to increases in the prevalence of obesity (Indicator 2.7), a major risk factor for the development of Type-2 diabetes. In 2011, the consumption of antidiabetics was highest in Finland, Germany and the United Kingdom, and lowest in Chile and Iceland.

The consumption of antidepressants has also increased significantly in most OECD countries since 2000 (Figure 4.10.4). Guidelines for the pharmaceutical treatment of depression vary across countries, and there is also great variation in prescribing behaviors among general practitioners and psychiatrists in each country. Iceland reported the highest level of consumption of antidepressants in 2011, followed by Australia, Canada, Denmark and Sweden. In 2008, almost 30% of women aged 65 and over had an antidepressant prescription in Iceland, compared with less than 15% in Norway (NOMESCO, 2010).

Greater intensity and duration of treatments are some of the factors explaining the general increase in antidepressant consumption across countries. In England, for example, the increase in antidepressant consumption has been associated with a longer duration of drug treatment (Moore et al., 2009). In addition, rising consumption levels can also be explained by the extension of the set of indications of some antidepressants to milder forms of depression, generalised anxiety disorders or social phobia (Hollingworth et al., 2010; Mercier et al., 2011). These extensions have raised concerns about appropriateness. Changes in the social acceptability and willingness to seek treatment during episodes of depression may also contribute to increased consumption.

Some of the increases in the use of antidepressants may also be linked to the insecurity created by the economic crisis (Gili et al., 2012). In Spain, the consumption of antidepressants per capita has increased by 23% between 2007 and 2011, although this increase was slightly lower than in the preceding four-year period (28% between 2003 and 2007). In Portugal, antidepressant consumption went up by 20% between 2007 and 2011. The consumption of antidepressants rose even more quickly in countries such as Germany (a rise of 46% between 2007 and 2011) which were less affected by the economic crisis and have experienced a more rapid economic recovery.

Definition and comparability

Defined daily dose (DDD) is the assumed average maintenance dose per day for a drug used for its main indication in adults. DDDs are assigned to each active ingredient(s) in a given therapeutic class by international expert consensus. For instance, the DDD for oral aspirin equals 3 grams, which is the assumed maintenance daily dose to treat pain in adults. DDDs do not necessarily reflect the average daily dose actually used in a given country. DDDs can be aggregated within and across therapeutic classes of the Anatomic-Therapeutic Classification (ATC). For more detail, see *www.whocc.no/atcddd*.

The volume of hypertension drugs consumption presented in Figure 4.10.1 refers to the sum of five ATC2 categories which can all be prescribed against hypertension (Antihypertensives, Diuretics, Beta-blocking agents, Calcium channel blockers and Agents acting on the Renin-Angiotensin system).

Data generally refer to outpatient consumption only, except for the Czech Republic, Estonia, Italy and Sweden where data also include hospital consumption. The data for Canada relate to two provinces only (Manitoba and Saskatchewan). The data for Spain refer to outpatient consumption for prescribed drugs covered by the National Health System (public insurance).

4.10.1. Hypertension drugs consumption, 2000 and 2011 (or nearest year)

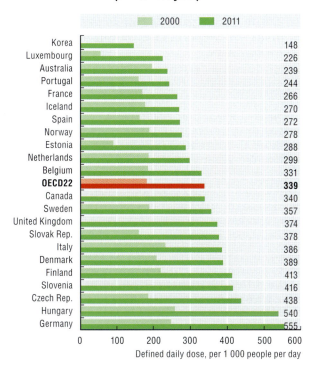

Korea	148
Luxembourg	226
Australia	239
Portugal	244
France	266
Iceland	270
Spain	272
Norway	278
Estonia	288
Netherlands	299
Belgium	331
OECD22	**339**
Canada	340
Sweden	357
United Kingdom	374
Slovak Rep.	378
Italy	386
Denmark	389
Finland	413
Slovenia	416
Czech Rep.	438
Hungary	540
Germany	555

Defined daily dose, per 1 000 people per day

Source: OECD Health Statistics 2013, http://dx.doi.org/10.1787/health-data-en.
StatLink http://dx.doi.org/10.1787/888932917693

4.10.2. Anticholesterols consumption, 2000 and 2011 (or nearest year)

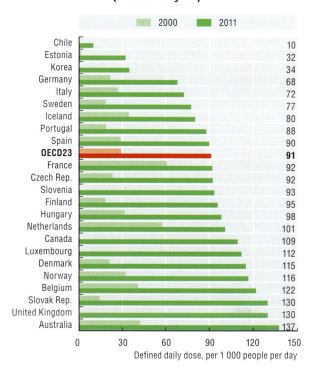

Chile	10
Estonia	32
Korea	34
Germany	68
Italy	72
Sweden	77
Iceland	80
Portugal	88
Spain	90
OECD23	**91**
France	92
Czech Rep.	92
Slovenia	93
Finland	95
Hungary	98
Netherlands	101
Canada	109
Luxembourg	112
Denmark	115
Norway	116
Belgium	122
Slovak Rep.	130
United Kingdom	130
Australia	137

Defined daily dose, per 1 000 people per day

Source: OECD Health Statistics 2013, http://dx.doi.org/10.1787/health-data-en.
StatLink http://dx.doi.org/10.1787/888932917712

4.10.3. Antidiabetics consumption, 2000 and 2011 (or nearest year)

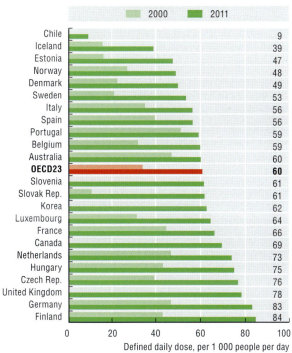

Chile	9
Iceland	39
Estonia	47
Norway	48
Denmark	49
Sweden	53
Italy	56
Spain	56
Portugal	59
Belgium	59
Australia	60
OECD23	**60**
Slovenia	61
Slovak Rep.	61
Korea	62
Luxembourg	64
France	66
Canada	69
Netherlands	73
Hungary	75
Czech Rep.	76
United Kingdom	78
Germany	83
Finland	84

Defined daily dose, per 1 000 people per day

Source: OECD Health Statistics 2013, http://dx.doi.org/10.1787/health-data-en.
StatLink http://dx.doi.org/10.1787/888932917731

4.10.4. Antidepressants consumption, 2000 and 2011 (or nearest year)

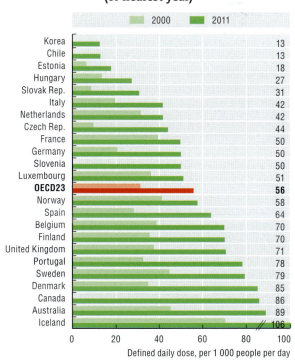

Korea	13
Chile	13
Estonia	18
Hungary	27
Slovak Rep.	31
Italy	42
Netherlands	42
Czech Rep.	44
France	50
Germany	50
Slovenia	50
Luxembourg	51
OECD23	**56**
Norway	58
Spain	64
Belgium	70
Finland	70
United Kingdom	71
Portugal	78
Sweden	79
Denmark	85
Canada	86
Australia	89
Iceland	106

Defined daily dose, per 1 000 people per day

Source: OECD Health Statistics 2013, http://dx.doi.org/10.1787/health-data-en.
StatLink http://dx.doi.org/10.1787/888932917750

4.11. Pharmaceutical generic market share

All OECD countries see the development of generic markets as a good opportunity to increase efficiency in pharmaceutical spending, by offering cheaper products than on-patent drugs for an equivalent health outcome. However, in 2011, generics accounted for about three-quarter of the volume of pharmaceuticals covered by basic health coverage in Germany, the United Kingdom, New Zealand and Denmark, while they represented less than one-quarter of the market in Luxembourg, Italy, Ireland, Switzerland, Japan and France (Figure 4.11.1).

The share of the generic market has increased significantly over the past decade in some countries that had low levels in 2000 (Figure 4.11.2). In Portugal, the generic market grew from virtually zero in 2000 to 30% in volume and 23% in value in 2011. In Spain, the generic market share reached 34% in volume and 15% in value in 2011, up from 3% in 2000. While this growth in the generic market share in Portugal and Spain preceded the 2008-09 economic recession, these efforts have been extended by policies recently implemented in these two countries to reduce their budgetary deficits.

Some of the differences in the share of the generic market across countries can be explained by market structures, notably the number of off-patent medicines or the preferences of doctors (who may be influenced by pharmaceutical representatives) for new on-patent medicines, but the generic take-up also very much depends on policies implemented by countries (OECD, 2010b; Vogler, 2012).

A majority of OECD countries allow physicians to prescribe in International Non-proprietary Names (INN), but professional behaviour is not only shaped by laws. While English doctors write 80% of their prescriptions in INN, French doctors do so for only 12% (OECD, 2010b). Similarly, pharmacists are allowed to substitute generics for brand-name drugs in a majority of OECD countries, and even mandated to do so in some countries (e.g., Denmark, Sweden). However, a mandate is not necessary for high generic penetration since countries like New Zealand and the United Kingdom have high penetration rates without mandate.

Financial incentives for physicians, pharmacists and patients have been implemented to foster the development of generic markets. For instance, in England, Primary Care Trusts were financially responsible for all health care spending for their patients and therefore had a direct interest to contain pharmaceutical costs. In France, social health insurance pays bonuses to physicians for high rates of generic prescription through a pay-for-performance scheme.

Patients have a financial interest to choose cheaper drugs when their co-payment is expressed as a percentage of the price or when fixed co-payments are lower for generics or in "reference price" systems. For example, in 2006, Switzerland increased the co-payment rate for brand-name drugs for which cheaper generics are available from 10 to 20%. In France, patients have to pay in advance for their drugs and be reimbursed later when they refuse generic substitution.

Pharmacists margins are set in relation to the price of medicines and are therefore higher (in absolute terms) for more expensive products. With such an incentive, pharmacists are penalised when they substitute a generic for a more expensive drug. Several countries have reversed or at least neutralised this incentive (e.g., France). Other countries have created positive incentives: in Switzerland for instance, pharmacists receive a fee for generic substitution. In several countries (e.g., Norway), pharmacists have the obligation to inform patients about the possibility of a cheaper alternative.

Beyond encouraging generic take-up, it is also important to promote the lowest possible price for generics if the purpose is to contain cost. Figure 4.11.1 suggests, for instance, that the differential between brand-name prices and generic prices is much higher in the United Kingdom than in Germany, since the generic share in value is much lower in the United Kingdom than in Germany while the generic share in volume is similar. One possible way to put pressure on generic prices is tendering. New Zealand introduced competitive tendering for generic drugs in 1997, which resulted in up to 84% to 96% price reductions within five years for a few products (OXERA, 2001).

Definition and comparability

A generic is defined as a pharmaceutical product which has the same qualitative and quantitative composition in active substances and the same pharmaceutical form as the reference product, and whose bioequivalence with the reference product has been demonstrated.

Generics can be classified in branded generics (generics with a specific trade name) and unbranded generics (which use the international non-proprietary name and the name of the company).

In most countries, the data cover all pharmaceutical consumption. However, in some countries, it only covers pharmaceuticals that are reimbursed by public insurance. In Chile, data refer only to sales in community pharmacies. In several countries, data only cover reimbursed pharmaceutical consumption.

4.11.1. Share of generics in the total pharmaceutical market, 2011 (or nearest year)

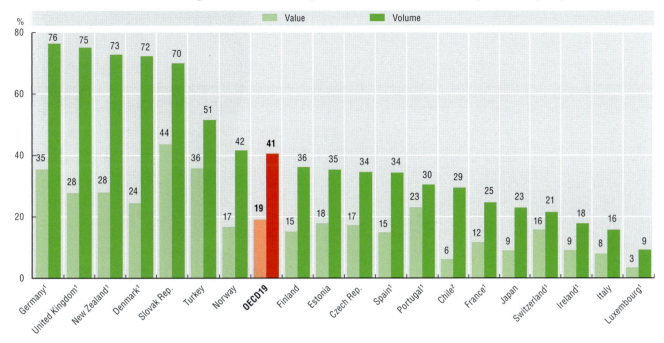

1. Reimbursed pharmaceutical market.
2. Community pharmacy market.
Source: OECD Health Statistics 2013, http://dx.doi.org/10.1787/health-data-en.

StatLink ⁊ᵯᵴᵇ http://dx.doi.org/10.1787/888932917769

4.11.2. Trend in share of generics in the pharmaceutical market, selected countries, 2000 to 2011

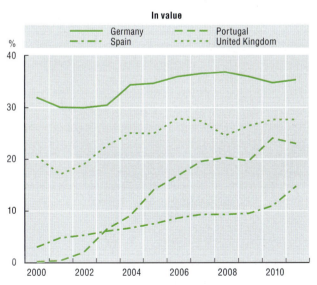

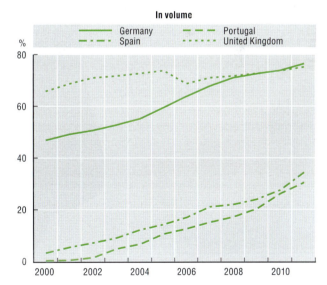

Source: OECD Health Statistics 2013, http://dx.doi.org/10.1787/health-data-en.

StatLink ⁊ᵯᵴᵇ http://dx.doi.org/10.1787/888932917788

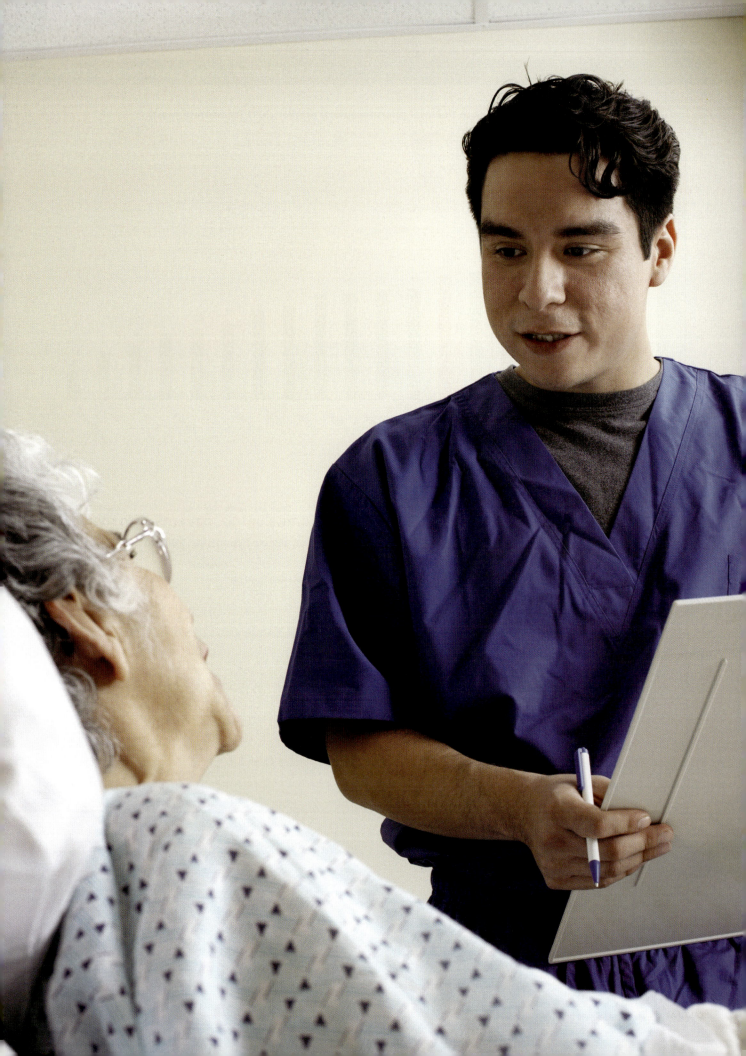

5. QUALITY OF CARE

The statistical data for Israel are supplied by and under the responsibility of the relevant Israeli authorities. The use of such data by the OECD is without prejudice to the status of the Golan Heights, East Jerusalem and Israeli settlements in the West Bank under the terms of international law.

5.1. Avoidable hospital admissions

Most health systems have developed a "primary level" of care whose functions include managing new health complaints that pose no immediate threat to life, managing long-term conditions and supporting the patient in deciding when referral to hospital-based services is necessary. A key aim is to keep people well, by providing a consistent point of care over the longer term, tailoring and co-ordinating care for those with multiple health care needs and supporting the patient in self-education and self-management (Kringos, 2010). In the context of increasing prevalence of chronic illnesses in many OECD countries (see Indicators 1.3, 1.4 and 1.10) achieving high quality primary care is a key priority in nearly every health system.

Asthma, chronic obstructive pulmonary disease (COPD) and diabetes are three widely prevalent long-term conditions. Both asthma and COPD limit the ability to breathe: asthma symptoms are usually intermittent and reversible with treatment, whilst COPD is a progressive disease that almost exclusively affects current or prior smokers. Asthma affects between 150 to 300 million people worldwide and causes some 250 000 deaths each year (WHO, 2011b). COPD affects around 64 million worldwide and currently is the fourth leading cause of death worldwide, responsible for around 3 million deaths each year (WHO, 2011c). Diabetes is a condition in which the body's ability to regulate excessive glucose levels in the blood is lost. This can lead to many complications over the longer term such as kidney failure or loss of sight; in the shorter term, loss of consciousness or coma can occur. Globally, around 180 million people are known to have diabetes (a similar number remain undiagnosed). The condition is estimated to have been responsible for 4.6 million deaths and 11% of total health expenditure in 2011 (IDF, 2011).

Common to all three conditions is the fact that the evidence base for effective treatment is well established and much of it can be delivered at a primary care level. A high-performing primary care system can, to a significant extent, avoid acute deterioration in people living with asthma, COPD or diabetes and prevent their admission to hospital. Avoiding hospital admission is not only cost-saving but often preferable to the patient as well. Many health care systems continue to struggle, however, in reducing use of the hospital sector for conditions which are largely manageable in primary care.

Figures 5.1.1 and 5.1.2 show hospital admission rates for asthma and COPD. Admission rates for the former vary 14-fold across countries. The Slovak Republic, the United States and Korea report rates two or three times greater than the OECD average; Italy, Canada and Mexico report the lowest rates. International variation in admission rates for COPD is similar, around 16-fold, with Hungary, Ireland and New Zealand reporting the highest rates and Japan, Portugal and Italy the lowest. Hospital admission rates for diabetes vary 8-fold, as shown in Figure 5.3.1. Italy, Iceland and Switzerland have the lowest rates, while Hungary, Mexico and Korea report rates at least double the OECD average.

Although disease prevalence may explain some, but not all, cross-country variation in admission rates, it is particularly noteworthy that the majority of countries report a reduction in admission rates for each of the three conditions over recent years. This may represent an improvement in access to and the quality of primary care. The approaches countries are taking to improve the quality of primary care, and the challenges faced, are described in a series of country reviews currently being undertaken by OECD. Israel's *Quality Indicators for Community Health Care* programme, for example, is one instance of how publicly reported information on the patterns and outcomes of care is used to incentivise providers to develop better services (OECD, 2012a).

Definition and comparability

The asthma and COPD indicators are defined as the number of hospital discharges of people aged 15 years and over per 100 000 population. The indicator for diabetes is based on the sum of three indicators: admissions for short-term and long-term complications and for uncontrolled diabetes without complications.

Rates were age-sex standardised to the 2010 OECD population aged 15 and over. Differences in coding practices among countries and the definition of an admission may affect the comparability of data. Differences in disease classification systems, for example between ICD-9-CM and ICD-10-AM, may also affect data comparability.

5.1.1. Asthma hospital admission in adults, 2006 and 2011 (or nearest year)

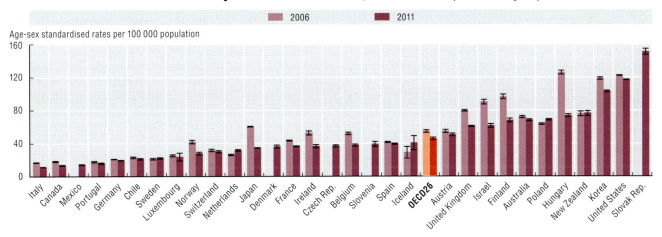

Note: 95% confidence intervals represented by |—|.
Source: OECD Health Statistics 2013, http://dx.doi.org/10.1787/health-data-en.

StatLink 🔗 http://dx.doi.org/10.1787/888932917807

5.1.2. COPD hospital admission in adults, 2006 and 2011 (or nearest year)

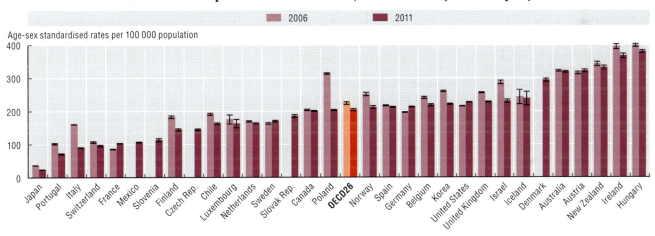

Note: 95% confidence intervals represented by |—|.
Source: OECD Health Statistics 2013, http://dx.doi.org/10.1787/health-data-en.

StatLink 🔗 http://dx.doi.org/10.1787/888932917826

5.1.3. Diabetes hospital admission in adults, 2006 and 2011 (or nearest year)

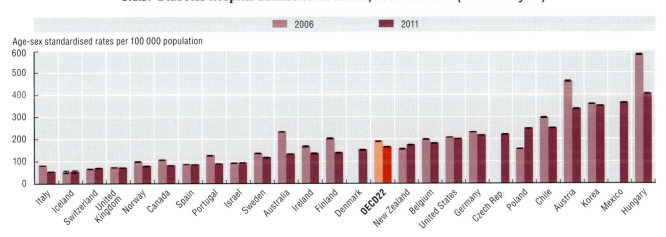

Note: 95% confidence intervals represented by |—|.
Source: OECD Health Statistics 2013, http://dx.doi.org/10.1787/health-data-en.

StatLink 🔗 http://dx.doi.org/10.1787/888932917845

5.2. Prescribing in primary care

Beyond consumption and expenditure (see Indicators 4.10 "Pharmaceutical consumption" and 7.4 "Pharmaceutical expenditure"), information on prescribing can be used as an indicator of health care quality. Two related indicators are shown: the total volume of antibiotics and, more specifically, the volume of quinolones and cephalosporins prescribed as a proportion of all antibiotics.

There is a clear correlation between the volume of antibiotics prescribed at community level and prevalence of resistant bacterial strains (Bronzwaer et al., 2002; Goosens et al., 2005). Infections caused by resistant microorganisms often fail to respond to conventional treatment, resulting in prolonged illness, greater risk of death, and higher costs. Reduced prescribing in primary care has been associated with reductions in antibiotic resistance (Butler et al., 2007). Antibiotics, therefore, should only be prescribed where there is an evidence-based need, avoiding use in mild throat infections, for example, which are nearly always viral (Cochrane Collaboration, 2013). Whilst an optimal level of prescribing is difficult to establish, variations in prescribing volume are a good indicator of health care quality in the primary care setting (Coenen et al., 2007).

Quinolones and cephalosporins are considered second-line antibiotics in most prescribing guidelines. Their use should be restricted to ensure availability of effective second-line therapy should first-line antibiotics fail. Again, although an optimal level of prescribing of these antibiotics is difficult to establish, there is widespread evidence that these antibiotics are prescribed unnecessarily where no, or a more standard, antibiotic would suffice. Their volume as a proportion of the total volume of antibiotics prescribed has also been validated as a marker of quality in the primary care setting (Adriaenssens et al., 2011).

Figure 5.2.1 shows volumes of antibiotics prescribed in primary care at national level. Volumes vary more than three-fold across countries, with Chile, Estonia and the Netherlands reporting the lowest volumes and Greece, Luxembourg and Belgium reporting volumes around 1.5 times the OECD average. Variation is likely to be explained, on the supply side, by differences in the regulation, guidelines and incentives that govern primary care prescribers and, on the demand side, by cultural differences in attitudes and expectations regarding the natural history and optimal treatment of infective illness (Akkerman et al., 2005; Koller et al., 2013).

Figure 5.2.2 shows the volume of quinolones and cephalosporins as a proportion of all antibiotics prescribed in primary care. The ten-fold variation across countries is much greater than for total antibiotic prescribing volume; Denmark, Norway and the United Kingdom report the lowest proportions, whilst Greece, Germany and the Slovak Republic report volumes approaching double that of the OECD average. There is some association in countries' ranking across these two indicators: Greece and Luxembourg report high volumes and the Nordic countries relatively low volumes, for example. Germany, Austria and Hungary, however, report low total prescribing volumes but relatively high proportions of quinolone and cephalosporin use.

Total use may well exceed the volumes reported here given that, in some countries, self-medication is prevalent (Grigoryan et al., 2006). Reducing use is a pressing, yet complex problem, likely to require multiple co-ordinated initiatives including surveillance, regulation and education of professionals and patients. Many such programmes are underway, including a European Union Joint Programme launched in 2008 (JPIAMR) and the World Health Organisation's Global Strategy for the Containment of Antimicrobial Resistance, as well as initiatives at national level, many of which have been shown to be effective (Huttner et al., 2010).

Definition and comparability

See Indicator 4.10 for a description of the defined daily dose (DDD). Data generally refer to outpatient consumption except for Chile, Canada, Greece, Korea, Israel, Iceland where data also include consumption in hospitals and other institutions beyond primary care. Data are from 2010 except for the United States (2004), Israel (2009) and the Slovak Republic (2009). Data for Chile only include drugs dispensed by private pharmacies. Data for Canada only cover Manitoba and Saskatchewan, provinces for which population level data were available, representing 6.7% of the population.

5.2.1. Overall volume of antibiotics prescribed, 2010 (or nearest year)

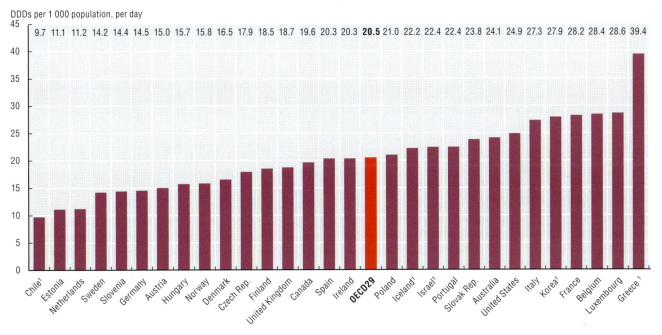

DDDs per 1 000 population, per day

1. Data refer to all sectors (not only primary care).
Source: OECD Health Statistics 2013, *http://dx.doi.org/10.1787/health-data-en, IMS for United States.*

StatLink ᴍˢᴸ *http://dx.doi.org/10.1787/888932917864*

5.2.2. Cephalosporins and quinolones as a proportion of all antibiotics prescribed, 2010 (or nearest year)

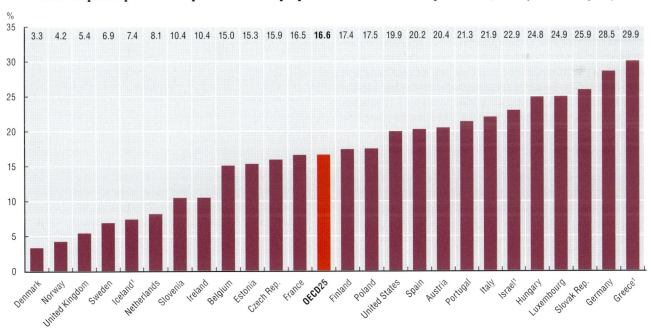

1. Data refer to all sectors (not only primary care).
Source: European Centre for Disease Prevention and Control 2013 and IMS for United States.

StatLink ᴍˢᴸ *http://dx.doi.org/10.1787/888932917883*

5.3. Mortality following acute myocardial infarction (AMI)

Mortality due to coronary heart disease has declined substantially since the 1970s (see Indicator 1.3 "Mortality from cardiovascular disease"). This reduction can, in part, be attributed to better treatments, particularly in the acute phases of myocardial infarction (AMI). Care for AMI has changed dramatically in recent decades, with the introduction of coronary care units and treatments aimed at rapidly restoring coronary blood flow (Khush et al., 2005). Clinical practice guidelines provide clinicians with information on how to optimise treatments and studies have shown that greater compliance with guidelines improve health outcomes (e.g., Schiele et al., 2005; Eagle et al., 2005). However, some AMI patients do not receive recommended care, raising concerns over the quality of care in some countries (Brekke and Gjelsvik, 2009; Kotseva et al., 2009).

A good indicator of acute care quality is the 30-day AMI case-fatality rate. This indicator measures the percentage of people who die within 30 days following admission to hospital for AMI. The measure reflects the processes of care, such as timely transport of patients and effective medical interventions. The indicator is influenced by not only the quality of care provided in hospitals but also differences in hospital transfers, average length of stay and AMI severity.

Figure 5.3.1 shows the case-fatality rates within 30 days of admission for AMI. The panel on the left reports the in-hospital case-fatality rate when the death occurs in the same hospital as the initial AMI admission. The lowest rate is found in Denmark (3%) and the highest rate is in Mexico (27%). Although Mexican case-fatality data only refer to public sector hospitals, the quality of pre-hospital emergency medical services is reportedly poor (Peralta, 2006). The high rate of uncontrolled diabetes in Mexico, Korea and Hungary may also be a contributing factor in explaining the high AMI case-fatality rates (see Indicators 1.10 "Diabetes prevalence and incidence" and 5.1 "Avoidable hospital admissions"). Patients with diabetes have worse outcomes after AMI compared to those without diabetes, particularly if the diabetes is poorly controlled (Norhammar et al., 2007; Ouhoummane et al., 2010; Yan et al., 2006). In Korea and Japan, people are less likely to die of heart disease overall, but are more likely to die once admitted into hospital for AMI compared to many other OECD countries. One possible explanation for this is that the severity of patients admitted to hospital with AMI may be more advanced among a smaller group of people across the population, but could also reflect underlying differences in emergency care, diag-

nosis, treatment patterns and even disease coding practices (OECD, 2012b).

The right-hand-side panel of Figure 5.3.1 shows 30-day AMI case-fatality rates where fatalities are recorded regardless of where they occur. This is a more robust indicator because it records deaths more widely than the same-hospital indicator, but it requires linked data which is not available in all countries. The average AMI case-fatality rate is 10.8% and ranges from 8.2% (Norway) to 18.8% (Hungary). The degree of cross-country variation is considerably less with the in- and out-of-hospital indicator compared to the same-hospital indicator. One potential reason for this is that patients may be more commonly transferred to other facilities in countries such as Denmark compared to countries such as Hungary.

Same-hospital case-fatality rates for AMI have decreased substantially over the ten year period between 2001 and 2011 (Figure 5.3.2). Across the OECD, case fatalities fell from 11.2% to 7.9%. Between 2006 and 2011, the rate of decline was particularly striking in Denmark, the Slovak Republic, Poland and Canada, where case-fatality rates fell by more than 30%. The improvements can at least be partially attributed to better and more reliable processes of care.

Definition and comparability

The admission-based case-fatality rate following AMI is defined as the number of people aged 45 and over who die within 30 days of being admitted to hospital with an AMI, where the death occurs in the same hospital as the initial AMI admission. The in- and out-of-hospital case-fatality rate is defined as the number of people who die within 30 days of being admitted to hospital with an AMI, where the death may occur in the same hospital, a different hospital, or out of hospital.

Rates were age-sex standardised to the 2010 OECD population aged 45+ admitted to hospital for AMI. The change in the population structure in this edition of *Health at a Glance* compared with previous editions (where rates were standardised using the 2005 OECD population of all ages) has led to a general increase in the standardised rates for all countries.

5.3.1. Case-fatality in adults aged 45 and over within 30 days after admission for AMI, 2011 (or nearest year)

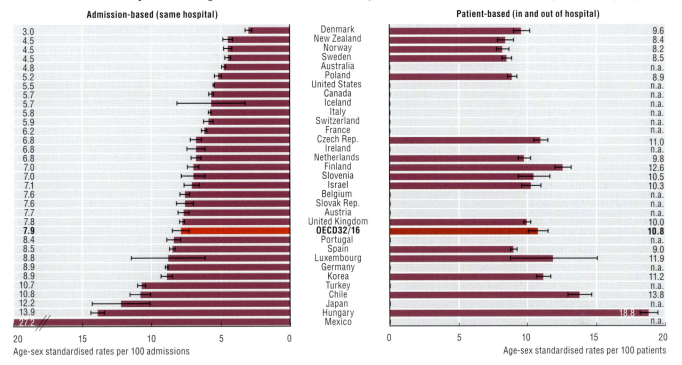

Note: 95% confidence intervals represented by |—|.
Source: OECD Health Statistics 2013, http://dx.doi.org/10.1787/health-data-en.

StatLink ᕝᕝᔍ http://dx.doi.org/10.1787/888932917902

5.3.2. Reduction in admission-based (same hospital) case-fatality in adults aged 45 and over within 30 days after admission for AMI, 2001-11 (or nearest year)

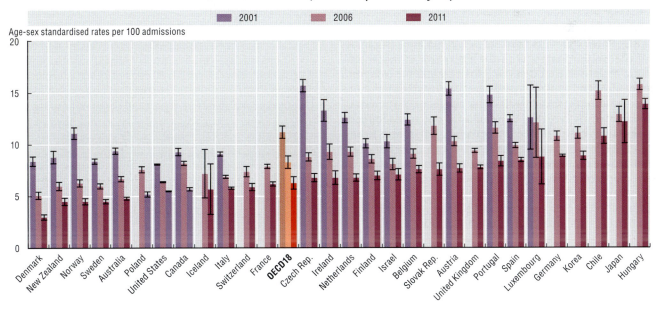

Note: 95% confidence intervals represented by |—|.
Source: OECD Health Statistics 2013, http://dx.doi.org/10.1787/health-data-en.

StatLink ᕝᕝᔍ http://dx.doi.org/10.1787/888932917921

5.4. Mortality following stroke

Stroke and other cerebrovascular diseases accounted for over 8% of all deaths in OECD countries. Ischemic stroke represents around 85% of all cerebrovascular disease cases. It occurs when the blood supply to a part of the brain is interrupted, leading to a necrosis (i.e. the cells that die) of the affected part. Treatment for ischemic stroke has advanced dramatically over the last decade. Clinical trials have demonstrated clear benefits of thrombolytic treatment for ischemic stroke as well as receiving care in dedicated stroke units to facilitate timely and aggressive diagnosis and therapy for stroke victims (Hacke et al., 1995; Seenan et al., 2007). Despite their clear clinical benefit, there is widespread variability in access to stroke units across and within countries (AIHW, 2013; Kapral et al., 2011; Indredavik, 2009).

Figure 5.4.1 shows the age-sex standardised case-fatality rates within 30 days of admission for ischemic stroke as an indicator of the quality of acute care received by patients. The left-hand-side panel reports the in-hospital case-fatality rate when the death occurs in the same hospital as the initial stroke admission. The panel on the right shows the case-fatality rate where deaths are recorded regardless of whether they occurred in or out of hospital. The indicator on the right hand side is more robust because it captures fatalities more comprehensively. Although more countries can report the more partial same-hospital measure, an increasing number of countries are investing in their data infrastructure and are able to provide more comprehensive measures.

Across OECD countries, 8.5% of patients died within 30 days in the same hospital in which the initial admission for ischemic stroke occurred. The case-fatality rates were highest in Mexico (19.6%), Slovenia (12.8%) and Turkey (11.8%). Rates were less than 5% in Japan, Korea, Denmark and the United States. With the exception of Japan and Korea, countries that achieve better results for ischemic stroke also tend to report good case-fatality rates for acute myocardial infarction (AMI). This suggests that certain aspects of acute care may be influencing outcomes for both stroke and AMI patients. By contrast, Japan and Korea report the lowest rates for ischemic stroke but high case-fatality rates for AMI. This somewhat paradoxical result requires further investigation but may be associated with the severity of disease in these two countries that is not captured in the data (see Indicator 5.3 "Mortality following acute myocardial infarction" for more details).

Across the 15 countries that reported in- and out-of-hospital case-fatality rates, 11.2% of patients died within 30 days of being admitted to hospital for stroke. This figure is higher than the same-hospital based indicator because it captures deaths that occur not just in the same hospital but also in other hospitals and out of hospital. The cross-country variation is substantially smaller for the in- and out-of-hospital measure compared to the same-hospital measure. This may be due to systematic differences between countries in the way that patients are transferred between hospitals and rehabilitative care facilities following stroke.

Between 2001 and 2011, same-hospital case-fatality rates for ischemic stroke declined by almost 25% across 19 OECD countries for which data were available over the entire period (Figure 5.4.2). However, the rate of decline was not uniform across countries. Between 2001 and 2011, improvements in case-fatality rates in Australia and Belgium, for example, were not as great as the OECD average. On the other hand, the Czech Republic, the Netherlands and Norway were able to reduce their case fatality rates in excess of 40% between 2001 and 2011. The improvements in case-fatality rates can at least be partially attributed to the degree of access to dedicated stroke units and the high quality of care provided there.

Definition and comparability

The admission-based case-fatality rates is defined as the number of people aged 45 and over who died within 30 days of being admitted to hospital for ischemic stroke, where the death occurs in the same hospital as the initial stroke admission. The in- and out-of-hospital case-fatality rate is defined as the number of people who die within 30 days of being admitted to hospital with a stroke, where the death may occur in the same hospital, a different hospital or out of hospital.

Rates were age-sex standardised to the 2010 OECD population aged 45+ admitted to hospital for stroke. The change in the population structure in this edition of *Health at a Glance* compared with previous editions (where rates were standardised using the 2005 OECD population of all ages) has led to a general increase in the standardised rates for all countries.

5.4.1. Case-fatality in adults aged 45 and over within 30 days after admission for ischemic stroke, 2011 (or nearest year)

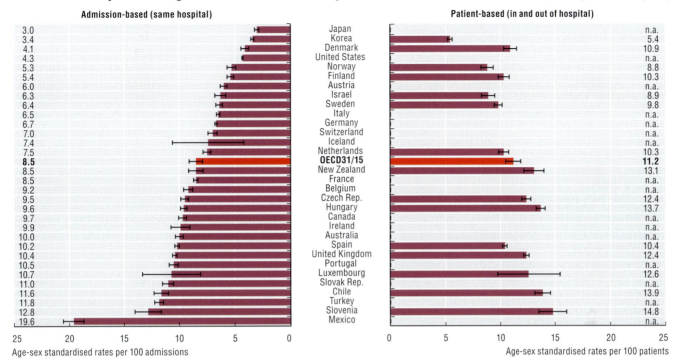

Note: 95% confidence intervals represented by |—|.
Source: OECD Health Statistics 2013, http://dx.doi.org/10.1787/health-data-en.

StatLink ⟨⟩ http://dx.doi.org/10.1787/888932917940

5.4.2. Reduction in admission-based (same hospital) case-fatality in adults aged 45 and over within 30 days after admission for ischemic stroke, 2001-11 (or nearest year)

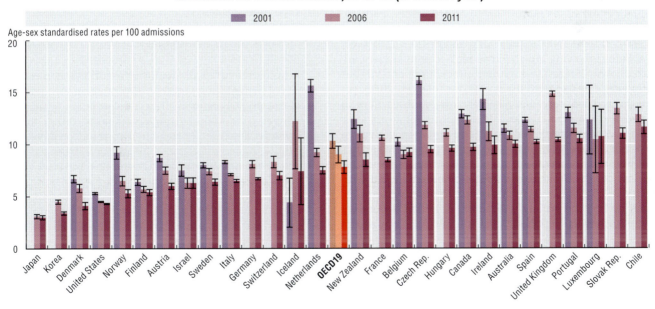

Note: 95% confidence intervals represented by |—|.
Source: OECD Health Statistics 2013, http://dx.doi.org/10.1787/health-data-en.

StatLink ⟨⟩ http://dx.doi.org/10.1787/888932917959

5.5. Surgical complications

Patient safety remains one of the most prominent issues in health policy and public debate. High rates of errors during the delivery of medical care have been demonstrated repeatedly, including the landmark report by the Institute of Medicine which estimated that more people die from medical errors than from traffic injuries or breast cancer (Kohn et al., 2000). Two types of patient safety event can be distinguished: *sentinel* events that should never occur such as failure to remove surgical foreign bodies (e.g. gauze swabs) at the end of a procedure; and *adverse* events, such as post-operative sepsis, which can never be fully avoided given the high-risk nature of some procedures, although increased incidence at an aggregate level may indicate a systemic failing.

Figures 5.5.1 and 5.5.2 show rates of two adverse events, post-operative pulmonary embolism (PE) or deep vein thrombosis (DVT) and post-operative sepsis. PE or DVT cause unnecessary pain and in some cases death, but can be prevented by anticoagulants and other measures before, during and after surgery. Likewise, sepsis after surgery, which may lead to organ failure and death, can in many cases be prevented by prophylactic antibiotics, sterile surgical techniques and good postoperative care. Figure 5.5.3 illustrates a sentinel event – rates of foreign body left in during procedure. The most common risk factors for this "never event" are emergencies, unplanned changes in procedure, patient obesity and changes in the surgical team; preventive measures include methodical wound exploration and effective communication among the surgical team (Gawande et al., 2003).

International variation in post-operative PE or DVT rates (all surgeries) varies more than 10-fold. Belgium, Portugal and Spain report the lowest rates, whilst Slovenia and Australia report rates approaching double the OECD average. Rates following hip and knee replacement surgery are also shown. These are high risk procedures and higher rates would be expected (Heit, 2012; Januel et al., 2012), yet this pattern is observed in relatively few countries. Several explanations are possible, including more careful care after hip and knee surgery. Differences in emergency/elective case mix across countries, in the mix of procedures across the public and private sectors if countries vary in the volume of hip and knee replacements undertaken in each sector, in how national databases link secondary complications back to the primary procedure, or in how secondary complications are reported to the national database, across surgical specialities within a country, are also possible explanations.

Variation in post-operative sepsis (all surgeries) is even greater, at around 20-fold. Rates following abdominal surgery, a high risk procedure (Bateman et al., 2010; Vogel et al., 2010) are higher, as expected, in almost all countries.

Variation in rates for the sentinel event is around 10-fold (Figure 5.5.3). Belgium, Denmark and Israel report the lowest rates and Switzerland, New Zealand and Australia the highest rates.

Caution is needed in interpreting the extent to which these indicators accurately reflect international differences in patient safety rather than differences in the way that countries report, code and calculate rates of adverse events (see *Definition and comparability* box). In some cases, higher adverse event rates may signal more developed patient safety monitoring systems rather than worse care. Nevertheless, these figures demonstrate how large numbers of patients suffer adverse events during medical care. International initiatives to make medical care safer, such as the European Union Joint Action on Patient Safety and Quality of Care, include efforts to improve the comparability of how countries document and report the occurrence of adverse events.

Definition and comparability

Surgical complications are defined as the number of discharges with ICD codes for the complication in any secondary diagnosis field, divided by the total number of discharges for patients aged 15 and older. The rates have been adjusted by the average number of secondary diagnoses (Drösler et al., 2011) in order to improve inter-country comparability. Despite this adjustment, results for countries that report less than 1.5 diagnoses per record may be underestimated. Rates have not been age-sex standardised, since this makes a marginal difference to countries' reported rate or ranking relative to other countries.

A fundamental challenge in international comparison of patient safety indicators centres on the quality of the underlying data. The indicators are typically derived from administrative databases, rather than systems specifically designed to monitor adverse events, hence differences in how countries record diagnoses and procedures and define hospital episodes can affect calculation of rates. Countries which rely on clinicians to report adverse events may record them less completely than countries which employ specially trained administrative staff to identify and code adverse events from patients' clinical records, for example. The extent to which national databases facilitate recording of secondary diagnoses or to which payments are determined by diagnosis or procedure lists may also influence recording.

5.5.1. Postoperative pulmonary embolism or deep vein thrombosis in adults, 2011 (or nearest year)

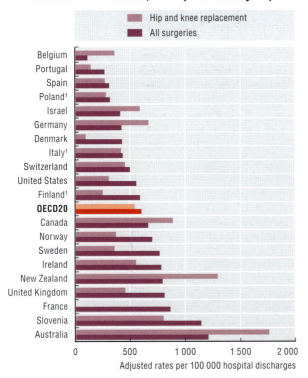

1. The average number of secondary diagnoses is < 1.5.
Source: OECD Health Statistics 2013, *http://dx.doi.org/10.1787/health-data-en.*
StatLink ⟨ms⟩ *http://dx.doi.org/10.1787/888932917978*

5.5.2. Postoperative sepsis in adults, 2011 (or nearest year)

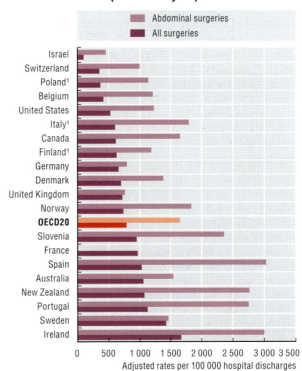

1. The average number of secondary diagnoses is < 1.5.
Source: OECD Health Statistics 2013, *http://dx.doi.org/10.1787/health-data-en.*
StatLink ⟨ms⟩ *http://dx.doi.org/10.1787/888932917997*

5.5.3. Foreign body left in during procedure in adults, 2011 (or nearest year)

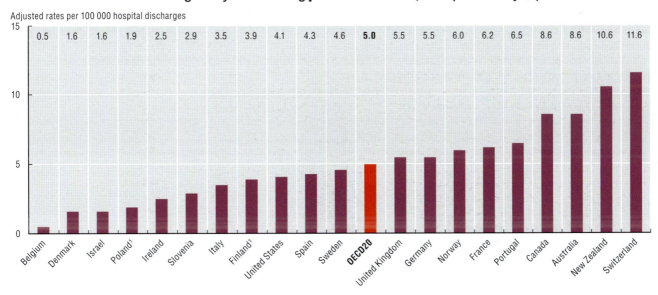

Note: Some of the variations across countries are due to different classification systems and recording practices.
1. The average number of secondary diagnoses is < 1.5.
Source: OECD Health Statistics 2013, *http://dx.doi.org/10.1787/health-data-en.*

StatLink ⟨ms⟩ *http://dx.doi.org/10.1787/888932918016*

Patient safety during childbirth can be assessed by looking at potentially avoidable tearing of the perineum during vaginal delivery. Such tears extend to the perineal muscles and bowel wall and require surgery. They are more likely to occur in the case of first vaginal delivery, high baby's birth weight, labour induction, occiput posterior baby position, prolonged second stage of labour and instrumental delivery. Possible complications include continued perineal pain and incontinence. A recent study found that around 10% of women who had such tears will suffer from faecal incontinence initially and almost 45% of women will have ongoing symptoms after four to eight years (Sundquist, 2012).

These types of tears are not possible to prevent in all cases, but can be reduced by employing appropriate labour management and high quality obstetric care. For example, findings from a recent study showed that enhanced midwifery skills in managing vaginal delivery reduce the risk of obstetric anal sphincter injuries (Hals et al., 2010). Hence, the proportion of deliveries involving higher degree lacerations is a useful indicator of the quality of obstetric care. Obstetric trauma indicators have been used by the US Joint Commission as well as by different international quality initiatives seeking to assess and improve obstetric care (AHRQ, 2006).

"Obstetric trauma with instrument" refers to deliveries using forceps or vacuum extraction. As the risk of a perineal laceration is significantly increased when instruments are used to assist the delivery, rates for this patient population are reported separately. Obstetric trauma indicators are considered as relatively reliable and comparable across countries. Nevertheless, differences in the consistency with which obstetric units report these complications may complicate international comparison. Fear of litigation, for example, may cause under-reporting; conversely, systems which facilitate recording of secondary diagnoses or rely on specially trained administrative staff to identify and code adverse events from patients' clinical records rather than clinicians to report procedures may produce more reliable data.

The rate of obstetric trauma after vaginal delivery *with* instrument (Figure 5.6.1) shows high variation across countries. Reported rates vary from below 2% in Poland, Israel, Italy, Slovenia and Portugal to more than 15% in Canada and Denmark. Rates of obstetric trauma after vaginal delivery *without* instrument (Figure 5.6.2) are considerably less but display equally large variation, from less than 0.5% in Poland, Israel, Italy and Slovenia to 3.5% or above in Sweden and Switzerland. There is a strong relationship between the two indicators: Poland, Israel, Italy, Slovenia, Portugal and Belgium report the lowest rates and Sweden, Canada and Denmark the highest rates for both indicators.

Definition and comparability

The two obstetric trauma indicators are defined as the proportion of instrument assisted/non-assisted vaginal deliveries with third- and fourth-degree obstetric trauma codes in any diagnosis and procedure field. Any differences in the definition of principal and secondary diagnoses have no influence on the calculated rates.

Differences in data reporting across countries may influence the calculated rates of obstetric patient safety indicators. These relate primarily to differences in coding practice and data sources. Some countries report obstetric trauma rates based on administrative hospital data and others based on obstetric register. There is some evidence that registries produce higher quality data and report a greater number of obstetric trauma events compared to administrative datasets (Baghestan et al., 2007).

5.6.1. Obstetric trauma, vaginal delivery with instrument, 2011 (or nearest year)

Crude rates per 100 instrument-assisted vaginal deliveries

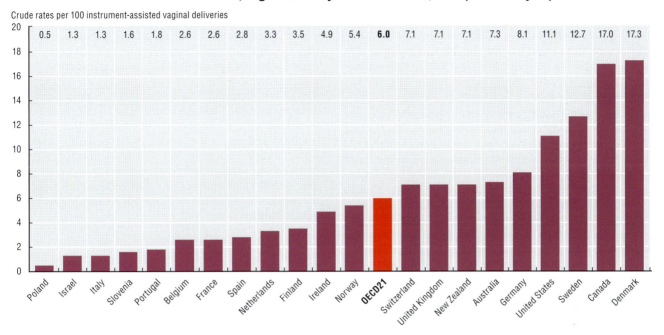

Source: OECD Health Statistics 2013, http://dx.doi.org/10.1787/health-data-en.

StatLink http://dx.doi.org/10.1787/888932918035

5.6.2. Obstetric trauma, vaginal delivery without instrument, 2011 (or nearest year)

Crude rates per 100 vaginal deliveries without instrument assistance

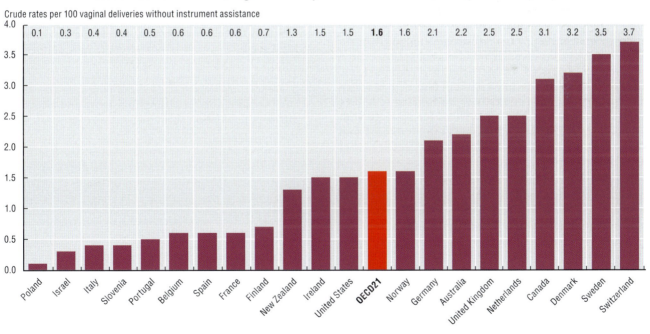

Source: OECD Health Statistics 2013, http://dx.doi.org/10.1787/health-data-en.

StatLink http://dx.doi.org/10.1787/888932918054

5.7. Unplanned hospital re-admissions for patients with mental disorders

The burden of mental illness is substantial. Mental and behavioural disorders, including major depressive disorder, anxiety disorders, and schizophrenia accounted for 7.4% of healthy years lost due to disability worldwide in 2010. Furthermore, the burden attributable for this group of diseases grew by 5.9% between 1990 and 2010, with schizophrenia and bipolar disorders among the major contributors to this growth (Murray et al., 2013).

Improving mental health care is a policy priority in many OECD countries, with countries seeking the most effective and efficient ways to deliver care to patients. Most OECD countries are moving away from hospital care as the main way of delivering care and towards community-based integrated care that involves a multidisciplinary team (OECD, forthcoming). Patients with severe mental disorders still receive specialised care at hospitals but, if deemed appropriate, coordinated follow-up is provided after discharge and patients are not usually re-admitted to hospital within 30 days without any prior plan to do so. The proportion of patients with within 30-day re-admissions is therefore used as an indicator of the lack of proper management of mental health conditions outside of hospital.

Over 15% of patients with schizophrenia were re-admitted to hospital within 30 days in 2011 in Israel, Korea, Australia, Denmark and Sweden, while the rate was around 5% in Mexico and Portugal (Figure 5.7.1). Relative positions of countries are similar between schizophrenia and bipolar disorder and the difference in re-admission rates was less than 3% in all countries except for Korea (Figure 5.7.2).

Countries show diverging trends over time for both schizophrenia and bipolar disorder re-admissions. The United Kingdom experienced an increase in re-admissions, whereas in Italy rates declined for both disorders between 2006 and 2011. In Italy, efforts have been made to reduce inappropriate use of inpatient services for patients with mental disorders, and re-admissions are monitored and used to improve organisation and clinical effectiveness of mental health care.

Mental health care systems have developed new organisational and delivery models over the past few decades. For example, community-based "crisis teams" are used to stabilise patients in outpatient settings in a number of countries such as Italy, Norway and the United Kingdom. Other countries, such as Denmark, use interval care protocols to place unstable patients in hospital for short periods, whilst being proactive in identifying patients in need of care through outreach teams following discharges. A more patient-centred approach is becoming commonplace, with patients involved in care and service plan development (OECD, forthcoming). The differences in mental health care delivery models may be a contributor to the cross-country variation in the proportion of re-admissions that are planned and unplanned, with only the latter indicating poor quality. However, our ability to identify between planned and unplanned re-admissions in the data is limited. At this stage, only a few countries have the capacity to distinguish between the two types of re-admissions in their administrative data.

Definition and comparability

The indicator uses within 30-day re-admissions as a proxy for unplanned re-admissions as many countries cannot differentiate these re-admissions. The denominator is the number of patients with at least one hospital admission during the year for schizophrenia or bipolar disorder as principal diagnosis or as one of the first two listed secondary diagnosis. The numerator is the number of these patients with at least one re-admission for any mental disorder to the same hospital within 30 days of discharge in the year. Patients with same-day admissions (less than 24 hours) are not included in the numerator. The data have been age-sex standardised based on the 2010 OECD population structure, to remove the effect of different population structures across countries.

Data presented in *Health at a Glance 2009* and *2011* refer to the number of within 30-day readmissions per 100 patients, which were slightly different from those presented in this edition of *Health at a Glance* which refer to the proportion of patients with at least one re-admission.

5.7.1. Schizophrenia re-admissions to the same hospital, 2006 and 2011 (or nearest year)

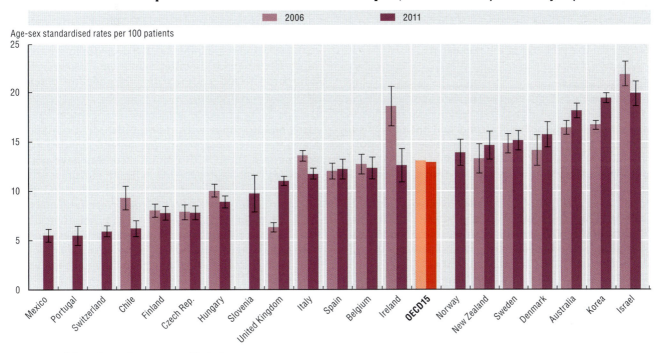

Note: 95% confidence intervals represented by |—|.
Source: OECD Health Statistics 2013, *http://dx.doi.org/10.1787/health-data-en.*

StatLink ⟨⟩ *http://dx.doi.org/10.1787/888932918073*

5.7.2. Bipolar disorder re-admissions to the same hospital, 2006 and 2011 (or nearest year)

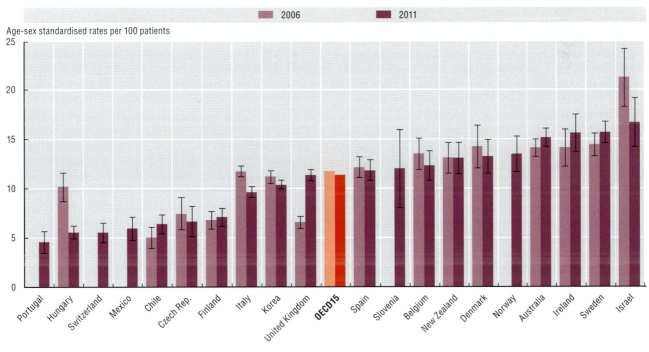

Note: 95% confidence intervals represented by |—|.
Source: OECD Health Statistics 2013, *http://dx.doi.org/10.1787/health-data-en.*

StatLink ⟨⟩ *http://dx.doi.org/10.1787/888932918092*

5.8. Excess mortality from mental disorders

Excess mortality is a ratio of the mortality rate for patients with a mental disorder compared with the mortality rate of the general population. A ratio value that is greater than one implies that people with mental disorders face a higher risk of death than the rest of the population.

There are a number of reasons why people with mental disorders have higher mortality rates than the general population. These include higher rates of suicide and accidents as well as a higher prevalence of co-morbidities or risk factors such as smoking, the abuse of alcohol and illicit drugs and side effects of psychotropic treatment (de Hert et al., 2011; Nordentoft et al., 2013; Björkenstam et al., 2012). Excess mortality among people with mental health disorders may also be partly due to lower access and use of health care as well as poorer quality of care provided to them. The quality of care may be compromised because these patients may have difficulties in effectively communicating their physical problems and providers may prioritise patient's psychiatric problem over their physical problems.

In 2011, excess mortality from schizophrenia and bipolar disorder ranges from 2.1 to 8.8 times greater than in the general population (Figures 5.8.1 and 5.8.2). Data are not available for all the United Kingdom. In England, data are not available for specific diagnostic categories of mental disorders, but excess mortality among all patients with serious mental illness is 3.3 times greater than in the general population in 2010.

For patients with schizophrenia, excess mortality ranges from 3.6 in Korea to 8.8 in Sweden (Figure 5.8.1). For patients with bipolar disorder, excess mortality is slightly lower in all countries, ranging from 2.1 in Denmark to 6.8 in Sweden in 2011 (Figure 5.8.2). The Swedish results are consistent with previous research which showed that death by suicide or other external causes, particularly among Swedish men with a mental disorder, are very high (Wahlbeck et al., 2011). For both disorders, Denmark, Korea and Slovenia have lower excess mortality than the OECD averages.

Previous studies have shown that excess mortality has increased across countries over the past decades (Saha et al., 2007). For schizophrenia, this trend has continued in most countries over recent years (Figure 5.8.1). The exception to this trend is in New Zealand where excess mortality has fallen between 2006 and 2011. New Zealand has strengthened mental health care systems in the past two decades by focusing on early intervention and assisting people to improve their own health and wellness and to live independent lives. It has improved access to specialist care and community-based services and involved patients and family in service planning and delivery (Ministry of Health, 2012).

Trends in excess mortality attributable to bipolar disorder vary across countries. Between 2006 and 2011, the ratio increased in Korea and Sweden, stayed fairly stable in Denmark and fell in the other countries (Figure 5.8.2). Similar to the schizophrenia indicator, the decrease in excess mortality from bipolar disorder was large in New Zealand. Compared to a decade earlier, the rate for Israel also declined substantially.

Despite some improvements over recent years, mortality rates among those with mental disorders remain well above the rates observed in the general population, suggesting that those with mental disorders have not fully benefited from improvements in health outcomes attained by the general population and the availability and quality of mental health care may be lagging behind (Saha et al., 2007; Tidemalm et al., 2008). Ensuring physical health and well-being in people with serious mental illness presents many challenges, and health services must proactively seek to address both the physical and mental health needs of this group.

Definition and comparability

The numerator for the excess mortality ratio is the overall mortality rate in a given year for persons aged between 15 and 74 years old diagnosed with schizophrenia/bipolar disorder. For Israel, New Zealand and Sweden, it refers to the mortality of person diagnosed in the same year but diagnosis year is not known for others. These differences may relate to variations shown in the figures to some extent. The denominator is the overall mortality rate for the general population aged between 15 and 74 years old in a given year.

Data coverage varies according to the place where mental disorders are diagnosed. In Israel and Korea patients can be identified in the data regardless of where diagnosis occurs while in New Zealand only diagnoses within the secondary care sector are included in the data, hence excess mortality appears to be high compared to other countries. For Finland and Sweden, data include only diagnosis within the hospital sector. The data have been age-sex standardised based on the 2010 OECD population structure, to remove the effect of different population structures across countries.

5.8.1. Excess mortality from schizophrenia, 2006 and 2011 (or nearest year)

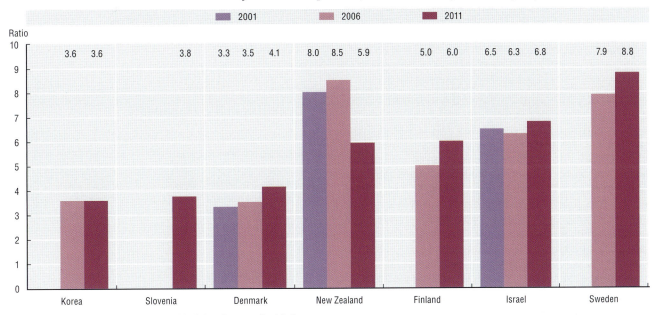

Source: OECD Health Statistics 2013, http://dx.doi.org/10.1787/health-data-en.

StatLink ᏧᏍ http://dx.doi.org/10.1787/888932918111

5.8.2. Excess mortality from bipolar disorder, 2006 and 2011 (or nearest year)

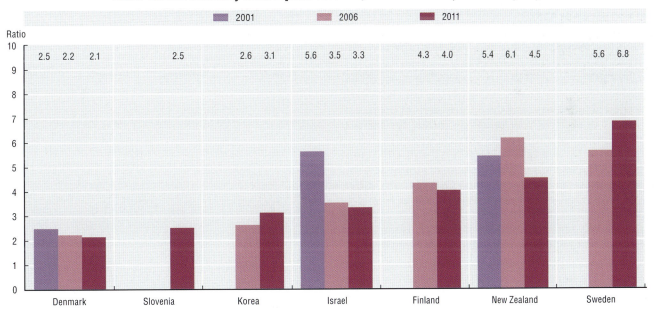

Source: OECD Health Statistics 2013, http://dx.doi.org/10.1787/health-data-en.

StatLink ᏧᏍ http://dx.doi.org/10.1787/888932918130

5.9. Screening, survival and mortality for cervical cancer

Cervical cancer is highly preventable if precancerous changes are detected and treated before progression occurs. The main cause of cervical cancer, which accounts for approximately 95% of all cases, is sexual exposure to the human papilloma virus (HPV) (IARC, 1995; Franco et al., 1999). Countries follow different policies with regards to the prevention and early diagnosis of cervical cancer.

About half of OECD countries have cervical cancer screening organised through population-based programmes but the periodicity and target groups vary (OECD, 2013e). Some countries with low cervical cancer incidence such as Israel and Switzerland do not have an organised screening programme, but in both countries women in the eligible age group can have a Pap smear test performed every three years for free. Since the development of a vaccine against some HPV types, vaccination programmes have been implemented in around half of OECD countries (Brotherton et al., 2011), although there is an ongoing debate about the impact of the vaccine on cervical cancer screening strategies (Goldhaber-Fiebert et al., 2008; Wheeler et al., 2009).

Screening rates for cervical cancer range from 15.5% in Turkey to 85.0% in the United States in 2011 (Figure 5.9.1). Austria, Germany, Sweden, Norway and New Zealand also achieved coverage above 75%. Screening rates in Iceland and the United Kingdom declined substantially over the decade. However, in each of these cases changes to programme eligibility and data capture may account for part of this decrease. On the other hand, Korea increased the screening coverage by four-fold, although the rate still remains well below the OECD average.

Cancer survival is one of the key measures of the effectiveness of cancer care systems, taking into account both early detection of the disease and the effectiveness of treatment. In recent years, five-year relative survival for cervical cancer improved in many countries, possibly due to improved effectiveness of screening and treatment (Figure 5.9.2). The most notable increase of almost 16% was observed in Iceland in recent years. Cross-country differences in cervical cancer range from 52.7% in Poland to 76.8% in Korea in the most recent period. Some countries with relatively high screening coverage such as the United States, Germany and New Zealand have lower survival.

Mortality rates reflect the effect of cancer care over the past years and the impact of screening, as well as changes in incidence (Dickman and Adami, 2006). The mortality rates for cervical cancer declined in most OECD countries between 2001 and 2011 (Figure 5.9.3), following the broad trend of an overall reduction in mortality from all types of cancer (see Indicator 1.4 "Mortality from cancer"). The decline was large in Denmark, Iceland, New Zealand and Norway. Mexico also experienced a sharp decrease in cervical

cancer mortality, although it still has the highest rate among OECD countries. However, in some countries, such as Greece and Estonia, mortality rates from cervical cancer increased.

Definition and comparability

Screening rates reflect the proportion of women who are eligible for a screening test and actually receive the test. Some countries ascertain screening based on surveys and other based on encounter data, which may influence the results. Survey-based results may be affected by recall bias. Programme data are often calculated for monitoring national screening programmes, and differences in target population and screening frequency may also lead to variations in screening coverage across countries.

Relative survival is the ratio of the observed survival experienced by cancer patients over a specified period of time after diagnosis to the expected survival in a comparable group from the general population in terms of age, sex and time period. Relative survival captures the excess mortality that can be attributed to the diagnosis. For example, relative survival of 80% mean that 80% of the patients that were expected to be alive after five years, given their age at diagnosis and sex, are in fact still alive. Survival data for Germany and Portugal are based on a sample of patients, representing 27% and 44% of the population respectively.

Cancer survival calculated through period analysis is up-to-date estimate of cancer patient survival using more recent incidence and follow-up periods than cohort analysis which uses survival information of a complete five-year follow-up period. In the United Kingdom, cohort analysis was used for 2001-06 data while 2006-11 data are calculated through period analysis. The reference periods vary slightly across countries. All the survival estimates presented here have been age-standardised using the International Cancer Survival Standard (ICSS) population (Corazziari et al., 2004). The survival is not adjusted for tumour stage at diagnosis, hampering assessment of the relative impact of early detection and better treatment.

See Indicator 1.4 "Mortality from cancer" for definition, source and methodology underlying cancer mortality rates.

5.9.1. Cervical cancer screening in women aged 20-69, 2001 to 2011 (or nearest year)

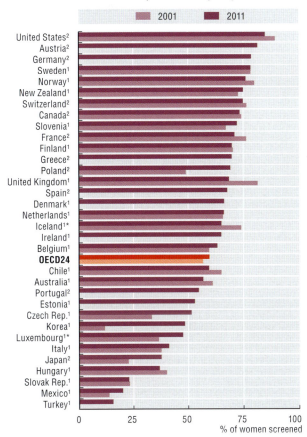

1. Programme.
2. Survey.
* Three-year average.
Source: OECD Health Statistics 2013, *http://dx.doi.org/10.1787/health-data-en.*
StatLink ⧉ *http://dx.doi.org/10.1787/888932918149*

5.9.2. Cervical cancer five-year relative survival, 2001-06 and 2006-11 (or nearest period)

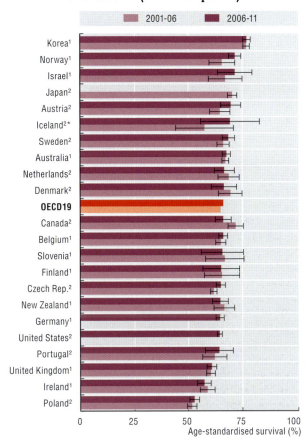

Note: 95% confidence intervals represented by |—|.
1. Period analysis.
2. Cohort analysis.
* Three-period average.
Source: OECD Health Statistics 2013, *http://dx.doi.org/10.1787/health-data-en.*
StatLink ⧉ *http://dx.doi.org/10.1787/888932918168*

5.9.3. Cervical cancer mortality, 2001 to 2011 (or nearest year)

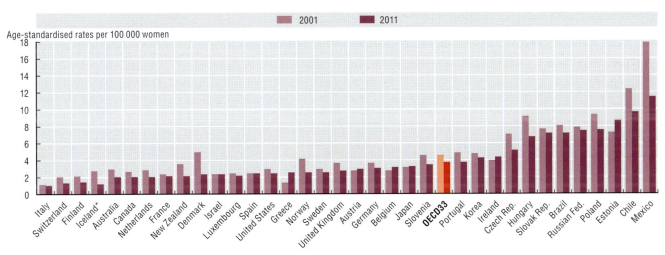

* Three-year average.
Source: OECD Health Statistics 2013, *http://dx.doi.org/10.1787/health-data-en.*

StatLink ⧉ *http://dx.doi.org/10.1787/888932918187*

5.10. Screening, survival and mortality for breast cancer

Breast cancer is the most prevalent form of cancer in women. One in nine women will acquire breast cancer at some point in their life and one in thirty will die from the disease. Risk factors that increase a person's chance of getting this disease include, but are not limited to, age, family history of breast cancer, oestrogen replacement therapy, lifestyle, diet, and alcohol.

Most OECD countries have adopted breast cancer screening programmes as an effective way for detecting the disease early. The periodicity and population target groups vary across countries and are still the subjects of debate. EU guidelines (European Commission, 2006) suggest a desirable target screening rate of at least 75% of eligible women in European countries. Screening rates vary widely across OECD countries in 2011, ranging from less than 10% in Chile to over 80% in Finland, the Netherlands, the United States and Austria (Figure 5.10.1). Some countries that had high screening rates ten years ago experienced some reductions over the past decade, including Finland, the United States, the United Kingdom, Norway, Ireland and Canada. On the other side, Korea, Poland and the Czech Republic showed substantial increases, although they still remain below the OECD average.

Breast cancer survival reflects advances in improved treatments as well as public health interventions to detect the disease early through screening programmes and greater awareness of the disease. The introduction of combined breast conserving surgery with local radiation and neoadjuvant therapy, for example, have increased survival as well as the quality of life of survivors (Mauri et al., 2008). The availability and use of newer and more effective chemotherapy agents for metastatic breast cancer have also been shown to improve survival among women (Chia et al., 2007).

The relative five-year breast cancer survival has improved in many countries in recent periods (Figure 5.10.2), attaining over 80% in all OECD countries except Poland. In part, this may be related to the access of care in Poland where the numbers of cancer care centres and radiotherapy facilities are limited (OECD, 2013e). Five-year survival for breast cancer has increased considerably in central and eastern European countries, where survival has historically been low, as well as in Belgium and Ireland (Verdecchia et al., 2007). Recent studies suggest that some of the differences in cancer survival could be due to variations in the implementation of screening programmes (Rosso et al., 2010). Countries such as Chile, Greece and the Slovak Republic have non-population-based breast cancer screening programmes.

In addition to well organised screening programmes, a recent OECD report on cancer care showed that shorter waiting times and the provision of evidence-based best practice are also associated with improved survival in OECD countries. Developing comprehensive cancer control plans, setting national targets with a specified time frame, having guidelines, using case management and having mechanisms for monitoring and quality assurance were found to be associated with improved cancer survival (OECD, 2013e).

Mortality rates have declined in most OECD countries over the past decade (Figure 5.10.3). The reduction in mortality rates are a reflection of improvements in early detection and treatment of breast cancer, and are also influenced by the incidence of the disease. Improvements were substantial in Norway, Ireland and the Czech Republic. Denmark also reported a considerable decline over the last decade, but its mortality rate was still the highest in 2011. In Korea and Japan, the mortality rate from breast cancer increased over the decade, although it remains the lowest among OECD countries.

Definition and comparability

Screening rates and survival are defined in Indicator 5.9 "Screening, survival and mortality for cervical cancer". See Indicator 1.4 "Mortality from cancer" for definition, source and methodology underlying cancer mortality rates.

5.10.1. Mammography screening in women aged 50- 69, 2001 to 2011 (or nearest year)

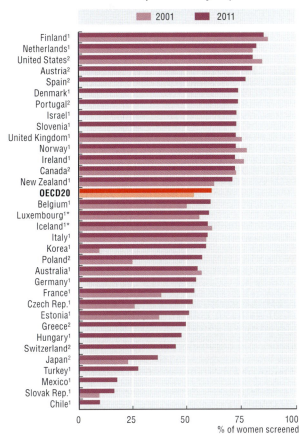

1. Programme.
2. Survey.
* Three-year average.
Source: OECD Health Statistics 2013, http://dx.doi.org/10.1787/health-data-en.

StatLink ᵐᵖ http://dx.doi.org/10.1787/888932918206

5.10.2. Breast cancer five-year relative survival, 2001-06 and 2006-11 (or nearest period)

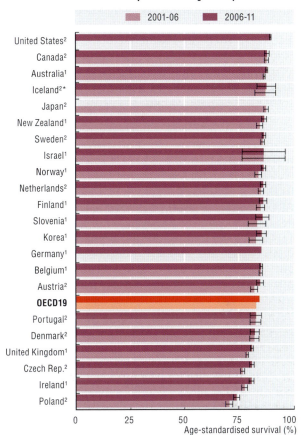

Note: 95% confidence intervals represented by |——|.
1. Period analysis.
2. Cohort analysis.
* Three-period average.
Source: OECD Health Statistics 2013, http://dx.doi.org/10.1787/health-data-en.

StatLink ᵐᵖ http://dx.doi.org/10.1787/888932918225

5.10.3. Breast cancer mortality in women, 2001 to 2011 (or nearest year)

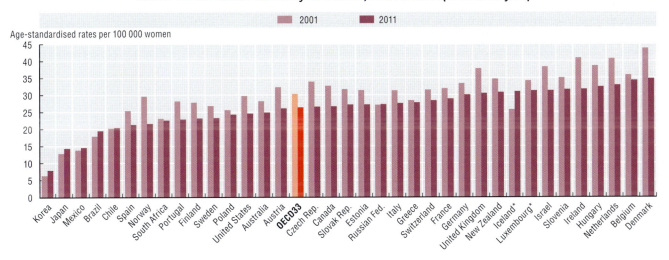

* Three-year average.
Source: OECD Health Statistics 2013, http://dx.doi.org/10.1787/health-data-en.

StatLink ᵐᵖ http://dx.doi.org/10.1787/888932918244

5.11. Survival and mortality for colorectal cancer

Colorectal cancer is the third most commonly diagnosed form of cancer worldwide, after lung and breast cancers, with over 1.2 million new cases diagnosed annually. Incidence rates are significantly higher for males than females (IARC, 2011). There are several factors that place certain individuals at increased risk for the disease, including age, the presence of polyps, ulcerative colitis, a diet high in fat and genetic background. The disease is more common in the United States and Europe, and is rare in Asia. But in countries where people have adopted western diets, such as Japan, the incidence of colorectal cancer is increasing. Total spending on the treatment of colorectal cancer in the United States is estimated at USD 14 billion per year (Mariotto et al., 2011).

Following screening for breast and cervical cancers, colorectal cancer screening has become available, and an increasing number of countries have introduced free population-based screening, targeting people in their 50s and 60s (OECD, 2013e). Partly because of uncertainties about the cost-effectiveness of screening (Lansdorp-Vogelaar et al., 2010), countries are using different methods (i.e. faecal occult blood test, colonoscopy and flexible sigmoidoscopy). Multiple methods are also available within the screening programme in some countries. In most countries that provide faecal occult blood test, screening is available every two years. The screening periodicity schedule is less frequent with colonoscopy and flexible sigmoidoscopy, generally every ten years, making it difficult to compare screening coverage across countries.

Advances in diagnosis and treatment of colorectal cancer have increased survival over the last decade. There is compelling evidence in support of the clinical benefit of improved surgical techniques, radiation therapy and combined chemotherapy. Most countries showed improvement in survival over recent periods (Figure 5.11.1). Across OECD countries, five-year survival improved from 58.0% to 61.3% for people with colorectal cancer during 2001-06 and 2006-11 respectively. Korea, Japan, Israel and Australia have attained five-year relative survival of over 65%. Poland and the Czech Republic, although having the lowest survival among OECD countries, improved considerably from 42.5% to 47.7% and from 48.2% to 53.4% respectively between 2001-06 and 2006-11.

Improvement in survival was observed for both men and women across countries. In all OECD countries, colorectal cancer survival is higher for women except in Korea and Japan where men have a slightly higher survival (Figure 5.11.2). The gender difference is the largest in Slovenia with the five-year relative survival of 58.9% for males and 67.2% for females. Denmark and Finland also have a comparatively large difference.

Most countries experienced a decline in mortality of colorectal cancer between 2001 and 2011, with the average rate across OECD countries falling from 28.3 to 25.0 deaths per 100 000 population over this period (Figure 5.11.3). The decline was particularly large in Australia, the Czech Republic and Austria. The main exceptions from the general trend were Brazil and Korea, where the mortality rate from colorectal cancer increased by about 20% in the last decade. Central and eastern European countries tend to have higher mortality rates than other OECD countries. Despite a decrease over time, Hungary and the Slovak Republic continue to have the highest mortality rate. Further gains in colorectal cancer mortality could be achieved through the strengthening of screening programmes and improving participation rates.

Definition and comparability

Survival and mortality rates are defined in Indicator 5.9. "Screening, survival and mortality for cervical cancer". See Indicator 1.4 "Mortality from cancer" for definition, source and methodology underlying cancer mortality rates. Survival and mortality rates of colorectal cancer are based on ICD-10 codes C18-C21 (colon, rectosigmoid junction, rectum, and anus).

5.11.1. Colorectal cancer, five-year relative survival, 2001-06 and 2006-11 (or nearest period)

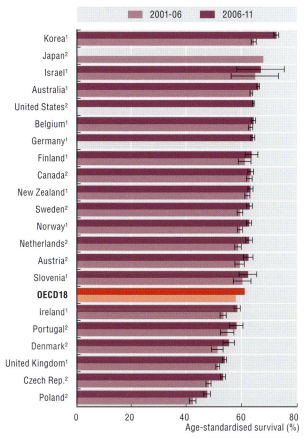

Note: 95% confidence intervals represented by |—|.
1. Period analysis.
2. Cohort analysis.
Source: OECD Health Statistics 2013, http://dx.doi.org/10.1787/health-data-en.

StatLink ᴍꜱ⊑ http://dx.doi.org/10.1787/888932918263

5.11.2. Colorectal cancer, five-year relative survival by gender, 2006-11 (or nearest period)

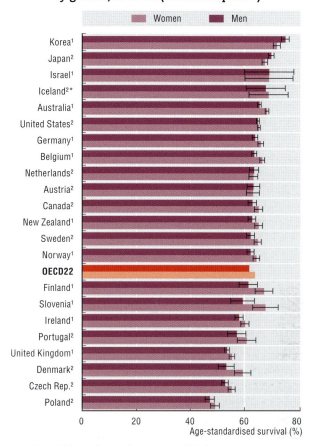

Note: 95% confidence intervals represented by |—|.
1. Period analysis.
2. Cohort analysis.
* Three-period average.
Source: OECD Health Statistics 2013, http://dx.doi.org/10.1787/health-data-en.

StatLink ᴍꜱ⊑ http://dx.doi.org/10.1787/888932918282

5.11.3. Colorectal cancer mortality, 2001 to 2011 (or nearest year)

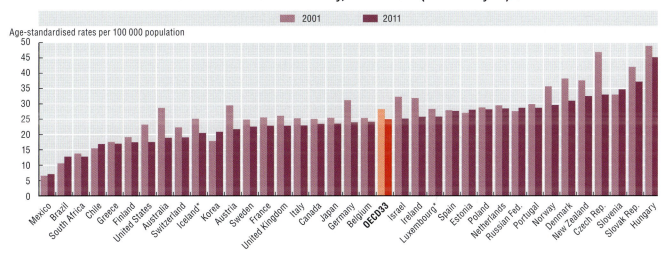

* Three-year average.
Source: OECD Health Statistics 2013, http://dx.doi.org/10.1787/health-data-en.

StatLink ᴍꜱ⊑ http://dx.doi.org/10.1787/888932918301

5.12. Childhood vaccination programmes

All OECD countries have established vaccination programmes based on their interpretation of the risks and benefits of each vaccine. There is strong evidence that vaccines provide safe and effective protection against diseases such as diphtheria, tetanus, pertussis (whooping cough), measles and hepatitis B. The percentage of children protected from these diseases can be considered as a quality of care indicator for such childhood vaccination programmes.

Vaccination against diphtheria, tetanus and pertussis (DTP) and measles are part of all national vaccination schedules in OECD countries. Figures 5.12.1 and 5.12.2 show that the overall vaccination of children against measles and DTP is high in OECD countries. On average, 96% of children receive the recommended DTP vaccination and 94% receive measles vaccinations in accordance with national immunisation schedules. Rates for DTP and/or measles vaccinations are below 90% only in Austria, Denmark, France, South Africa, India and Indonesia.

While national coverage rates are high, some parts of the population remain exposed to certain diseases. In 2013, for example, there was a measles outbreak in the north of England as well as parts of Wales. The outbreak has been linked to a time in the early 2000s when vaccination rates fell to 80% among a cohort of children. During this period there was intense media coverage of the safety of the measles, mumps and rubella (MMR) vaccine, leading many parents to decide not to immunise their child. Although these safety concerns have since been refuted, large numbers of children in this age cohort remain unimmunised, raising the likelihood of outbreaks such as the one experienced in 2013 (Elliman and Bedford, 2013; Sengupta et al., 2004).

Figure 5.12.3 shows the percentage of children aged one year who are vaccinated for hepatitis B. The hepatitis B virus is transmitted by contact with blood or body fluids of an infected person. A small proportion of infections become chronic, and these people are at high risk of death from cancer or cirrhosis of the liver. A vaccination has been available since 1982 and is considered to be 95% effective in preventing infection and its chronic consequences. Since a high proportion of chronic infections are acquired during early childhood, the WHO recommends that all infants should receive their first dose of hepatitis B vaccine as soon as possible after birth, preferably within 24 hours (WHO, 2009).

Most countries have followed the WHO recommendation to incorporate hepatitis B vaccine as an integral part of their national infant immunisation programme (WHO/Unicef, 2013). For these countries, the immunisation coverage is averaging 93%. However, a number of countries do not currently require children to be vaccinated and consequently the rates for these countries are significantly lower than in other countries. For example, in Denmark and Sweden, vaccination against hepatitis B is not part of the general infant vaccination programme, but is provided to high risk groups such as children with mothers who are infected by the hepatitis B virus. Other OECD countries that do not include vaccination against hepatitis B in their infant programmes are Iceland, Finland, Hungary, Japan, Slovenia, Switzerland and the United Kingdom. In Canada, hepatitis B vaccination is universally included for adolescents but not all provinces and territories include it in their infant vaccine schedules (Public Health Agency of Canada, 2009; Mackie et al., 2009). In the Netherlands, hepatitis B vaccines were recently added to the schedule for children born after August 2011 (WHO/Unicef, 2013).

Definition and comparability

Vaccination rates reflect the percentage of children that receive the respective vaccination in the recommended timeframe. The age of complete immunisation differs across countries due to different immunisation schedules. For those countries recommending the first dose of a vaccine after age one, the indicator is calculated as the proportion of children less than two years of age who have received that vaccine. Thus, these indicators are based on the actual policy in a given country.

Some countries administer combination vaccines (e.g. DTP for diphtheria, tetanus and pertussis) while others administer the vaccinations separately. Some countries ascertain vaccinations based on surveys and others based on encounter data, which may influence the results.

5.12.1. Vaccination against diphteria, tetanus and pertussis, children aged 1, 2011

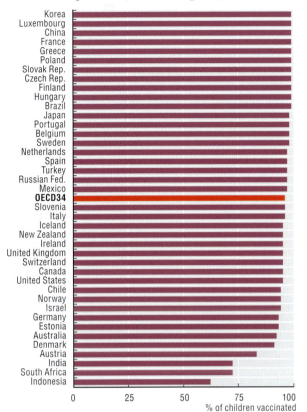

Source: WHO/Unicef, http://dx.doi.org/10.1787/health-data-en.
StatLink http://dx.doi.org/10.1787/888932918320

5.12.2. Vaccination against measles, children aged 1, 2011

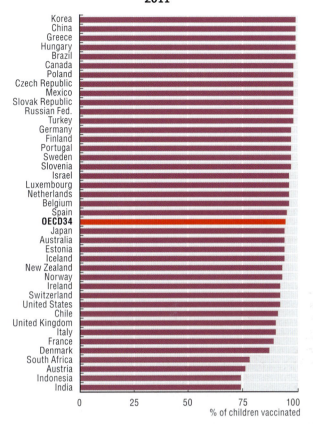

Source: WHO/Unicef, http://dx.doi.org/10.1787/health-data-en.
StatLink http://dx.doi.org/10.1787/888932918339

5.12.3. Vaccination against hepatitis B, children aged 1, 2011

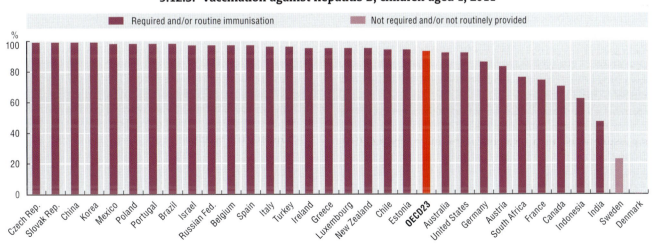

Note: OECD average only includes countries with required or routine immunisation.
Source: WHO/Unicef and OECD Health Statistics 2013 for Sweden and Denmark, http://dx.doi.org/10.1787/health-data-en.
StatLink http://dx.doi.org/10.1787/888932918358

5.13. Influenza vaccination for older people

Influenza is a common infectious disease that affects between 5 and 15% of the population each year (WHO, 2009). Most people with the illness recover quickly, but elderly people and those with chronic medical conditions are at higher risk of complications and even death. Influenza can also have a major impact on the health care system. In the United Kingdom, an estimated 779 000 general practice consultations and 19 000 hospital admissions were attributable to influenza per year (Pitman et al., 2006). At certain times of the year, influenza can place health systems under enormous stress. For example, in Toronto, Canada, every 100 local cases of influenza resulted in an increase of 2.5 hours per week of ambulance diversion; this is a clear sign of emergency department overcrowding (Hoot et al., 2008; Schull et al., 2004).

Vaccines have been used for more than 60 years and provide a safe means of preventing influenza. While influenza vaccines have shown positive results in clinical trials and observational studies, there is a need for more high quality studies on the effectiveness of influenza vaccines for the elderly (Jefferson et al., 2010). Nevertheless, appropriate influenza vaccines have been shown to reduce the risk of death by up to 55% among healthy older adults as well as reduce the risk of hospitalisation by between 32% and 49% among older adults (Lang et al., 2012; Nichols et al., 2007).

In 2003, countries participating in the World Health Assembly committed to the goal of attaining vaccination coverage of the elderly population of at least 50% by 2006 and 75% by 2010 (WHA, 2003). Figure 5.13.1 shows that in 2011 the average influenza vaccination rate for people aged 65 and over was 50%. Vaccination rates range from 1% in Estonia to 94% in Mexico. Whilst there is still some uncertainty about the reasons for the cross-national differences, personal contact with a doctor, better communication, patient and provider education initiatives, and recall and reminder systems as well as insurance coverage can play important roles in improving vaccination rates (Kohlhammer et al., 2007; Mereckiene et al., 2008; Kroneman et al., 2003; Kunze et al., 2007). In Estonia, for example, influenza vaccination is not publicly covered.

Figure 5.13.2 indicates that between 2005 and 2011, the average vaccination rates across all OECD countries fell marginally from 58.2% to 56.6% of the elderly population among the group of countries that have data for these two years, with no uniform trend among countries. Only Mexico and Korea attained the 75% coverage target in 2011, and targets were nearly met in Australia, the Netherlands and the United Kingdom. Changes over time should be interpreted with some caution because of changes to the way vaccination rates were calculated in some countries (see box on "Definition and comparability").

In June 2009, the WHO declared an influenza pandemic (WHO, 2009c). The H1N1 influenza virus (also referred to as "swine flu") infected an estimated 11% to 18% of the population (Kelly et al., 2011). Mexico was at the centre of the pandemic, being among the first countries where swine flu was detected and also where mortality rates were reportedly higher than those in many other countries (Echevarría-Zuno et al., 2010). The high rate of seasonal vaccinations that are still being observed in Mexico may be the result of the H1N1 experiences in that country. In other countries, however, the take-up rate of H1N1 vaccine was lower than expected, despite the vaccine being included in most 2009-10 vaccination programmes (Valenciano et al., 2011; Poland, 2011; Mereckiene et al., 2012). In part, this may be due to the easing of concerns about the threat of H1N1 amongst the general population by the time the vaccine became available. Studies have shown that the most important determinant for individuals to take-up H1N1 vaccine was previous exposure to seasonal flu vaccine, leading some researchers to argue that higher vaccination rates for seasonal flu may help uptake during potential future pandemics (Poland, 2011; Nguyen et al., 2011).

Definition and comparability

Influenza vaccination rate refers to the number of people aged 65 and older who have received an annual influenza vaccination, divided by the total number of people over 65 years of age. The main limitation in terms of data comparability arises from the use of different data sources, whether survey or programme, which are susceptible to different types of errors and biases. For example, data from population surveys may reflect some variation due to recall errors and irregularity of administration. A number of countries changed the way in which influenza vaccination rates were calculated between 2005 and 2011. These countries are: Chile, Denmark, Germany, Israel, Luxembourg, New Zealand, Slovenia, Switzerland and the United Kingdom.

5.13.1. Influenza vaccination coverage, population aged 65 and over, 2011 (or nearest year)

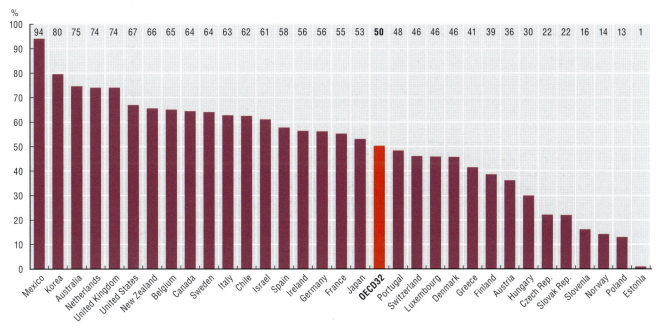

Source: OECD Health Statistics 2013, http://dx.doi.org/10.1787/health-data-en.

StatLink ᕦᗑᓆ http://dx.doi.org/10.1787/888932918377

5.13.2. Influenza vaccination coverage, population aged 65 and over, 2005-11 (or nearest year)

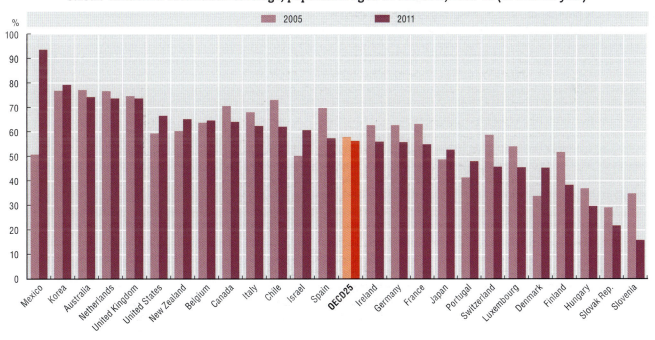

Source: OECD Health Statistics 2013, http://dx.doi.org/10.1787/health-data-en.

StatLink ᕦᗑᓆ http://dx.doi.org/10.1787/888932918396

5.14. Patient experience with ambulatory care

Delivering health care that is responsive and patient-centered is playing a greater role in health care policy across OECD countries. Measuring and monitoring patient experiences empowers patients and the public, involves them in decisions on health care delivery and governance, and provides insight to the extent that they are health-literate and have control over the treatment they receive.

Since the mid-1990s, there have been efforts to institutionalise measurement and monitoring of patient experiences. A number of countries have developed survey instruments for regular data collection and monitoring and in several countries, including the United Kingdom, the Netherlands and Norway, responsible organisations have recently been established. In these countries, patient experiences are reported in periodic national health system reports or on public websites, demonstrating differences across providers, regions and over time. There is evidence that such reporting has actually triggered improvements by providers (Iversen et al., 2011). In the United Kingdom, it is also used in the payment mechanism to reward providers for delivering patient-centered care (Department of Health, 2011).

Patients generally report positive experiences when it comes to communication and autonomy in the ambulatory health care system. Patients report positively on time spent with the doctor (Figure 5.14.1), explanations given (Figure 5.14.2), opportunities to ask questions or raise concerns (Figure 5.14.3), as well as involvement in care and treatment decisions (Figure 5.14.4). But there are some differences across countries, and the proportion of patients reporting positive experiences ranges from around 75% in Sweden to over 95% in certain countries, depending on the indicator. There is no clear gender difference in patient experiences across countries, but in the Netherlands higher proportions of men consistently report positive experiences than women. The proportion of patients with positive experiences has increased in recent years in countries such as Australia, Canada and New Zealand. The improvement was large in the United States while it was modest in the United Kingdom (Commonwealth Fund, 2004, 2007, 2010).

Generally, when a country scores relatively well on one dimension of patient experience, it scores relatively well on others. For example, Luxembourg scores high for all four aspects of patient experiences. However, the Czech Republic is an exception with relatively low scores on patient involvement in decision-making, but high scores on all the communication indicators.

Various health system characteristics and policies influence doctors' behaviour towards patients and hence have an impact on patient experiences, including the organisation of health care delivery, remuneration methods, systematic monitoring and reporting of patient experiences and the medico-legal policies for protecting patients' interests. Based on the data currently available, it is not yet possible to conclude that a particular policy is associated with improved patient experiences. There is a need for more comparable data from countries on measures of patient experiences across a broader array of health services.

Definition and comparability

Since the late 1990s, international efforts have been made to collect patient experience measures through surveys developed by the Picker Institute, and Consumer Assessment of Healthcare Providers and Systems (CAHPS) surveys by the US Agency for Healthcare Research and Quality (AHRQ). WHO also collected different dimensions of patient experience in its 2000/01 World Health Survey, and the Commonwealth Fund's *International Health Policy Survey* has been collecting patient experience data every three years since 1998.

Since 2006, the OECD has been involved in developing and validating a tool to measure patient experiences systematically. In order to measure general patient experiences in health care system, the OECD recommends monitoring patient experiences with any doctor rather than asking patients about their experiences with their regular doctor.

For most of the countries, the Commonwealth Fund's *International Health Policy Survey 2010* was used as the data source, even though there are a number of critiques relating to the sample size, representativeness and response rates. Further efforts are needed to improve international comparability of these indicators. Data presented refer to patient experiences with their regular doctor rather than any doctor. Data collected through other national surveys were reported here for Australia (for Figure 5.14.1), the Czech Republic, Israel, Luxembourg and New Zealand (for Figures 5.14.1, 5.14.2 and 5.14.4). Reference periods are sometimes different across countries. For example, New Zealand data are for doctors' visits in previous three months only. For all countries, rates are age-sex standardized to the 2010 OECD population, to remove the effect of different population structures across countries.

5.14.1. Regular doctor spending enough time with patient in consultation, 2010 (or nearest year)

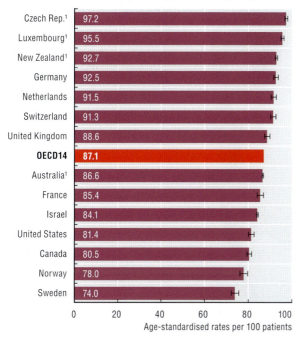

Czech Rep.[1]	97.2
Luxembourg[1]	95.5
New Zealand[1]	92.7
Germany	92.5
Netherlands	91.5
Switzerland	91.3
United Kingdom	88.6
OECD14	87.1
Australia[1]	86.6
France	85.4
Israel	84.1
United States	81.4
Canada	80.5
Norway	78.0
Sweden	74.0

Age-standardised rates per 100 patients

Note: 95% confidence intervals represented by |—|.
1. Patient experience with any doctor.
Source: The Commonwealth Fund International Health Policy Survey 2010 and other national sources.

StatLink ⟫ *http://dx.doi.org/10.1787/888932918415*

5.14.2. Regular doctor providing easy-to-understand explanations, 2010 (or nearest year)

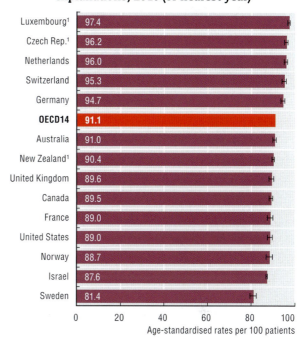

Luxembourg[1]	97.4
Czech Rep.[1]	96.2
Netherlands	96.0
Switzerland	95.3
Germany	94.7
OECD14	91.1
Australia	91.0
New Zealand[1]	90.4
United Kingdom	89.6
Canada	89.5
France	89.0
United States	89.0
Norway	88.7
Israel	87.6
Sweden	81.4

Age-standardised rates per 100 patients

Note: 95% confidence intervals represented by |—|.
1. Patient experience with any doctor.
Source: The Commonwealth Fund International Health Policy Survey 2010 and other national sources.

StatLink ⟫ *http://dx.doi.org/10.1787/888932918434*

5.14.3. Regular doctor giving opportunity to ask questions or raise concerns, 2010 (or nearest year)

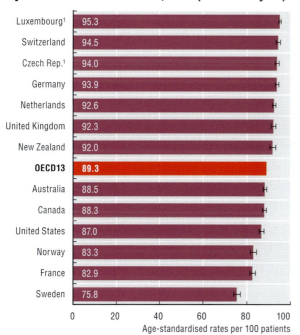

Luxembourg[1]	95.3
Switzerland	94.5
Czech Rep.[1]	94.0
Germany	93.9
Netherlands	92.6
United Kingdom	92.3
New Zealand	92.0
OECD13	89.3
Australia	88.5
Canada	88.3
United States	87.0
Norway	83.3
France	82.9
Sweden	75.8

Age-standardised rates per 100 patients

Note: 95% confidence intervals represented by |—|.
1. Patient experience with any doctor.
Source: The Commonwealth Fund International Health Policy Survey 2010 and other national sources.

StatLink ⟫ *http://dx.doi.org/10.1787/888932918453*

5.14.4. Regular doctor involving patient in decisions about care and treatment, 2010 (or nearest year)

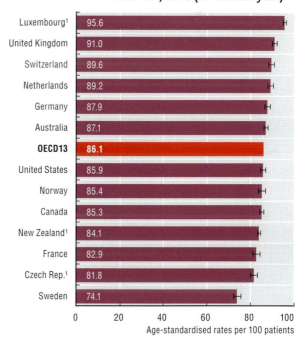

Luxembourg[1]	95.6
United Kingdom	91.0
Switzerland	89.6
Netherlands	89.2
Germany	87.9
Australia	87.1
OECD13	86.1
United States	85.9
Norway	85.4
Canada	85.3
New Zealand[1]	84.1
France	82.9
Czech Rep.[1]	81.8
Sweden	74.1

Age-standardised rates per 100 patients

Note: 95% confidence intervals represented by |—|.
1. Patient experience with any doctor.
Source: The Commonwealth Fund International Health Policy Survey 2010 and other national sources.

StatLink ⟫ *http://dx.doi.org/10.1787/888932918472*

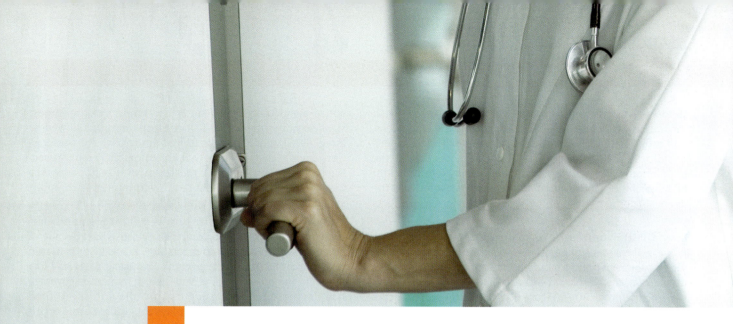

6. ACCESS TO CARE

The statistical data for Israel are supplied by and under the responsibility of the relevant Israeli authorities. The use of such data by the OECD is without prejudice to the status of the Golan Heights, East Jerusalem and Israeli settlements in the West Bank under the terms of international law.

6.1. Coverage for health care

Health care coverage through public or private health insurance promotes access to medical goods and services, and provides financial security against unexpected or serious illness (OECD, 2004a). However, the percentage of the population covered does not provide a complete indicator of accessibility, since the range of services covered and the degree of cost-sharing applied to those services also affects access to care.

Most OECD countries have achieved universal (or near-universal) coverage of health care costs for a core set of services, which usually include consultations with doctors and specialists, tests and examinations, and surgical and therapeutic procedures (Figure 6.1.1). Generally, dental care and pharmaceutical drugs are partially covered, although there are a number of countries where these services are not covered at all (Paris, Devaux and Wei, 2010).

Two OECD countries do not have universal health coverage. In Mexico, the "Seguro Popular" voluntary health insurance scheme was introduced in 2004 to provide coverage for the poor and uninsured, and has grown rapidly so that by 2011, nearly 90% of the population was covered. In the United States, coverage is provided mainly through private health insurance, and 53% of the population had this for their basic coverage in 2011. Publicly financed coverage insured 32% of the population (the elderly, people with low income or with disabilities), leaving 15% of the population without health coverage. The problem of persistent un-insurance is a major barrier to receiving health care, and more broadly, to reducing health inequalities among population groups (AHRQ, 2011b). The Affordable Care Act, adopted in 2010, will expand health insurance coverage in the United States, which will become mandatory for nearly all citizens and legal residents from January 2014.

Basic primary health coverage, whether provided through public or private insurance, generally covers a defined "basket" of benefits, in many cases with cost-sharing. In some countries, additional health coverage can be purchased through private insurance to cover any cost-sharing left after basic coverage (complementary insurance), add additional services (supplementary insurance) or provide faster access or larger choice to providers (duplicate insurance). Among the 34 OECD countries, ten have private coverage for over half of the population (Figure 6.1.2).

Private health insurance offers 96% of the French population *complementary* insurance to cover cost-sharing in the social security system. The Netherlands has the largest *supplementary* market (89% of the population), followed by Israel (80%), whereby private insurance pays for prescription drugs and dental care that are not publicly reimbursed. *Duplicate* markets, providing faster private-sector access to medical services where there are waiting times in public systems, are largest in Ireland (48%) and Australia (45%).

The population covered by private health insurance has increased in some OECD countries over the past decade. It has doubled in Belgium to reach 80%. It has also increased in Mexico and Turkey, although it remains at a very low level. On the other hand, private health insurance coverage has decreased at least slightly in Chile and the United States, two countries where it plays a significant role in primary coverage for health care (Figure 6.1.3).

The importance of private health insurance is not linked to a countries' economic development. Other factors are more likely to explain market development, including gaps in access to publicly financed services, the way private providers are financed, government interventions directed at private health insurance markets, and historical development (OECD, 2004b).

Definition and comparability

Coverage for health care is defined here as the share of the population receiving a core set of health care goods and services under public programmes and through private health insurance. It includes those covered in their own name and their dependents. Public coverage refers both to government programmes, generally financed by taxation, and social health insurance, generally financed by payroll taxes. Take-up of private health insurance is often voluntary, although it may be mandatory by law or compulsory for employees as part of their working conditions. Premiums are generally non-income-related, although the purchase of private coverage can be subsidised by government.

Private health insurance can be both complementary and supplementary in Denmark, Korea and New Zealand.

6.1.1. Health insurance coverage for a core set of services, 2011

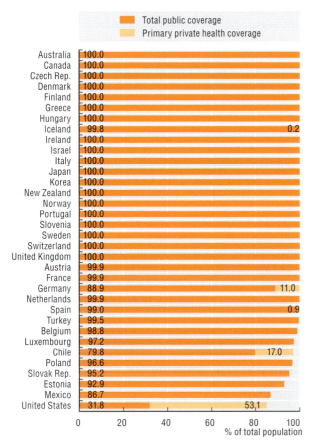

Source: OECD Health Statistics 2013, http://dx.doi.org/10.1787/health-data-en.

StatLink ᴹˢᴸ http://dx.doi.org/10.1787/888932918491

6.1.2. Private health insurance coverage, by type, 2011 (or nearest year)

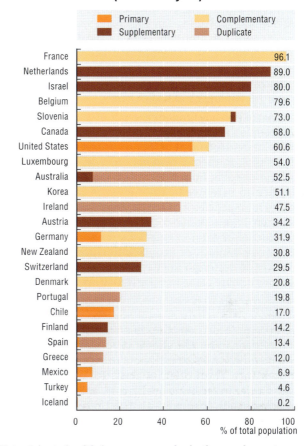

Note: Private health insurance can be both complementary and supplementary in Denmark, Korea and New Zealand; and duplicate, complementary and supplementary in Israel.

Source: OECD Health Statistics 2013, http://dx.doi.org/10.1787/health-data-en.

StatLink ᴹˢᴸ http://dx.doi.org/10.1787/888932918510

6.1.3. Evolution in private health insurance coverage, 2000 to 2011

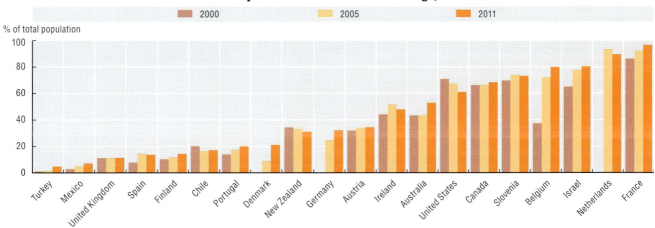

Source: OECD Health Statistics 2013, http://dx.doi.org/10.1787/health-data-en.

StatLink ᴹˢᴸ http://dx.doi.org/10.1787/888932918529

6.2. Out-of-pocket medical expenditure

Financial protection through public or private health insurance substantially reduces the amount that people pay directly for medical care, yet in some countries the burden of out-of-pocket spending can still create barriers to health care access and use. Households that have difficulties paying medical bills may delay or forgo needed health care (Banthin et al., 2008). On average across OECD countries, 20% of health spending is paid directly by patients (see Indicator 7.6 "Financing of health care").

In contrast to publicly funded care, out-of-pocket payments rely on people's ability to pay. If the financing of health care becomes more dependent on out-of-pocket payments, the burden shifts, in theory, towards those who use services more, and possibly from high to low-income households, where health care needs are higher. In practice, many countries have policies in place to protect vulnerable populations from excessive out-of-pocket payments. These consist of partial or total exemptions for social assistance beneficiaries, seniors, or people with chronic conditions, and in caps on out-of-pocket payments, defined in absolute terms or as a share of income (Paris, Devaux and Wei, 2010).

The burden of out-of-pocket medical spending can be measured either by its share of total household income or its share of household consumption. In 2011, the share of household consumption allocated to medical spending represented only 1.5% of total household consumption in countries such as the Netherlands, Turkey, the United Kingdom and France, but more than 4% in Portugal, Korea, Mexico and Chile (Figure 6.2.1). The United States, with 2.9% of household consumption spent on medical care, is on the OECD average.

Health systems in OECD countries differ in the degree of coverage for different health services and goods. In most countries, the degree of coverage for hospital care and doctor consultations is generally higher than for pharmaceuticals, dental care and eye care (Paris et al., 2010). Taking into account these differences as well as the relative importance of these different spending categories, it is not surprising to note some significant variations between OECD countries in the breakdown of the medical costs that households have to bear themselves.

In most OECD countries, curative care (including both inpatient and outpatient care) and pharmaceuticals are the two main spending items for out-of-pocket expenditure (Figure 6.2.2). On average, these two components account for 70% of all medical spending by households. In Belgium, Switzerland, New Zealand and Korea, household payments for inpatient and outpatient curative care account for about 50% or more of total household outlays. In other countries such as Poland, Estonia and the Czech Republic, half of out-of-pocket payments or more are for pharmaceuticals. In these countries, in addition to co-payments for prescribed pharmaceuticals, spending on over-the-counter medicines for self-medication has historically been high.

Payments for dental treatment also play a significant part in household medical spending. Around 19% of all out-of-pocket expenditure across OECD countries goes on dental care. In Denmark and Spain, this figure reaches 30%. This can be explained at least partly by the relatively low public coverage for dental care in these countries (see Indicator 6.5). The significance of therapeutic appliances (eye-glasses, hearing aids, etc.) in households' total medical spending is around 30% in the Netherlands and in the Slovak Republic. The average across OECD countries is 12%. More than half of this relates to eye-care products. In many countries, public coverage is limited to a contribution to the cost of lenses. Frames are often exempt from public coverage, leaving private households to bear the full cost if they are not covered by complementary private insurance.

Definition and comparability

Out-of-pocket payments are expenditures borne directly by a patient where neither public nor private insurance cover the full cost of the health good or service. They include cost-sharing and other expenditure paid directly by private households, and also include estimations of informal payments to health care providers in some countries. Only expenditure for medical spending (i.e. current health spending less expenditure for the health part of long-term care) is presented here, because the capacity of countries to estimate private long-term care expenditure varies widely.

6.2.1. Out-of-pocket medical spending as a share of final household consumption, 2011 (or nearest year)

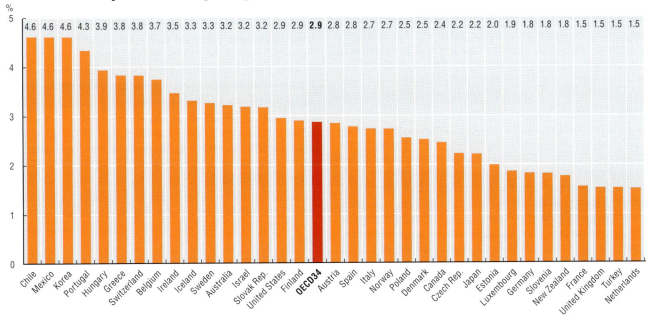

Note: This indicator relates to current health spending excluding long-term care (health) expenditure.
Source: OECD Health Statistics 2013, http://dx.doi.org/10.1787/health-data-en.

StatLink ᵐˢᵖ http://dx.doi.org/10.1787/888932918548

6.2.2. Shares of out-of-pocket medical spending by services and goods, 2011 (or nearest year)

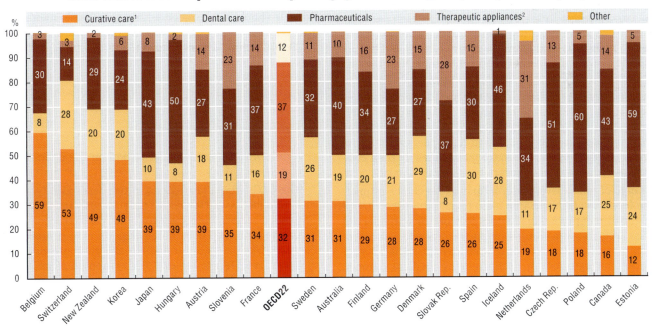

Note: This indicator relates to current health spending excluding long-term care (health) expenditure.
1. Including rehabilitative and ancillary services.
2. Including eye care products, hearing aids, wheelchairs, etc.
Source: OECD Health Statistics 2013, http://dx.doi.org/10.1787/health-data-en.

StatLink ᵐˢᵖ http://dx.doi.org/10.1787/888932918567

6.3. Geographic distribution of doctors

Access to medical care requires an adequate number and proper distribution of physicians in all parts of the country. Shortages of physicians in certain regions can increase travel times or waiting times for patients, and result in unmet care needs. The uneven distribution of physicians is an important concern in most OECD countries, especially in those countries with remote and sparsely populated areas, and those with deprived urban regions which may also be underserved.

The overall number of doctors per capita varies across OECD countries from lows of about two per 1 000 population in Chile, Turkey and Korea, to highs of four and more in Greece, Austria and Italy (Indicator 3.1). Beyond these cross-country differences, the number of doctors per capita also often varies widely across regions within the same country (Figure 6.3.1). A common feature in many countries is that there tends to be a concentration of physicians in capital cities. In the Czech Republic, for example, the density of physicians in Prague is almost twice the national average. Austria, Belgium, Greece, Portugal, the Slovak Republic and the United States also have a much higher density of physicians in their national capital region.

The density of physicians is consistently greater in urban regions, reflecting the concentration of specialised services such as surgery and physicians' preferences to practice in urban settings. Differences in the density of doctors between predominantly urban regions and rural regions in 2011 was highest in the Slovak Republic, Czech Republic and Greece, driven to a large extent by the strong concentration of doctors in their national capital region. The distribution of physicians between urban and rural regions was more equal in Japan and Korea (Figure 6.3.2).

Doctors may be reluctant to practice in rural and disadvantaged urban regions due to various concerns about their professional life (e.g. income, working hours, opportunities for career development, isolation from peers) and social amenities (such as educational opportunities for their children and professional opportunities for their spouse).

A range of policy levers may influence the choice of practice location of physicians, including: 1) the provision of financial incentives for doctors to work in underserved areas; 2) increasing enrolments in medical education programmes of students coming from specific social or geographic background, or decentralising medical schools; 3) regulating the choice of practice location of doctors (for all new medical graduates or possibly targeting more specifically international medical graduates); and 4) re-organising health service delivery to improve the working conditions of doctors in underserved areas and find innovative ways to improve access to care for the population.

In many OECD countries, different types of financial incentives have been provided to doctors to attract and retain them in underserved areas, including one-time subsidies to help them set up their practice and recurrent payments such as income guarantees and bonus payments.

In Canada, the province of Ontario provides an example of an attempt to decentralise medical schools. A new medical school was created in the Northern part of the province in 2005, far from the main urban centres, with the objective of increasing access to physician services in rural and remote parts (NOSM, 2012).

In Germany, the number of practice permits for new ambulatory care physicians in each region is regulated, based on a national service delivery quota (Federal Joint Committee, 2012).

In France, new multi-disciplinary medical homes (Maisons de Santé Pluridisciplinaires) were introduced a few years ago as a new form of group practices in underserved areas, allowing physicians and other health professionals to work in the same location while remaining self-employed.

The effectiveness and costs of different policies to promote a better distribution of doctors can vary significantly, with the impact likely to depend on the characteristics of each health system, the geography of the country, physician behaviours, and the specific policy and programme design. Policies should be designed with a clear understanding of the interests of the target group in order to have any significant and lasting impact (Ono et al., forthcoming).

Definition and comparability

Indicators 3.1 provides information on the definition of doctors.

The OECD classifies regions in two territorial levels. The higher level (Territorial Level 2) consists of large regions corresponding generally to national administrative regions. These broad regions may contain a mixture of urban, intermediate and rural areas. The lower level (Territorial level 3) is composed of smaller regions which are classified as predominantly urban, intermediate or predominantly rural regions (OECD, 2011a).

6.3.1. Physician density, by Territorial Level 2 regions, 2011 (or nearest year)

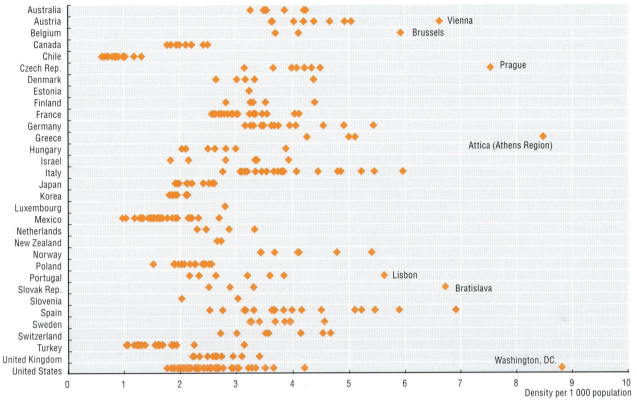

Source: OECD Regions at a Glance 2013.

StatLink ⌗ http://dx.doi.org/10.1787/888932918586

6.3.2. Physicians density in predominantly urban and rural regions, selected countries, 2011 (or nearest year)

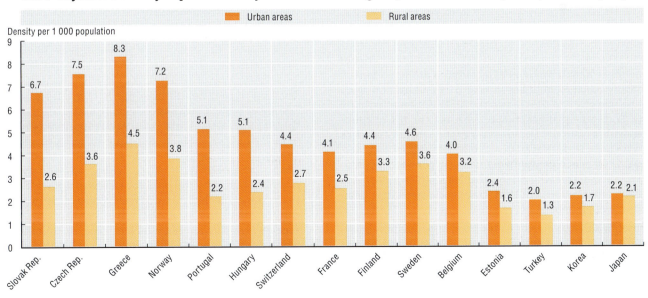

Source: OECD Regions at a Glance 2013.

StatLink ⌗ http://dx.doi.org/10.1787/888932918605

6.4. Inequalities in doctor consultations

Problems of access to health care can be measured by the actual utilisation of health care services and reported unmet health care needs. Any inequalities in health care utilisation and unmet care needs may result in poorer health status and increase health inequalities.

Inequalities in the probability and the number of doctor consultations across different socio-economic groups must take into account differences in need, because health problems are more frequent and more severe among lower socio-economic groups. The adjustment for need provides a better measure of inequity.

Figure 6.4.1 shows the degree of inequities for the probability of a doctor visit in the past year in 17 OECD countries and Brazil through the horizontal inequity index. If this index is greater than zero, then high income groups access doctors more than low income groups, after adjusting for relative need. Doctor visits were more likely among higher income persons in 15 out of 18 countries, although in most countries the degree of inequity is low. This is not the case in the United States, Brazil, Chile and Mexico, where richer people are significantly more likely to visit doctors.

In many countries, there are significant differences in the probability of GP and specialist visits. While the probability of a GP visit tends to be equally distributed in most countries, a different pattern emerges for specialist visits. In nearly all countries, higher income people are more likely to see a specialist than those with low income, and also more frequently. The only exceptions were the United Kingdom, the Czech Republic and Slovenia, where there was no statistically significant difference (Devaux and de Looper, 2012).

Consistent with these findings, an earlier European study found that people with higher education tend to use specialist care more, and the same was true for GP use in several countries (France, Portugal and Hungary) (Or et al., 2008). The study suggests that, beyond the direct cost of care, other health system characteristics are important in reducing social inequalities in health care utilisation, such as the role given to the GP and the organisation of primary care. Social inequalities in specialist use are less in countries with a National Health System and where GPs act as gatekeepers. Countries with established primary care networks may place greater emphasis on deprived populations, and gatekeeping often provides simpler access and better guidance for people in lower socio-economic positions (Or et al., 2008).

Unmet health care needs, as reported in population-based health surveys, is another way of assessing any access problems for certain population groups. A European-wide survey, conducted on an annual basis, provides information on the proportion of people reporting having some unmet needs for medical examination for different reasons. In all countries, people with low incomes are more likely to report unmet care needs than people with high incomes (Figure 6.4.2). The gap was particularly large in Hungary, Italy and Greece. The most common reason reported by low income people for unmet needs for medical examination is cost. In contrast, high income people report that their unmet care needs are due to a lack of time and a willingness to wait and see if the problem would simply go away.

It is important to consider self-reported unmet care needs in conjunction with other indicators of potential barriers to access, such as the extent of health insurance coverage and the amount of out-of-pocket payments. Germany, for example, reports above average levels of unmet care needs, yet it has full insurance coverage, low out-of-pocket payments, and a high density of doctors (Indicators 6.1, 6.2 and 3.1).

Definition and comparability

Consultations with doctors refer to the probability of visiting a doctor in the past 12 months, including both generalists and specialists. Data for Brazil, Chile and Mexico come from different studies. They relate to the probability of a doctor visit in the past three months in Chile and the past two weeks in Mexico.

Estimates of the horizontal inequity indices are derived from health interview or household surveys conducted around 2009. Inequalities in doctor consultations are assessed in terms of household income. The probability of doctor visits is adjusted for need, based on self-reported information about health status.

Differing survey questions and response categories may affect cross-national comparisons, and the measures used to grade income can also vary.

Data on unmet health care needs come from the European Union Statistics on Income and Living Conditions survey (EU-SILC). Survey respondents are asked whether there was a time in the previous 12 months when they felt they needed a medical examination but did not receive it, followed by a question as to why the need for care was unmet. The reasons include that care was too expensive, the waiting time was too long, the travelling distance to receive care was too far, a lack of time, or that they wanted to wait and see if the problem got better on its own. Figures presented here cover unmet care needs for any reason. Cultural factors, public expectations and policy debates may affect attitudes to unmet care. Caution is needed in comparing the results across countries.

6.4.1. Horizontal inequity indices for probability of a doctor visit in the past 12 months (with 95% confidence interval), selected OECD countries, 2009 (or nearest year)

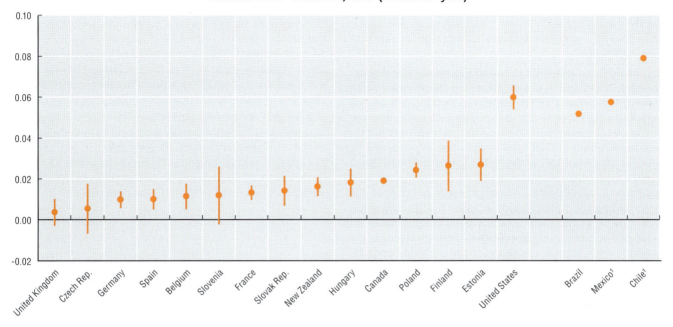

Note: The probability of a doctor, GP or specialist visit is inequitable if the horizontal inequity index is significantly different from zero. It favours high income groups when it is above zero. The index is adjusted for need.

1. Any physician visits in the past thee months in Chile and in the past two weeks in Mexico.

Source: Devaux and de Looper (2012); Almeida et al. (2013); Vasquez et al. (2013); Barraza-Lloréns et al. (2013).

StatLink ᵃˢᵖ *http://dx.doi.org/10.1787/888932918624*

6.4.2. Unmet care needs for medical examination by income level, European countries, 2011

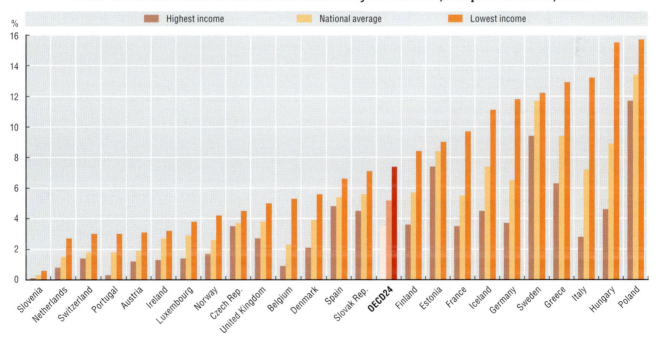

Source: EU-SILC 2011.

StatLink ᵃˢᵖ *http://dx.doi.org/10.1787/888932918643*

6.5. Inequalities in dentist consultations

Problems in access to dentists persist in many countries, most commonly among disadvantaged and low income groups. For example, in the United States, over 40% of low income persons aged 20-64 years had untreated dental caries in 2005-08, compared with only 16% of high income persons (NCHS, 2011).

Oral health care is mostly provided by private dental practitioners. Treatment is costly, averaging 5% of total health expenditure across OECD countries, with most of the spending paid for privately in many countries. On average across OECD countries, out-of-pocket payment for dental care represented 55% of total dental care expenditure in 2011, ranging from 18% in the Netherlands to 97% in Spain (Figure 6.5.1). In countries such as Spain, Israel and Switzerland, adult dental care is generally not part of the basic package of public health insurance, although some care may be provided for certain population groups. In most other countries, prevention and treatment are covered, but a significant share of the costs is borne by patients, and this may create access problems for low-income groups.

Recent OECD findings show that high income persons were more likely to visit a dentist within the last 12 months than low income persons (Figure 6.5.2). Inequalities are larger in countries with a lower probability of a dental visit such as Hungary, Poland, and the United States. Denmark and France have different recall periods, which affect the average probability of a dental visit but not the level of inequality. Both countries are among the most equitable for the probability of a dental visit, although the share of out-of-pocket payments in Denmark is much greater than in France.

There are also differences in the types of dental care received across different socio-economic groups. A Canadian study showed that access to preventive care is more common among higher income persons (Grignon et al., 2010). Income-related inequalities in dental service utilisation have also been found among Europeans aged 50 years and over, mostly due to inequalities in preventive dental visits (Listl, 2011).

A significant proportion of the population in different countries reports some unmet needs for dental care. Iceland (13.7%), Italy (11.5%) and Portugal (11.4%) reported the highest rates among EU countries in 2011, according to the European Union "Statistics on Income and Living Conditions survey" (Figure 6.5.3). In these three countries, there were large inequalities in unmet dental care needs between high and low income groups. On average across those European countries covered under this survey,

slightly more than 10% of low income people reported having some unmet care needs for dental care, compared with 3.4% for high income people. The most common reason reported by low income people for unmet needs for dental care was cost (for 68% of respondents), followed by fear of dentists (9%). A much lower proportion of high income people reported that their unmet needs for dental care was due to cost (30%), while a higher share responded that this was due to a lack of time (17%), fear (15%) or waiting times to get an appointment (13%).

Strategies to improve access to dental care for disadvantaged or underserved populations need to include both reducing financial and non-financial barriers, as well as promoting an adequate supply of dentists and other dental care practitioners to respond to the demand.

Definition and comparability

Data on the probability of a dentist visit come from health interview or household surveys, and rely on self-report. Inequalities in dental consultations are here assessed in terms of household income.

Differing survey questions and response categories may affect cross-national comparisons, and the measures used to grade income level can also vary. Most countries refer to dental consultations during the past 12 months, except for France (past 24 months) and Denmark (past three months). The difference in recall periods is likely to have an impact on the average probability of dentist visits, but not on the level of inequality.

Data on unmet health care needs come from the European Union Statistics on Income and Living Conditions survey (EU-SILC). No single survey or study on unmet care needs has been conducted across all OECD countries. To determine unmet dental care, EU-SILC asks whether there was a time in the previous 12 months when people felt they needed dental examinations but did not receive them. Cultural factors and policy debates may affect attitudes to unmet care. Caution is needed in comparing the magnitude of inequalities in unmet dental care needs across countries.

6.5.1. Out-of-pocket dental expenditure, 2011 (or nearest year)

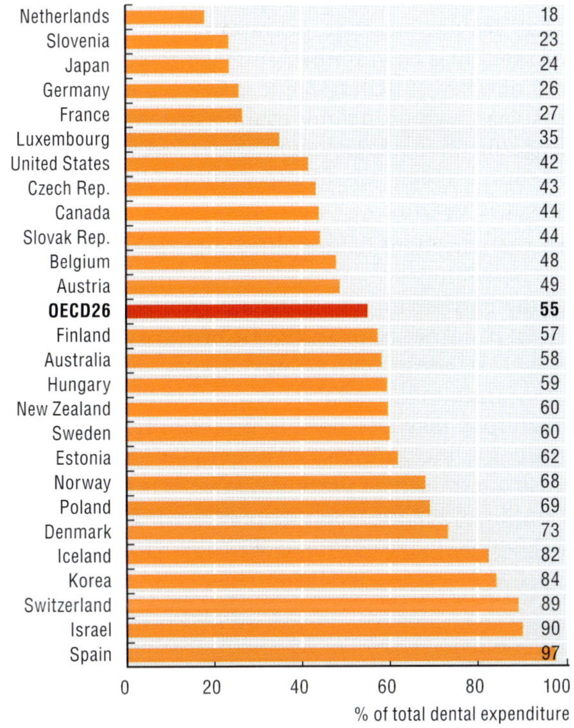
Netherlands 18
Slovenia 23
Japan 24
Germany 26
France 27
Luxembourg 35
United States 42
Czech Rep. 43
Canada 44
Slovak Rep. 44
Belgium 48
Austria 49
OECD26 55
Finland 57
Australia 58
Hungary 59
New Zealand 60
Sweden 60
Estonia 62
Norway 68
Poland 69
Denmark 73
Iceland 82
Korea 84
Switzerland 89
Israel 90
Spain 97
0 20 40 60 80 100
% of total dental expenditure

Source: OECD Health Statistics 2013, http://dx.doi.org/10.1787/health-data-en.

StatLink http://dx.doi.org/10.1787/888932918662

6.5.2. Probability of a dental visit in the past 12 months, by income group, 16 OECD countries, 2009 (or nearest year)

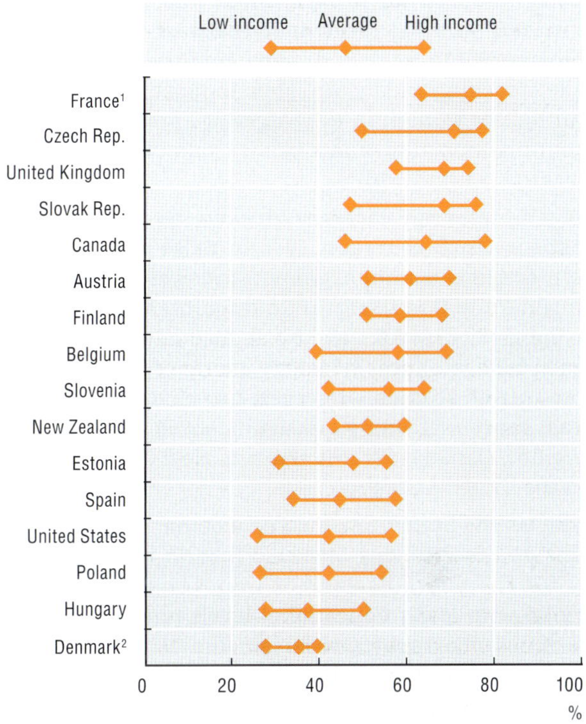
Low income
Average
High income
France[1]
Czech Rep.
United Kingdom
Slovak Rep.
Canada
Austria
Finland
Belgium
Slovenia
New Zealand
Estonia
Spain
United States
Poland
Hungary
Denmark[2]
0 20 40 60 80 100
%

1. Visits in the past two years.
2. Visits in the past three months.

Source: Devaux and de Looper (2012).

StatLink http://dx.doi.org/10.1787/888932918681

6.5.3. Unmet need for a dental examination, by income quintile, European countries, 2011

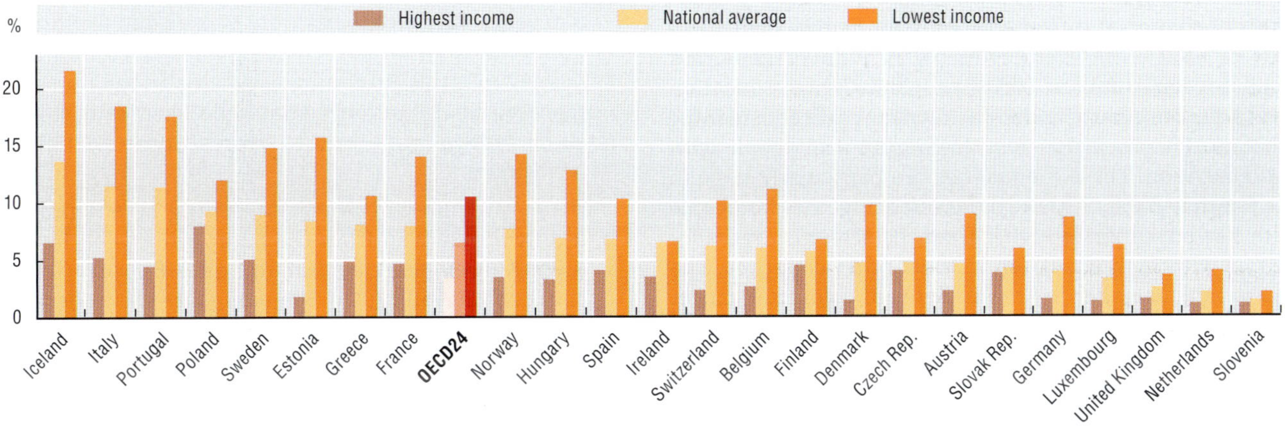
%
Highest income
National average
Lowest income
0
5
10
15
20
Iceland
Italy
Portugal
Poland
Sweden
Estonia
Greece
France
OECD24
Norway
Hungary
Spain
Ireland
Switzerland
Belgium
Finland
Denmark
Czech Rep.
Austria
Slovak Rep.
Germany
Luxembourg
United Kingdom
Netherlands
Slovenia

Source: EU-SILC 2011.

StatLink http://dx.doi.org/10.1787/888932918700

6.6. Inequalities in cancer screening

Cancer is the second most common cause of death in OECD countries, responsible for 26% of all deaths in 2011. The early detection of breast, cervical, and colorectal cancers through screening programmes has contributed to increased survival rates over the past five years (see Indicators 5.9 to 5.11), and many countries have opted to make screening widely available. In most countries, more than half of women in the target age groups have had a recent mammogram, and a pelvic exam or Pap smear (see Indicators 5.9 and 5.10).

Screening rates vary widely by education and socio-economic groups in OECD countries. Even in those countries where the practice is common, women in lower income groups are generally less likely to undergo breast and cervical screening (Figures 6.6.1 and 6.6.2). Income-related inequalities in cervical cancer screening are significant in 15 of the 16 countries studied. However, pro-rich inequalities in breast cancer screening are significant in fewer countries (Belgium, Canada, Estonia, France, New Zealand, Poland and the United States).

In the United States, low-income women, women who are uninsured or receiving Medicaid (health insurance coverage for the poor, disabled or impoverished elderly) or women with lower educational levels report much lower use of mammography and Pap smears (NCHS, 2011). There is additional evidence in European countries for significant social inequalities in utilisation of early detection and prevention services (von Wagner et al., 2011). In particular, women in higher socio-economic groups are more likely to have mammograms (Sirven and Or, 2010). However, in most OECD countries, income should not be a barrier to accessing screening mammography or Pap smears, since the services are provided free of charge, or at the cost of a doctor consultation.

Rates of colorectal cancer screening for people aged 50-75 vary by education level (Figure 6.6.3). On average across ten European countries, 22% of people with high education level have once participated in colorectal cancer screening whereas this proportion goes down to 14% for people with low education. These inequalities are particularly large in the Czech Republic, although the screening rates for people with low education is higher than the screening rates for people with high education in most other countries. The gap is much smaller in France. Rates of colorectal cancer screening vary across countries, with the highest rates in the Czech Republic and France. The Czech Republic and France completed nationwide rollout of colorectal cancer screening earlier than other countries (OECD, 2013e).

The utilisation of cancer screening services may largely depend on the availability of national public screening programmes. For instance, findings in Europe highlight that inequalities are larger in countries without population-based screening programmes (Palència et al., 2010). In addition, a number of demographic and socio-economic characteristics – such as income, ethnicity, younger age, higher level of education, employment status – as well as having a usual source of care are all important predictors of participation in screening.

Given the variety of factors affecting the use of different cancer screening, no single action can be expected to overcome the barriers for all population groups (Gakidou et al., 2008). In countries with sufficient health system capacity, increased screening can be encouraged by ensuring services are free and available where needed. Some policy interventions may also need to be better targeted in order to overcome inequalities. As a complementary tool, the promise of new cancer preventing vaccines also has important implications for resource-poor settings where maintaining screening programmes is challenging.

Definition and comparability

Breast and cervical screening rates measure the proportion of women of a given age who have received a recent mammogram, breast exam, pap smear or pelvic exam. Rates by income group were derived from national health surveys. For cervical cancer, women aged 20-69 years were asked whether they had been screened in the three years prior to the survey, and for breast cancer, women aged 50-69 years in the past two years. The exceptions were Mexico and Denmark (for breast only), where screening was reported for the past 12 months. Screening estimates based on self-reported health surveys should be used cautiously, since respondents tend to overestimate desirable behaviours.

Rates of colorectal cancer screening by education level were derived from the European Health Interview Survey (carried out in some EU countries between 2006 and 2009). Screening rate was collected for people aged 50-75, based on the following question: "Have you ever had a faecal occult blood test (FOBT)?". However, in some countries, other types of tests (e.g. colonoscopy, flexible sigmoidoscopy) may be used (see Indicator 5.11).

6.6.1. Cervical cancer screening in past three years by income level, selected OECD countries, 2009 (or nearest year)

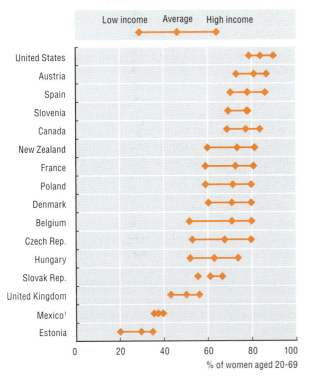

% of women aged 20-69

6.6.2. Breast cancer screening in past two years by income level, selected OECD countries, 2009 (or nearest year)

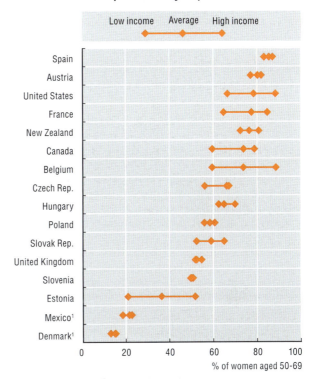

% of women aged 50-69

Note: The data source for some countries may be different to that used for reporting breast and cervical cancer screening in Chapter 5.
1. Visits in the past 12 months.
Source: Devaux and de Looper (2012).

StatLink *http://dx.doi.org/10.1787/888932918719*

Note: The data source for some countries may be different to that used for reporting breast and cervical cancer screening in Chapter 5.
1. Visits in the past 12 months.
Source: Devaux and de Looper (2012).

StatLink *http://dx.doi.org/10.1787/888932918738*

6.6.3. Colorectal cancer screening once in lifetime by educational level, European countries, 2009 (or nearest year)

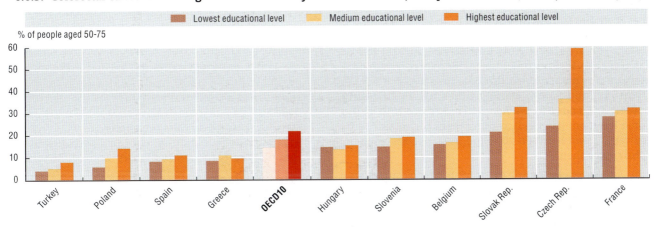

Source: Eurostat Statistics Database 2013.

StatLink *http://dx.doi.org/10.1787/888932918757*

6.7. Waiting times for elective surgery

Long waiting times for health services is an important health policy issue in many OECD countries (Siciliani et al., 2013). Long waiting times for elective (non-emergency) surgery, such as cataract surgery, hip and knee replacement, generates dissatisfaction for patients because the expected benefits of treatments are postponed, and the pain and disability remains. While long waiting times is considered an important policy issue in many countries, this is not the case in others (e.g., Belgium, France, Germany, Japan, Korea, Luxembourg, Switzerland, United States).

Waiting times is the result of a complex interaction between the demand and supply of health services, where doctors play a critical role on both sides. The demand for health services in general and elective surgery specifically is determined by the health status of the population, progress in medical technologies (including the increase ease of many procedures like cataract which can now be performed as day surgery), patient preferences (including their weighting of the expected benefits and risks), and the extent of cost-sharing for patients. However, doctors play a crucial role in converting the demand for better health from patients in a demand for medical care. On the supply side, the availability of different categories of surgeons, anaesthesists and other staff involved in surgical procedures, as well as the supply of the required medical and hospital equipment is likely to influence surgical activity rates.

The measure presented here focuses on waiting times from the time that a medical specialist adds a patient to the waiting list to the time that the patient receives the treatment. Both the average waiting time and the median are presented. Because some patients wait for very long times, the average is usually greater than the median.

In 2012, the average waiting times for cataract surgery was just over 30 days in the Netherlands, but more than three-times higher in Finland and Spain (Figure 6.7.1). Within the United Kingdom (in England), the average waiting times for cataract surgery was slightly over 60 days in 2011 (latest year available). Waiting times for cataract surgery has come down over the past few years in some countries, but not all. In Portugal and Spain, waiting times fell significantly between 2006 and 2010, but has increased since 2010. In the United Kingdom (England), waiting times for cataract surgery came down between 2006 and 2008, but has gone up slightly since then.

In 2012, the average waiting times for hip replacement was about 40 days in the Netherlands, but above 120 days in Spain, Portugal and Finland (Figure 6.7.2). The median waiting times was between 80 to 90 days in the United Kingdom (England) and Canada, but above 100 days in Estonia,

Australia, Finland and Portugal. As was the case for cataract surgery, waiting times for hip replacement fell sharply in the United Kingdom (England) between 2006 and 2008, but has gone up slightly since then. Similarly, following significant reduction between 2006 and 2010, waiting times for hip replacement in Portugal and Spain has increased since 2010. It has also increased slightly in Canada, and more so in New Zealand.

Waiting times for knee replacement has come down over the past few years in the Netherlands, Finland and Estonia, although it remains very long in Estonia (Figure 6.7.3). In the United Kingdom (England), it fell between 2006 and 2008, but has risen slightly since then. In Canada, New Zealand and Australia, waiting times for knee replacement has also increased at least slightly between 2008 and 2012.

Over the past decade, waiting time guarantees have become the most common policy tool to tackle long waiting times in several countries. This has been the case for instance in Finland where a National Health Care Guarantee was introduced in 2005 and led to a reduction in waiting times for elective surgery (Jonsson et al., 2013). However, these guarantees are only effective if they are enforced. There are two main approaches to enforcement: setting waiting time targets and holding providers accountable for achieving these targets; or allowing patients to choose alternative health providers (including the private sector) if they have to wait beyond a maximum amount of time (Siciliani et al., 2013).

Definition and comparability

There are at least two ways of measuring waiting times for elective procedures: 1) measuring the waiting times for patients treated in a given period; or 2) measuring waiting times for patients still on the list at a point in time. The data reported here relate to the first measure (data on the second measure are available in the OECD health database). The data come from administrative databases (not surveys). Waiting times are reported both in terms of the average and the median. The median is the value which separates a distribution in two equal parts (meaning that half the patients have longer waiting times and the other half lower waiting times). Compared with the average, the median minimises the influence of outliers (patients with very long waiting times). The data for the United Kingdom relate only to England.

6.7.1. Cataract surgery, waiting times from specialist assessment to treatment, 2006 to 2012 (or 2011)

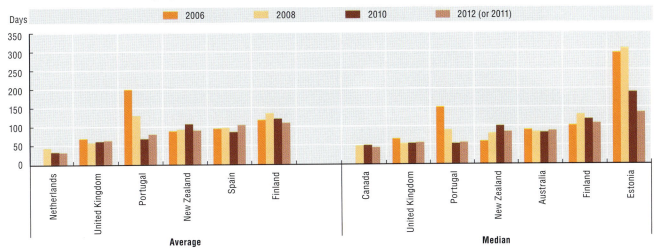

Source: OECD Health Statistics 2013, *http://dx.doi.org/10.1787/health-data-en.*

StatLink ᴹˢᴾ *http://dx.doi.org/10.1787/888932918776*

6.7.2. Hip replacement, waiting times from specialist assessment to treatment, 2006 to 2012 (or 2011)

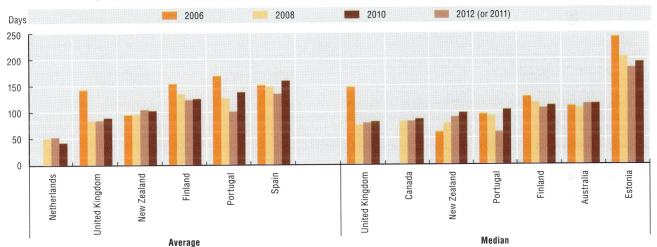

Source: OECD Health Statistics 2013, *http://dx.doi.org/10.1787/health-data-en.*

StatLink ᴹˢᴾ *http://dx.doi.org/10.1787/888932918795*

6.7.3. Knee replacement, waiting times from specialist assessment to treatment, 2006 to 2012 (or 2011)

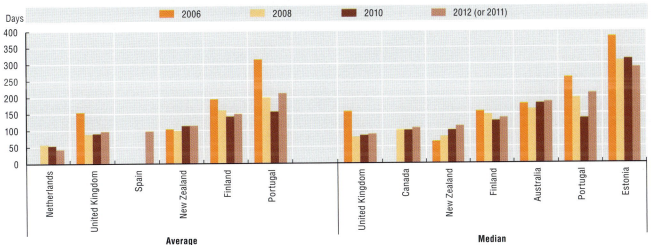

Source: OECD Health Statistics 2013, *http://dx.doi.org/10.1787/health-data-en.*

StatLink ᴹˢᴾ *http://dx.doi.org/10.1787/888932918814*

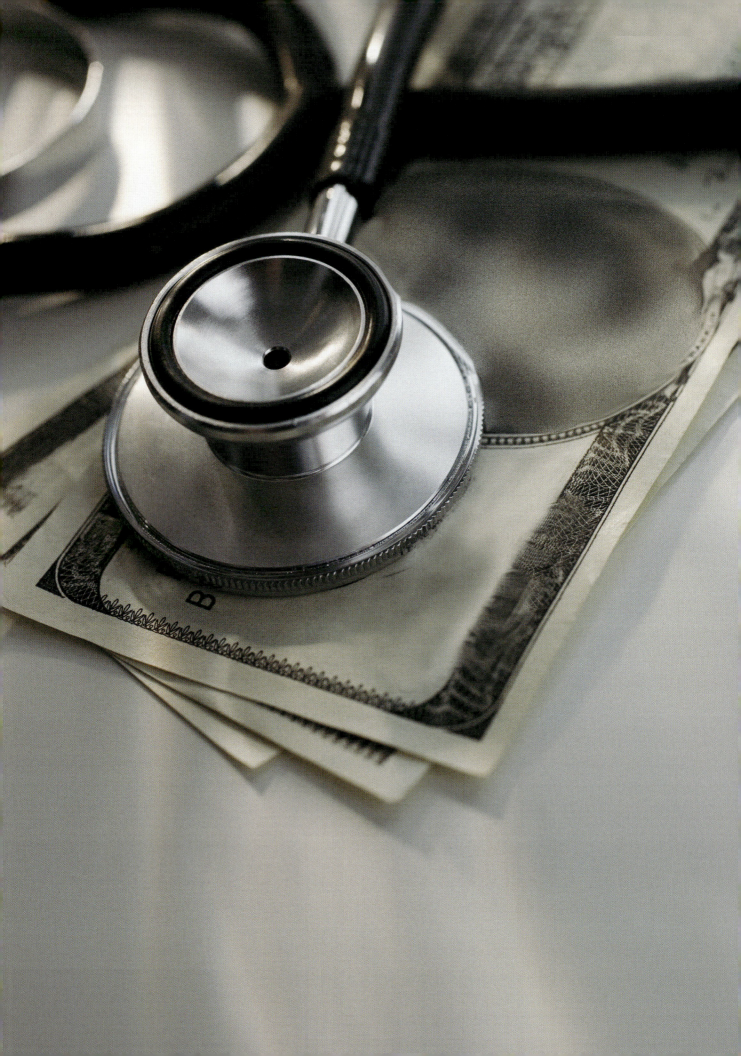

7. HEALTH EXPENDITURE AND FINANCING

The statistical data for Israel are supplied by and under the responsibility of the relevant Israeli authorities. The use of such data by the OECD is without prejudice to the status of the Golan Heights, East Jerusalem and Israeli settlements in the West Bank under the terms of international law.

7.1. Health expenditure per capita

How much OECD countries spend on health and the rate at which it grows reflects a wide array of market and social factors, as well as countries' diverse financing and organisational structures of their health systems.

In 2011, the United States continued to outspend all other OECD countries by a wide margin, with the equivalent of USD 8 508 for each person (Figure 7.1.1). This level of health spending is two-and-a-half times the average of all OECD countries and 50% higher than Norway and Switzerland, which were the next biggest spending countries. Compared with large European economies such as France and Germany, the United States spends around twice as much on health care per person. Around half of OECD countries fall within a per capita spending of between USD 3 000 and USD 4 500 (adjusted for countries' different purchasing powers – see Definition and Comparability). Countries spending below USD 3 000 include most of the southern and central European members of the OECD, together with Korea and Chile. The lowest per capita spenders on health in the OECD were Mexico and Turkey with levels of less than a third of the OECD average. Outside of the OECD, among the key emerging economies, China and India spent 13% and 4% of the OECD average on health per capita in 2011.

Figure 7.1.1 also shows the breakdown of per capita spending on health into public and private sources (see also Indicator 7.6 "Financing of health care"). In general, the ranking according to per capita public expenditure remains comparable to that of total spending. Even if the private sector in the United States continues to play the dominant role in financing, public spending on health per capita is still greater than that in all other OECD countries, with the exception of Norway and the Netherlands.

Since 2009, health spending has slowed markedly or fallen in many OECD countries after years of continuous growth. However, health spending patterns across the 34 OECD countries have been affected to varying degrees. On average across the OECD, per capita health spending over the period 2000-09 is estimated to have grown, in real terms, by 4.1% annually (Figure 7.1.2). In stark contrast, over the subsequent two years (2009-11), average health spending across the OECD grew at only 0.2% as the effects of the economic crisis took hold.

The extent of the slowdown has varied considerably across the OECD. While a number of European countries have experienced drastic cuts in spending, other countries out-

side of Europe have continued to see health spending grow albeit in many cases at a reduced pace.

Some of the European countries hardest hit by the economic downturn saw dramatic reversals in health spending compared with the period before the crisis. Greece, for example, saw per capita health spending falling by 11% in 2010 and 2011 after a yearly growth rate of more than 5% between 2000 and 2009. Ireland and Estonia also suffered significant falls in per capita health spending after previously strong growth.

Away from Europe, health spending growth also slowed significantly in most countries between 2009 and 2011, notably in Canada (0.8%) and the United States (1.3%). Only two OECD countries – Israel and Japan – saw the rate of health spending growth accelerate since 2009 compared with the period before. Health spending in Korea has continued to grow at more than 6% per year since 2009, albeit at a slower rate than in previous years.

Definition and comparability

Total expenditure on health measures the final consumption of health goods and services (i.e. current health expenditure) plus capital investment in health care infrastructure. This includes spending by both public and private sources on medical services and goods, public health and prevention programmes and administration.

To compare spending levels between countries, per capita health expenditures are converted to a common currency (US dollar) and adjusted to take account of the different purchasing power of the national currencies, in order to compare spending levels. Economy-wide (GDP) PPPs are used as the most available and reliable conversion rates.

To compare spending over time, figures are deflated using the economy-wide GDP implicit deflator for each country. In the case of Chile, the Consumer Price Index (CPI) is preferred since it is considered more representative of price changes in the health sector in recent years.

7.1.1. Health expenditure per capita, 2011 (or nearest year)

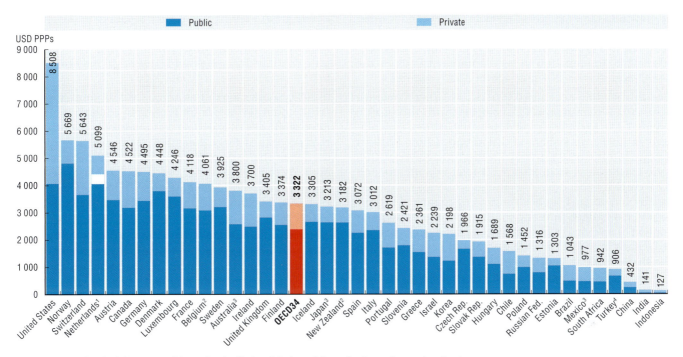

1. In the Netherlands, it is not possible to clearly distinguish the public and private share related to investments.
2. Current health expenditure.
3. Data refers to 2010.
4. Data refers to 2008.

Source: OECD Health Statistics 2013, http://dx.doi.org/10.1787/health-data-en; WHO Global Health Expenditure Database.

StatLink 🔢 *http://dx.doi.org/10.1787/888932918833*

7.1.2. Annual average growth rate in per capita health expenditure, real terms, 2000 to 2011 (or nearest year)

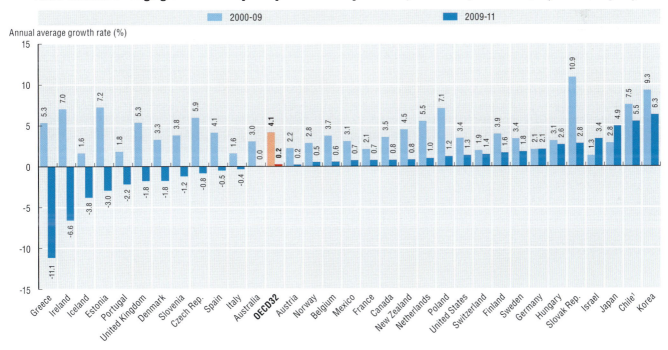

1. CPI used as deflator.
Source: OECD Health Statistics 2013, http://dx.doi.org/10.1787/health-data-en.

StatLink 🔢 *http://dx.doi.org/10.1787/888932918852*

7.2. Health expenditure in relation to GDP

Changes in the health spending to GDP ratio are the result of both fluctuations in the rate of health spending as well as growth in the economy as a whole. The economic crisis that began in 2008 ended a long period during which health spending had grown faster than GDP in many OECD countries. This has resulted in very different trends in the health-spending-to-GDP ratio across OECD countries.

Health spending accounted for 9.3% of GDP on average across OECD countries in 2011, compared with 9.4% in 2010 (Figure 7.2.1). Excluding capital spending, current expenditure on health as a share of GDP dropped from 9.1% on average in 2010 to 8.9% in 2011. The health spending to GDP ratio reached a peak in 2009 (9.6% total expenditure and 9.2% current expenditure) as overall economic conditions rapidly deteriorated but health spending continued to grow or was maintained in many countries. In the subsequent context of reducing public deficits and falling incomes, the reductions in (public) spending on health have resulted in the share of GDP falling since 2009.

In 2011, the United States spent 17.7% (17.0% for current expenditure on health) of GDP on health, remaining well above the OECD average and around six percentage points above the next group of countries, which include the Netherlands, France, Germany, Canada and Switzerland. The health spending to GDP ratio in the United States has remained at the same level since 2009, after years of continuous increases. It is not clear yet whether this levelling-off reflects cyclical factors and may start to grow again once the economy picks up, or whether it reflects more structural changes such as a slower diffusion of new technologies and pharmaceuticals, and changes in provider payments resulting in greater efficiency. Of the OECD countries, Mexico, Turkey and Estonia devoted only around 6% of GDP to health – around two-thirds of the OECD average. Outside of the OECD, China and India spent 5.2% and 3.9% of GDP respectively in 2011, while Brazil devoted 8.9% of GDP to health – close to the OECD average.

During the pre-crisis period up to 2009, all OECD countries saw health spending outpace economic growth resulting in an increasing share of GDP allocated to health (Figures 7.2.2 and 7.2.3). Average annual growth in health spending in real terms between 2000 and 2009 was 4.1% compared to GDP growth of only 1.5%. For example, Ireland saw health spending grow much more rapidly than the rate of economic growth during this period, resulting in the share of GDP rising from just over 6% in 2000 to 10% by 2009. France also, where economic growth in this period was more sluggish, continued to see a trend increase in the health share to GDP ratio between 2000 and 2009.

In 2009, health spending as a share of GDP jumped in many OECD countries as overall economic conditions deteriorated while health spending was essentially maintained in many countries. Since then, OECD countries have typically seen their share of health spending to GDP stabilise or fall. Some European countries, such as Estonia, Greece and Ireland saw health spending growth decline much more than GDP, resulting in a rapidly decreasing health spending to GDP ratio.

Away from Europe, Japan has continued to see its ratio to GDP grow such that by 2010 (latest figure available), the health spending to GDP ratio in Japan climbed above the OECD average for the first time. In Canada, after a sharp increase in 2009, the share of GDP devoted to health remained stable in 2010 and declined slightly in 2011.

Definition and comparability

See Indicator 7.1 "Health expenditure per capita" for a definition of total and current expenditure on health.

Gross Domestic Product (GDP) = final consumption + gross capital formation + net exports. Final consumption of households includes goods and services used by households or the community to satisfy their individual needs. It includes final consumption expenditure of households, general government and non-profit institutions serving households.

In countries such as Ireland and Luxembourg, where a significant proportion of GDP refers to profits exported and not available for national consumption, GNI may be a more meaningful measure than GDP.

7.2.1. Health expenditure as a share of GDP, 2011 (or nearest year)

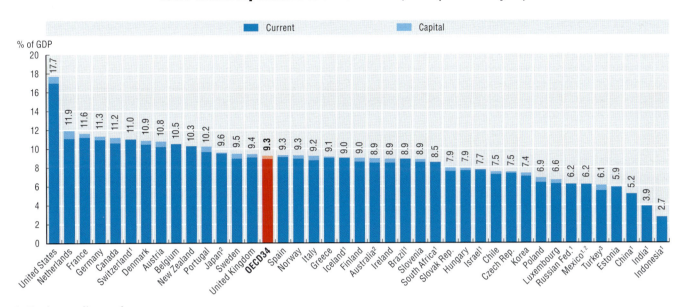

1. Total expenditure only.
2. Data refers to 2010.
3. Data refers to 2008.

Source: OECD Health Statistics 2013, http://dx.doi.org/10.1787/health-data-en; WHO Global Health Expenditure Database.

StatLink ⁜ᔆᖶ *http://dx.doi.org/10.1787/888932918871*

7.2.2. Health expenditure as a share of GDP, 2000-11, selected G7 countries

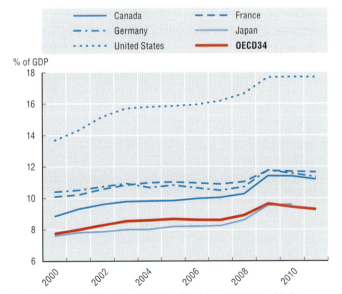

Source: OECD Health Statistics 2013, http://dx.doi.org/10.1787/health-data-en.

StatLink ⁜ᔆᖶ *http://dx.doi.org/10.1787/888932918890*

7.2.3. Health expenditure as a share of GDP, 2000-11, selected European countries

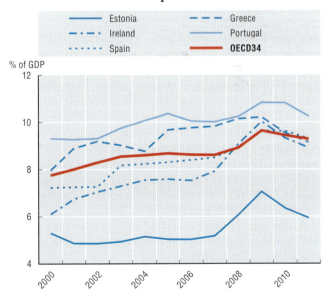

Source: OECD Health Statistics 2013, http://dx.doi.org/10.1787/health-data-en.

StatLink ⁜ᔆᖶ *http://dx.doi.org/10.1787/888932918909*

7.3. Health expenditure by function

Spending on inpatient care and outpatient care combined accounts for a large proportion of health expenditure across OECD countries – around 62% of current health expenditure on average in 2011 (Figure 7.3.1). A further 20% of health spending was allocated to medical goods (mainly pharmaceuticals, which accounted for 17% of total health spending), 12% on long-term care and the remaining 6% on collective services, such as public health and prevention services and administration.

Spending on inpatient care (including day care in hospitals) was the biggest costing component for a number of countries, including France and Greece where it accounted for 37% of total spending. While the United States consistently reports the highest share of outpatient care (and by consequence the lowest inpatient share), it should be noted that this figure includes remunerations of physicians who independently bill patients for hospital care. Other countries with a high share of outpatient spending include Israel and Portugal (48% and 45%).

The other major category of health spending is medical goods. In the Slovak Republic and Hungary, medical goods represent the largest spending category at 38% and 37% of current health expenditure respectively. In Denmark, New Zealand, Norway and Switzerland, on the other hand, spending on medical goods represents only 11% of total health spending. Differences in the consumption pattern of pharmaceuticals and relative prices are some of the main factors explaining the variations between countries.

There are also differences between countries in their expenditure on long-term care (see Indicator 8.9). Countries such as Norway, Denmark and the Netherlands, which have established formal arrangements for the elderly and the dependent population, allocate more than 20% of current health spending to long-term care. In countries with less comprehensive formal long-term care services such as Portugal, the expenditure on long-term care accounts for a much smaller share of total spending.

The slowdown in health spending experienced in many OECD countries in recent years has affected all spending categories, but to varying degrees (Figure 7.3.2). In more than half of OECD countries, total pharmaceutical spending fell in 2011 (see also Indicator 7.4). Many OECD countries have reduced their spending on prevention and public health services, with the reduction averaging 1.5% in 2010 and 1.7% in 2011 across all OECD countries. Whereas the decrease in 2010 can to some extent be explained by the

H1N1 influenza pandemic in 2009 which led to significant one-off expenditures for the purchase of large stocks of vaccines in many countries, the reduction in 2011 is mainly due to more general cuts to public health budgets. Expenditure growth for administration also slowed down. It was negative in 2010 and went up slightly in 2011, but the growth rate was lower than in 2008 and 2009. Cuts in administrative budgets were frequently an initial response to the financial crisis in many countries, such as in the Czech Republic where the budget of the Ministry of Health was reduced by 30% between 2008 and 2010.

Although remaining positive, growth rates for inpatient care, outpatient care and long-term care spending decreased significantly in 2010 and 2011 compared to 2008 and 2009. Many governments introduced measures to curb public spending on these health care functions, such as cuts in salaries of health workers and the reduction of health workforce, reductions in the fees to health providers and increases in co-payments for patients to ease mounting budget pressures (Morgan and Astolfi, 2013).

Definition and comparability

The *System of Health Accounts* (OECD, 2000; OECD, Eurostat, WHO, 2011) defines the boundaries of the health care system. Current health expenditure comprises personal health care (curative care, rehabilitative care, long-term care, ancillary services and medical goods) and collective services (prevention and public health services as well as health administration). Curative, rehabilitative and long-term care can also be classified by mode of production (inpatient, day care, outpatient and home care). Concerning long-term care, only the health aspect is normally reported as health expenditure, although it is difficult in certain countries to separate out clearly the health and social aspects of long-term care. Some countries with comprehensive long-term care packages focusing on social care might be ranked surprisingly low based on SHA data because of the exclusion of their social care. Thus, estimations of long-term care expenditure are one of the main factors limiting comparability across countries.

7.3.1. Current health expenditure by function of health care, 2011 (or nearest year)

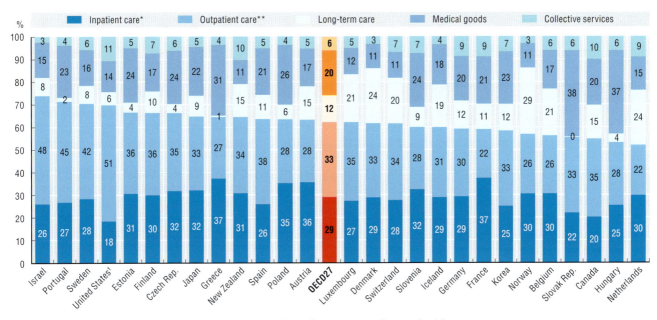

Note: Countries are ranked by curative-rehabilitative care as a share of current expenditure on health.
* Refers to curative-rehabilitative care in inpatient and day care settings.
** Includes home-care and ancillary services.
1. Inpatient services provided by independent billing physicians are included in outpatient care for the United States.
Source: OECD Health Statistics 2013, http://dx.doi.org/10.1787/health-data-en.

StatLink ⟨𝖬𝗦𝖫⟩ http://dx.doi.org/10.1787/888932918928

7.3.2. Average annual growth rates of health spending for selected functions, in real terms, OECD average, 2008 to 2011

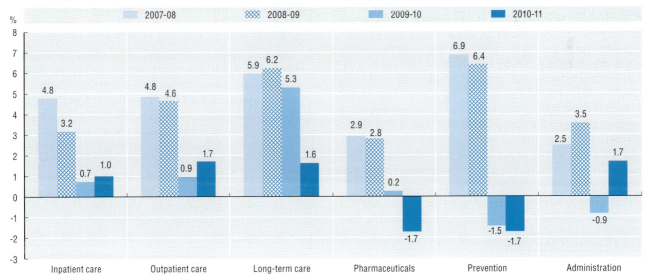

Source: OECD Health Statistics 2013, http://dx.doi.org/10.1787/health-data-en.

StatLink ⟨𝖬𝗦𝖫⟩ http://dx.doi.org/10.1787/888932918947

7.4. Pharmaceutical expenditure

Spending on pharmaceuticals accounted for more than a sixth (17%) of all health expenditure on average across OECD countries in 2011, making it the third largest spending component after inpatient and outpatient care.

The total pharmaceutical bill across OECD countries was around USD 800 billion in 2011. However, there are wide variations in pharmaceutical spending per capita across countries, reflecting differences in volume, structure of consumption and pharmaceutical prices (Figure 7.4.1, left panel). At almost USD 1 000 in 2011, the United States spent far more on pharmaceuticals than any other OECD country on a per capita basis. Canada (USD 701) and Greece (USD 673) also spent significantly more on medicines than the OECD average. At the other end of the scale, Chile and Mexico had relatively low spending levels.

Pharmaceutical spending accounted for 1.5% of GDP on average across OECD countries with around 0.8% of GDP financed publicly and the rest from private sources. Across OECD countries, the share of pharmaceutical spending in GDP ranges from less than 1% in Luxembourg, Norway, Denmark and Chile, to more than 2.5% in Hungary and Greece (Figure 7.4.1, right panel).

The economic crisis has had a significant effect on the growth in pharmaceutical spending in many OECD countries (Figure 7.4.2). Between 2000 and 2009, annual pharmaceutical expenditure per capita grew by 3.5% in real terms on average in OECD countries, but in the two years since 2009, the average growth became negative (-0.9%). Annual growth rates in pharmaceutical spending were lower between 2009 and 2011 than in the 2000-09 period in all OECD countries, apart from Chile and Australia. The reduction was particularly steep in those countries that were hit hardest by the recession. In Greece, pharmaceutical spending per capita decreased by 10% in both 2010 and 2011, following high growth rates in the preceding years. Estonia (-7.2%), Portugal (-5.9%), Iceland (-4.7%) and Ireland (-4.4%) also experienced substantial reductions in pharmaceutical spending between 2009 and 2011. In some of the larger OECD economies, spending growth per capita was also negative: annual growth rates decreased on average in Germany (-0.7%), France (-0.6%), the United States (-0.5%) and Canada (-0.3%) between 2009 and 2011.

OECD countries have introduced a series of measures to reduce pharmaceutical spending, including: price cuts (achieved through negotiations with pharmaceutical manufacturers, introduction of reference pricing, application of compulsory rebates, decrease of pharmacy margins, reductions of the value added tax applicable for pharmaceuticals), centralized public procurement of pharmaceuticals, promoting the use of generics, reduction in coverage (excluding pharmaceuticals from reimbursement) and increases in co-payments by households.

For example, Spain introduced a general rebate applicable for all medicines prescribed by NHS physicians in 2010. In addition, it mandated price reductions for generics which is one of the factors explaining the growth in the consumption of generics in that country (see Indicator 4.11). In Germany, compulsory rebates for manufacturers were raised in 2011 and prices frozen until 2013. From 2011 on, pharmaceutical companies were also mandated to enter into reimbursement price negotiations based on benefit evidence with the national association of health insurance funds for innovative drugs, which put an end to the previous free-pricing regime. In the United States, the Medicaid drug rebate percentage was increased and an annual fee imposed on manufacturers and importers of branded pharmaceuticals (OECD, 2010b). In Canada, the spending halt was due partly to patent expirations of brand name drugs for cholesterol and hypertension and the reduction of generic prices in many provinces (CIHI, 2012).

Definition and comparability

Pharmaceutical expenditure covers spending on prescription medicines and self-medication, often referred to as over-the-counter products, as well as other medical non-durable goods. It also includes pharmacists' remuneration when the latter is separate from the price of medicines. Pharmaceuticals consumed in hospitals are excluded (data available suggests that their inclusion would add another 15% to pharmaceutical spending approximately). Final expenditure on pharmaceuticals includes wholesale and retail margins and value-added tax.

7.4.1. Expenditure on pharmaceuticals per capita and as a share of GDP, 2011 (or nearest year)

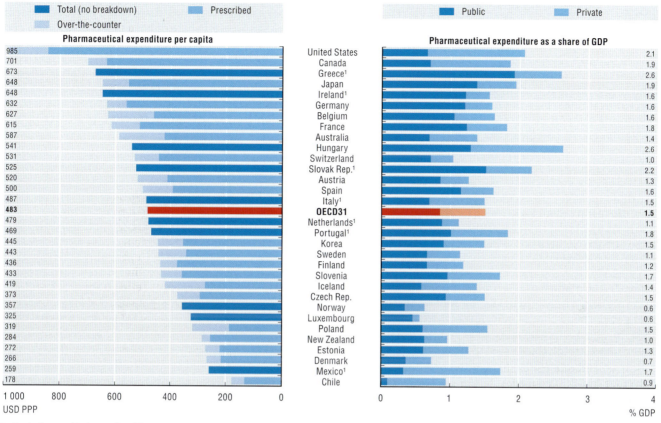

1. Includes medical non-durables.
Source: OECD Health Statistics 2013, http://dx.doi.org/10.1787/health-data-en.

StatLink http://dx.doi.org/10.1787/888932918966

7.4.2. Average annual growth in pharmaceutical expenditure per capita, in real terms, 2000 to 2011 (or nearest year)

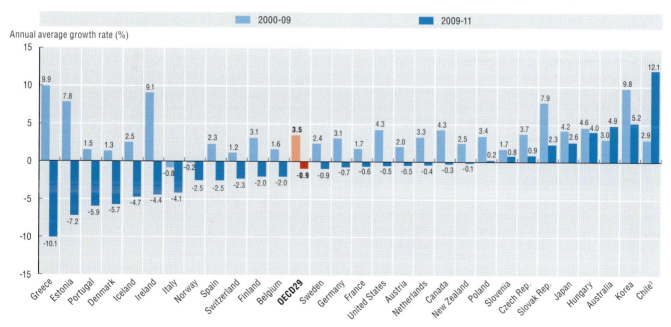

1. CPI used as deflator.
Source: OECD Health Statistics 2013, http://dx.doi.org/10.1787/health-data-en.

StatLink http://dx.doi.org/10.1787/888932918985

7. HEALTH EXPENDITURE AND FINANCING

7.5. Expenditure by disease and age

Attributing health care expenditure by disease and age is important for health policy makers in order to analyse resource allocations in the health care system. This information can also play a role in assessing the recent and possible future impact of ageing populations and changing disease patterns on spending. Furthermore, the linking of health expenditure by disease to appropriate measures of outputs (e.g. hospital discharges by disease) and outcomes (e.g. survival rates after heart attack or cancer) helps in monitoring the performance of health care systems at a disease-based level (Heijink et al., 2006).

Figure 7.5.1 shows the distribution of hospital acute inpatient expenditure according to six main diagnostic categories. These categories account for between 51% and 73% of all acute inpatient care expenditure in this group of countries. Circulatory diseases account for the highest share of inpatient spending in each of the countries except for Korea and the Netherlands, where spending on cancer and mental and behavioural disorders is the largest category, respectively. The differences between countries can be influenced by a number of factors, including demographic structure and disease patterns, as well as institutional arrangements and clinical guidelines for treating different diseases. Japan allocates more than 22% of hospital inpatient expenditure to the treatment of circulatory diseases, which is somewhat surprising given that discharges related to circulatory diseases only account for 12% of all discharges – a proportion similar to other countries. The high share of expenditure allocated to circulatory diseases may be explained by longer than average lengths of stay in Japan, particularly for some specific circulatory diseases such as cerebrovascular disease (stroke). In the Netherlands, mental and behavioral disorders account for 19% of all inpatient spending – around twice the level of the other countries shown. This may be partly explained by the large number of acute mental health hospitals with very long average lengths of stay.

Figure 7.5.2 compares expenditure per hospital discharge for circulatory diseases and cancer. Generally, the cost per discharge between these two main disease categories is similar in all countries, apart from Japan where spending per discharge for circulatory diseases is more than twice that of cancer. Japan also has the highest expenditure per discharge compared to the other countries, again likely due to the much longer lengths of stay, while Australia and the Netherlands have the highest expenditure per discharge for cancer treatment.

The different cost patterns may also be due partly to demographic factors. Figure 7.5.3 shows the share of hospital spending for people aged 65 and over compared with the share of the population aged 65 and over. As expected, this age group consumes proportionally more hospital resources compared to their share of the population. Japan allocates the greatest share of hospital expenditure to people aged 65 and over (64%), associated with the fact that it also has the highest share of people in that age group (23%). By contrast, Israel, Korea, and the Netherlands allocate only a third of all expenditure to those aged 65 and over, reflecting, at least partly, the fact that the proportion of the population in this age-group in these countries is only between 10% and 15%.

Definition and comparability

Expenditure by disease and age allocates current health expenditure by patient characteristics. Disease categories are based on ICD-10. To ensure comparability between countries, expenditures are linked to the System of Health Accounts (SHA) framework and a common methodology is proposed advocating primarily a top-down allocation of expenditure based on principal diagnosis.

The main comparability issues relate to the treatment of non-allocated and non-disease-specific expenditure. In the former case this is due to data limitations (often in outpatient and pharmaceutical expenditure) and in the latter case mainly prevention and administration expenditure. For more meaningful comparisons a subset of expenditure can be used, such as acute inpatient hospital care – an area where administrative records are generally complete with the necessary diagnostic and patient information.

The data presented here come primarily from data provided by countries as part of the OECD project of Estimating Expenditures by Disease, Age and Gender, supplemented by additional country data where similar methodologies have been used. Note that Figures 7.5.1-7.5.3 represent allocated spending only, and the following limitations apply: Canada excludes acute inpatient hospitalisations in Quebec and all inpatient hospitalisations in designated psychiatric hospitals; the Czech Republic refers to expenditure by the Health Insurance Fund only; Germany refers to total hospital expenditure; and the Netherlands refers to curative care in general and specialty hospitals.

7.5.1. Share of hospital inpatient expenditure by main diagnostic category, 2011 (or nearest year)

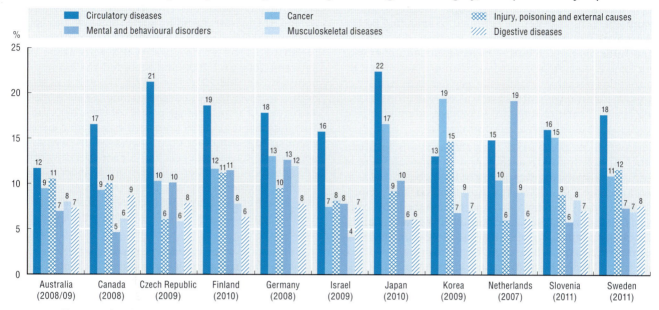

Source: Australia: AIHW (2012); Canada, Czech Republic, Finland, Israel, Korea, Slovenia and Sweden: unpublished data; Germany: Federal Statistical Office (2013); Japan, Netherlands: OECD calculations using published data.

StatLink 🔗 http://dx.doi.org/10.1787/888932919004

7.5.2. Expenditure per hospital discharge for two diagnostic categories, 2011 (or nearest year)

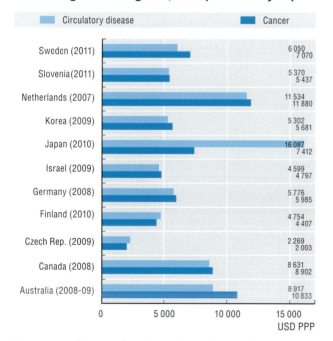

Source: Australia: AIHW (2012); Canada, Czech Republic, Finland, Israel, Korea, Slovenia and Sweden: unpublished data; Germany: Federal Statistical Office (2013); Japan, Netherlands: OECD calculations using published data.

StatLink 🔗 http://dx.doi.org/10.1787/888932919023

7.5.3. Hospital inpatient expenditure for those aged 65 and over, 2011 (or nearest year)

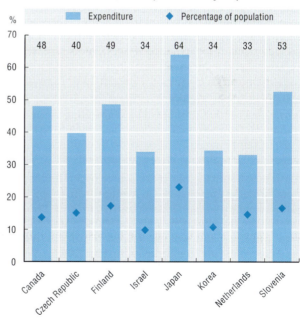

Source: Australia: AIHW (2012); Canada, Czech Republic, Finland, Israel, Korea, Slovenia and Sweden: unpublished data; Germany: Federal Statistical Office (2013); Japan, Netherlands: OECD calculations using published data.

StatLink 🔗 http://dx.doi.org/10.1787/888932919042

7.6. Financing of health care

Across all OECD countries, health care is financed by a mix of public and private spending. In some countries, public health spending is generally confined to spending by the government using general revenues. In others, social insurance funds finance the bulk of health expenditure. Private financing of health care consists mainly of payments by households (either as standalone payments or as part of co-payment arrangements) as well as various forms of private health insurance intended to replace, complement or supplement publicly financed coverage.

In nearly all OECD countries, the public sector is the main source of health care financing. Around three-quarters of health care spending was publicly financed in 2011. In Denmark, the United Kingdom and Sweden, the central, regional or local governments finance more than 80% of all health spending. In the Czech Republic, the Netherlands, Luxembourg, Japan, France, Slovenia and Germany, social insurance finances 70% or more of all health expenditure making it the dominant financing scheme. Only in Chile (45%), Mexico (47%) and the United States (49%) was the share of public spending on health below 50%. In these countries, a great proportion of health spending is financed either directly by households (Chile and Mexico) or by private insurance (United States).

Although public funds are the main source of financing for health spending in the majority of OECD countries, this does not imply that the public sector plays the dominant financing role for all health services and goods. On average across OECD countries, the public sector covered a much higher proportion of the costs of medical services (78%) compared with medical goods (54%) in 2011 (Figure 7.6.2). This is true for all countries with the exception of Switzerland, Greece and Korea where public coverage for medical goods is greater. For medical services, public sources covered 90% or more of total spending in the Czech Republic, the Netherlands and Estonia. Concerning medical goods, Luxembourg and Greece were the countries with the highest public spending shares (above 70%).

After public financing, the main source of funding tends to be out-of-pocket payments. On average it financed 20% of health spending across OECD countries in 2011. The share of out-of-pocket payments was above 30% in Mexico, Chile, Korea and Greece. It was the lowest in the Netherlands (6%), France (8%) and the United Kingdom (10%).

The share of out-of-pocket spending has changed in many countries over the past decade (Figure 7.6.3). While out-of-pocket spending decreased overall in Iceland and Spain between 2000 and 2011, the share has increased by nearly 2 percentage points since 2009 as public coverage for certain services was reduced as a result of the crisis and a growing share of payments was transferred to households. In Ireland, the private spending share remained flat between 2000 and 2009 but has since grown by 2 percentage points. In Portugal, the share grew by 1.5 percentage points between 2000 and 2009 and recorded the same growth between 2009 and 2011. The Slovak Republic has seen the biggest increase in the household share of health spending, with a rise of 15 percentage points between 2000 and 2010. This increase took place prior to the economic crisis, and was due to a combination of increased co-payments on prescribed pharmaceuticals and higher spending on non-prescribed drugs, greater use of private providers as well as informal payments to public providers (Szalay et al., 2011). Out-of-pocket payments also increased substantially in the Czech Republic between 2000 and 2008 with a slight drop since.

In a number of other countries, spending by private households has fallen sharply in the last decade as more services were covered by public sources or private insurance schemes. In Turkey, the reliance on private spending has been significantly reduced in the past decade as universal health care coverage has been expanded. In Switzerland the share of out-of-pocket spending also fell notably between 2000 and 2011 by around 7 percentage points, with most of this drop occurring between 2000 and 2008.

Definition and comparability

The financing of health care can be analysed from the point of view of the sources of funding (households, employers and the state), financing schemes (e.g., compulsory or voluntary insurance), and financing agents (organisations managing the financing schemes). Here "financing" is used in the sense of financing schemes as defined in the *System of Health Accounts* (OECD, 2000; OECD, Eurostat and WHO, 2011). Public financing includes expenditure by the general government and social security funds. Private financing covers households' out-of-pocket payments, private health insurance and other private funds (NGOs and private corporations). Out-of-pocket payments are expenditures borne directly by patients. They include cost-sharing and, in certain countries, estimations of informal payments to health care providers.

7.6.1. Expenditure on health by type of financing, 2011 (or nearest year)

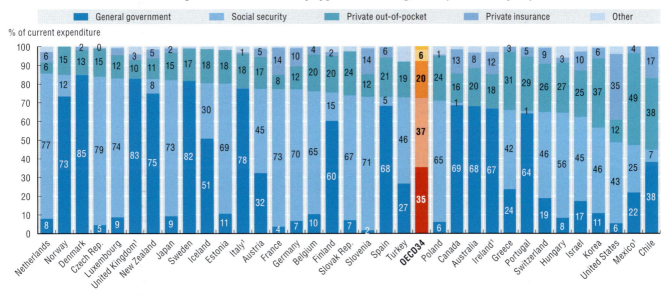

1. Data refer to total health expenditure.
Source: OECD Health Statistics 2013, http://dx.doi.org/10.1787/health-data-en.

StatLink http://dx.doi.org/10.1787/888932919061

7.6.2. Public share of expenditure on medical services and goods, 2011 (or nearest year)

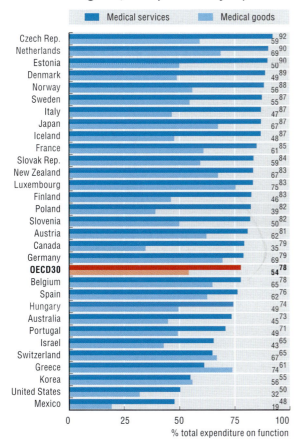

Source: OECD Health Statistics 2013, http://dx.doi.org/10.1787/health-data-en.
StatLink http://dx.doi.org/10.1787/888932919080

7.6.3. Change in out-of-pocket expenditure as share of total expenditure on health, 2000 to 2011 (or nearest year)

1. Data refer to current expenditure.
Source: OECD Health Statistics 2013, http://dx.doi.org/10.1787/health-data-en.
StatLink http://dx.doi.org/10.1787/888932919099

7.7. Trade in health services

Trade in health services and its most high-profile component, medical tourism, has attracted a great deal of media attention in recent years. The growth in "imports" and "exports" has been fuelled by a number of factors. Technological advances in information systems and communication allow patients or third party purchasers of health care to seek out quality treatment at lower cost and/or more immediately from health care providers in other countries. An increase in the portability of health coverage, whether as a result of regional arrangements with regard to public health insurance systems, or developments in the private insurance market, are also poised to further increase patient mobility. All this is coupled with a general increase in the temporary movement of populations for business, leisure or specifically for medical reasons between countries.

While the major part of international trade in health services does involve the physical movement of patients across borders to receive treatment, to get a full measure of imports and exports, there is also a need to consider goods and services delivered remotely such as pharmaceuticals ordered from another country or diagnostic services provided from a doctor in one country to a patient in another. The magnitude of such trade remains small, but advances in technology mean that this area also has the potential to grow rapidly.

Data on imports of health services and goods are available for most OECD countries and amounted to more than USD 7 billion in 2011. The vast majority of the trade recorded is between OECD countries. However, due to data gaps and under-reporting, this is likely to be a significant underestimate. With health-related imports of nearly USD 2.3 billion, Germany is the greatest importer in absolute terms, followed by the United States and the Netherlands. Nevertheless, in comparison to the size of the health sector, trade in health goods and services remains marginal for most countries. Even in the case of Germany, reported imports represent only around 0.6% of Germany's current health expenditure. The share rises above 1% of health spending only in Iceland and Portugal, as these smaller countries see a higher level of cross-border movement of patients. Luxembourg is a particular case because a large part of its insured population is living and consuming health services in neighbouring countries. In the majority of OECD countries reporting imports of health care goods and services, these have been increasing in the last five years, in many cases with double-digit annual growth rates.

A smaller number of countries can quantify total exports of health-related travel expenditure and other health services totalling around USD 6.9 billion in 2011 (Figure 7.7.2). For many countries these figures are, again, likely to be significant underestimates. In absolute values, the United States reported exports around USD 3 billion, while the exports of France and the Czech Republic exceeded USD 500 million. In relation to overall health spending, health-related exports remain marginal in most countries, except for the Czech Republic where they account for 3.6%. Slovenia, Poland and Hungary have also recorded shares above 1%. These countries have become popular destinations for patients from other European countries, particularly for services such as dental surgery. The growth rate in health-related exports has been around 20% per year over the past five years in Slovenia and Poland, but also in Korea.

Patient mobility in Europe may see further growth since the adoption of a EU directive in 2011 (Directive 2011/24/EU). The directive supports patients in exercising their right to cross border health care and promotes co-operation between health systems.

Definition and comparability

The *System of Health Accounts* includes imports within current health expenditure, defined as imports of medical goods and services for final consumption. Of these the purchase of medical services and goods, by resident patients while abroad, is currently the most important in value terms.

In the balance of payments, trade refers to goods and services transactions between residents and non-residents of an economy. According to the *Manual on Statistics of International Trade in Services*, "Health-related travel" is defined as "goods and services acquired by travellers going abroad for medical reasons". This category has some limitations in that it covers only those persons travelling for the specific purpose of receiving medical care, and does not include those who happen to require medical services when abroad. The additional item "Health services" covers those services delivered across borders but can include medical services delivered between providers as well as to patients.

7.7.1. Imports of health care services as share of health expenditure, 2011 and annual growth rate in real terms, 2006-2011 (or nearest year)

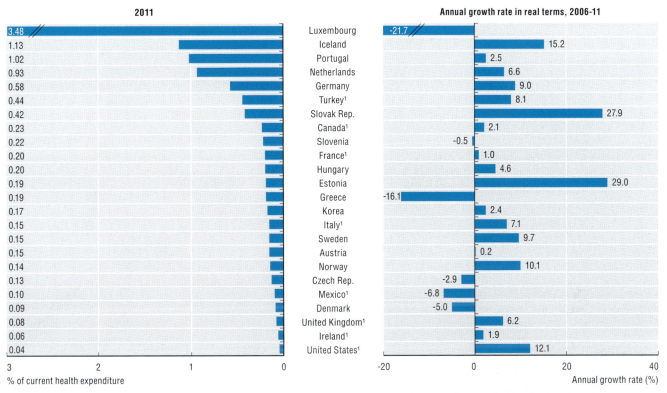

1. Refers to balance of payments concept of health-related travel plus health services within personal, recreational and cultural services.

Source: OECD Health Statistics 2013, http://dx.doi.org/10.1787/health-data-en; OECD-Eurostat Trade in Services Database.

StatLink ᴍˢᴾ *http://dx.doi.org/10.1787/888932919118*

7.7.2. Exports of health-related travel or other services as share of health expenditure, 2011 and annual growth rate in real terms, 2006-2011 (or nearest year)

Note: Health-related exports occur when domestic providers supply medical services to non-residents.

Source: OECD-Eurostat Trade in Services Database; Hungarian Central Statistical Office – Tourism Statistics.

StatLink ᴍˢᴾ *http://dx.doi.org/10.1787/888932919137*

8. AGEING AND LONG-TERM CARE

The statistical data for Israel are supplied by and under the responsibility of the relevant Israeli authorities. The use of such data by the OECD is without prejudice to the status of the Golan Heights, East Jerusalem and Israeli settlements in the West Bank under the terms of international law.

8.1. Demographic trends

Population ageing is characterised by a rise in the share of the elderly population resulting from longer life expectancy (see Indicator 1.1) and declining fertility rates (OECD, 2011b).

On average across OECD countries, the share of the population aged over 65 years has increased from less than 9% in 1960 to 15% in 2010 and is expected to nearly double in the next four decades to reach 27% in 2050 (Figure 8.1.1, left panel). In about two-thirds of OECD countries, at least one-quarter of the population will be over 65 years of age by 2050. This proportion is expected to be especially large in Japan, Korea and Spain where nearly 40% of the population will be aged over 65 years by 2050. Population ageing will also occur rapidly in China where the share of the population over 65 is expected to more than triple between 2010 and 2050, to reach the same level as the OECD average. Conversely, Israel and the United States will see a more gradual increase in the share of the elderly population due to significant inflows of migrants and higher fertility rates.

The increase in the share of the population aged 80 years and over will be even more dramatic (Figure 8.1.1, right panel). On average across OECD countries, 4% of the population were 80 years old and over in 2010. By 2050, the percentage will increase to 10%. In Japan, Spain and Germany, the proportion of the population aged over 80 is expected to nearly triple between 2010 and 2050 (rising from 6% to 16% in Japan, and from 5% to 15% in Spain and Germany). The rise will be even faster in Korea where the share of the population aged over 80 years will grow from 2% to 14% over the next four decades. Similarly, in China, the share of the population aged over 80 will rise from 1% to 8%.

Population ageing is a phenomenon affecting most countries around the world, but the speed of the process varies (Figure 8.1.2). The speed of population ageing is particularly rapid in the European Union, where the share of the popu-

lation aged 80 years and over increased from 1.5% in 1960 to nearly 5% in 2010, and is expected to rise to 11% by 2050. The pace of population ageing is slower in other parts of the world, although it is expected to accelerate in coming decades. In large emerging countries including Brazil, China, India, Indonesia and South Africa, only 1% of the population was 80 years and over in 2010, but this share is expected to reach around 5% by 2050.

Although the pressure that this growing proportion of people aged 65 and 80 over will put on long-term care systems will depend on the health status of people as they reach these ages, population ageing is likely to lead, all other things being equal, to greater demand for elderly care. As the share of the economically active population is expected to decline, it will also affect the financing of social protection systems and the potential supply of labour in the economy. On average across OECD countries, there were slightly more than four people of working age (15-64 years) for every person 65 years and older in 2012. This rate is projected to halve from 4.2 in 2012 to 2.1 on average across OECD countries over the next 40 years (OECD, 2013c).

Definition and comparability

Data on the population structure have been extracted from the OECD Historical Population Data and Projections (1950-2050). The projections are based on the most recent "medium-variant" population projections from the United Nations, World Population Prospects – 2012 Revision.

8.1.1. Share of the population aged over 65 and 80 years, 2010 and 2050

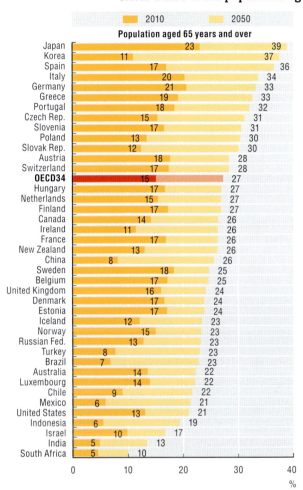

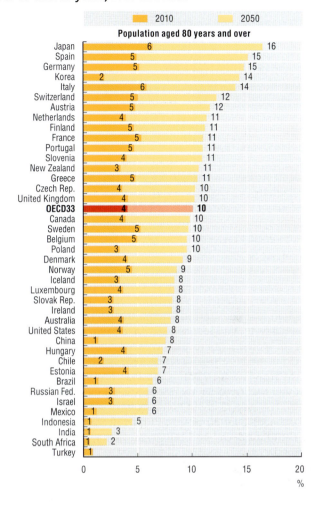

Source: OECD Historical Population Data and Projections Database, 2013.

StatLink http://dx.doi.org/10.1787/888932919156

8.1.2. Trends in the share of the population aged over 80 years, 1960-2050

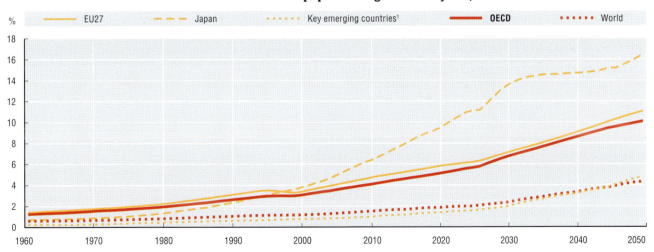

1. Emerging economies include Brazil, China, India, Indonesia and South Africa.
Source: OECD Historical Population Data and Projections Database, 2013.

StatLink http://dx.doi.org/10.1787/888932919175

8.2. Life expectancy and healthy life expectancy at age 65

Life expectancy at age 65 has increased significantly for both men and women during the past 50 years across both OECD countries and emerging economies. Some of the factors explaining these gains in life expectancy at age 65 include advances in medical care combined with greater access to health care, healthier lifestyles and improved living conditions before and after people reach age 65.

In 2011, women at age 65 could expect to live for another 20.9 years on average across OECD countries, while men could expect to live 17.6 years (Figure 8.2.1). Life expectancy at age 65 was the highest in France for both women (23.8 years) and men (19.3 years), followed by Japan. It was lower in Turkey (16.1 years for women and 14.1 years for men), where life expectancy at age 65 is similar to that of other major emerging countries such as South Africa.

On average across OECD countries, life expectancy at age 65 has increased by six years for women and 4.8 years for men since 1960. While the gender gap in life expectancy at age 65 widened in many countries in the 1960s and the 1970s, it has slightly narrowed over the past 30 years. In some countries such as Australia, New Zealand, United Kingdom and the United States, the overall gains in life expectancy at age 65 since 1960 have been greater for men than for women. Japan has achieved the highest gains in life expectancy at age 65 since 1960, with an increase of almost ten years for women and over seven years for men, although the increase has slowed down over the past few years. The gains in life expectancy have been more modest in some central and eastern European countries, such as the Slovak Republic and Hungary, especially for men, and in Mexico.

Countries relative position with respect to life expectancy at age 65 mirrors closely their relative position with regard to life expectancy at age 80. Life expectancy at age 80 is the highest in France (11.8 for women, 9.2 for men), followed by Japan (11.4 for women, 8.4 for men) and Italy (10.7 for women, 8.5 for men). Turkey has the lowest life expectancy at age 80 among OECD countries (6.7 for women and 6.2 for men). While life expectancy at age 65 in the United Kingdom is around the OECD average, it is much higher than the OECD average at age 80 (10.2 for women, 8.8 for men).

Increased life expectancy at age 65 does not necessarily mean that the extra years lived are in good health. In Europe, an indicator of disability-free life expectancy known as "healthy life years" is calculated regularly, based on a general question about disability in the European Survey of Income and Living Conditions (EU-SILC). Given that this indicator has only recently been developed, long-time series are not yet available and efforts continue to improve its comparability.

Among European countries participating in the survey, the average number of healthy life years at age 65 was almost the same for women and men, at 9.5 years for women and 9.4 years for men in 2011 (Figure 8.2.2). The absence of any significant gender gap in healthy life years means that women are more likely to live with some type of activity limitation after age 65 than men. Norway and Sweden had the highest number of healthy life years at age 65 in 2011, with over 15 years free of disability for women and about 14 years for men.

Definition and comparability

Life expectancy measures how long on average a person of a given age can expect to live, if current death rates do not change. However, the actual age-specific death rate of any particular birth cohort cannot be known in advance. If rates are falling, as has been the case over the past decades in OECD countries, actual life spans will be higher than life expectancy calculated using current death rates. The methodology used to calculate life expectancy can vary slightly between countries. This can change a country's estimates by a fraction of a year.

Disability-free life expectancy (or "healthy life years") is defined as the number of years spent free of activity limitation. In Europe, this indicator is calculated annually by Eurostat for EU countries and some EFTA countries using the Sullivan method (Sullivan, 1971). The disability measure is the Global Activity Limitation Indicator (GALI) which comes from the EU-SILC survey. The GALI measures limitation in usual activities due to health problems.

8.2.1. Life expectancy at age 65, 2011 and years gained since 1960 (or nearest year)

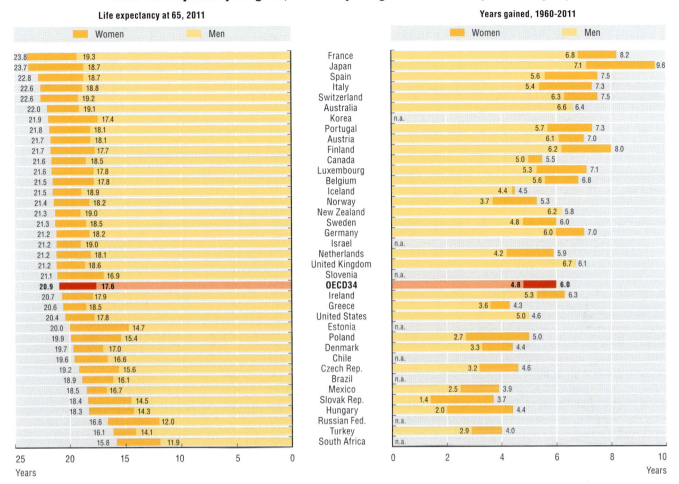

Life expectancy at 65, 2011 — Women / Men

Years gained, 1960-2011 — Women / Men

Country	Women	Men		Women gained	Men gained
France	23.8	19.3		6.8	8.2
Japan	23.7	18.7		7.1	9.6
Spain	22.8	18.7		5.6	7.5
Italy	22.6	18.8		5.4	7.3
Switzerland	22.6	19.2		6.3	7.5
Australia	22.0	19.1		6.6	6.4
Korea	21.9	17.4		n.a.	
Portugal	21.8	18.1		5.7	7.3
Austria	21.7	18.1		6.1	7.0
Finland	21.7	17.7		6.2	8.0
Canada	21.6	18.5		5.0	5.5
Luxembourg	21.6	17.8		5.3	7.1
Belgium	21.5	17.8		5.6	6.8
Iceland	21.5	18.9		4.4	4.5
Norway	21.4	18.2		3.7	5.3
New Zealand	21.3	19.0		6.2	5.8
Sweden	21.3	18.5		4.8	6.0
Germany	21.2	18.2		6.0	7.0
Israel	21.2	19.0		n.a.	
Netherlands	21.2	18.1		4.2	5.9
United Kingdom	21.2	18.6		6.7	6.1
Slovenia	21.1	16.9		n.a.	
OECD34	**20.9**	**17.6**		**4.8**	**6.0**
Ireland	20.7	17.9		5.3	6.3
Greece	20.6	18.5		3.6	4.3
United States	20.4	17.8		5.0	4.6
Estonia	20.0	14.7		n.a.	
Poland	19.9	15.4		2.7	5.0
Denmark	19.7	17.0		3.3	4.4
Chile	19.6	16.6		n.a.	
Czech Rep.	19.2	15.6		3.2	4.6
Brazil	18.9	16.1		n.a.	
Mexico	18.5	16.7		2.5	3.9
Slovak Rep.	18.4	14.5		1.4	3.7
Hungary	18.3	14.3		2.0	4.4
Russian Fed.	16.6	12.0		n.a.	
Turkey	16.1	14.1		2.9	4.0
South Africa	15.8	11.9		n.a.	

25 20 15 10 5 0 Years

0 2 4 6 8 10 Years

Source: OECD Health Statistics 2013, *http://dx.doi.org/10.1787/health-data-en*; national sources for non-OECD countries.

StatLink 🔗 *http://dx.doi.org/10.1787/888932919194*

8.2.2. Healthy life years at age 65, European countries, 2011

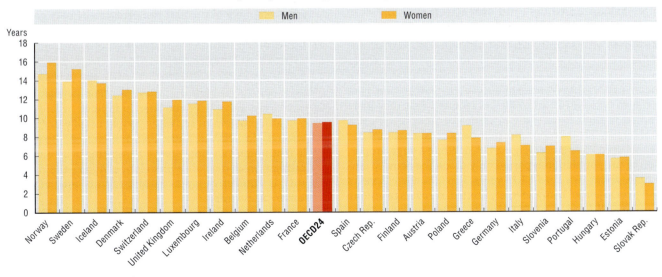

Men / Women

Source: Eurostat Statistics Database 2013.

StatLink 🔗 *http://dx.doi.org/10.1787/888932919213*

8.3. Self-reported health and disability at age 65

Most OECD countries conduct regular health surveys which allow respondents to report on different aspects of their health. A question that is often found among such surveys is usually similar to: "How is your health in general?". Although these questions are subjective, indicators of perceived general health have been found to be a good predictor of people's future health care use and mortality (DeSalvo, 2005; Bond et al., 2006). However, cross-country differences in perceived health status may be difficult to interpret as survey questions may differ slightly, and cultural factors can affect responses.

Keeping these limitations in mind, more than half of the population aged 65 years and over rate their health to be good in 12 of the 34 OECD countries (Figure 8.3.1). New Zealand, Canada and the United States have the highest percentage of older people assessing their health to be good, with at least three out of four people reporting to be in good health. However, the response categories offered to survey respondents in these three countries are different from those used in most other OECD countries, introducing an upward bias in the results (see box on "Definition and comparability" below).

In Finland, France, Germany, Greece and Spain, only between 35% and 40% of people aged 65 years and over rate their health to be good. And in Portugal, Hungary, Poland, Estonia, the Slovak Republic, Turkey, Japan and the Czech Republic, less than 20% of people aged 65 and over report being in good health. In nearly all countries, men over 65 were more likely than women to rate their health to be good, the exception being Australia. On average across OECD countries, 45.6% of men aged over 65 rated their health to be good, while 39.5% of women did so.

The percentage of the population aged 65 years and over who rate their health as being good has remained fairly stable over the past 30 years in most countries where long time series are available. There has been significant improvement however in the United States, where the share has increased from just over 60% in 1982 to 75% in 2011.

Measures of disability are not yet standardised across countries, limiting the possibility for comparisons across all OECD countries. In Europe, based on the EU Statistics on Income and Living Conditions survey (EU-SILC), 42% of people aged between 65 and 74 years reported that they were limited in their usual daily activities because of a health problem in 2011. The proportion rises to almost 60% for people aged 75 and over (Figure 8.3.2). While a large proportion of the population reported only moderate activity limitation, about 14% aged 65-74 years, and 25% aged 75 years and over reported being severely limited, on average among a group of 25 European OECD countries. Severe activity lim-

itations are more likely to create needs for long-term care, whether formal or informal.

People in Nordic countries reported the lowest level of moderate or severe disability, with the exception of Finland, where self-reported disability rates are higher and close to the European average. The highest rate of self-reported disability is in the Slovak Republic, followed by Estonia.

Definition and comparability

Self-reported health reflects people's overall perception of their own health, including both physical and psychological dimensions. Typically, survey respondents are asked a question such as: "How is your health in general? Very good, good, fair, poor, very poor". *OECD Health Statistics* provides figures related to the proportion of people rating their health to be "good/very good" combined.

Caution is required in making cross-country comparisons of perceived health status, for at least two reasons. First, people's assessment of their health is subjective and can be affected by cultural factors. Second, there are variations in the question and answer categories used to measure perceived health across surveys/countries. In particular, the response scale used in Australia, Canada, New Zealand and the United States is asymmetric (skewed on the positive side), including the following response categories: "excellent, very good, good, fair, poor". The data reported in *OECD Health Statistics* refer to respondents answering one of the three positive responses ("excellent, very good or good"). By contrast, in most other OECD countries, the response scale is symmetric, with response categories being: "very good, good, fair, poor, very poor". The data reported from these countries refer only to the first two categories ("very good, good"). Such difference in response categories biases upward the results from those countries that are using an asymmetric scale.

Perceived general disability is measured in the EU-SILC survey through the question: "For at least the past six months, have you been hampered because of a health problem in activities people usually do? Yes, strongly limited/Yes, limited/No, not limited". Persons in institutions are not surveyed, resulting in an underestimation of disability prevalence. Again, the measure is subjective, and cultural factors may affect survey responses.

8.3.1. Population aged 65 years and over reporting to be in good health, 2011 (or nearest year)

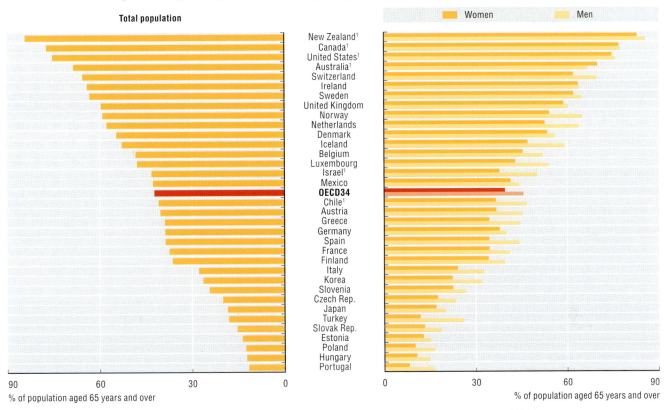

1. Results not directly comparable with other countries due to methodological differences (resulting in an upward bias).
Source: OECD Health Statistics 2013, http://dx.doi.org/10.1787/health-data-en.

StatLink 🔗 http://dx.doi.org/10.1787/888932919232

8.3.2. Limitations in daily activities, population aged 65-74 and 75 years and over, European countries, 2011

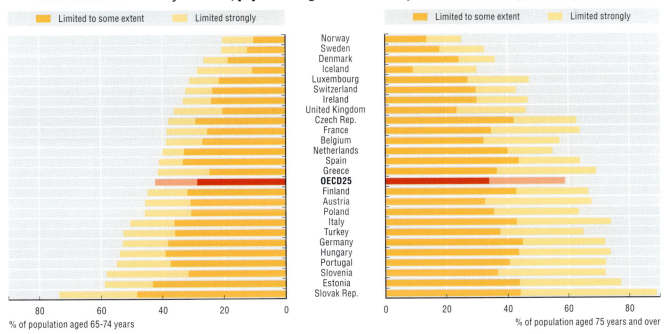

Source: Eurostat Database 2013.

StatLink 🔗 http://dx.doi.org/10.1787/888932919251

8.4. Dementia prevalence

Dementia describes a variety of brain disorders which progressively lead to brain damage, and cause a gradual deterioration of the individual's functional capacity and social relations. Alzheimer's disease is the most common form of dementia, representing about 60% to 80% of cases. Currently, there is no treatment that can halt dementia, but pharmaceutical drugs and other interventions can slow the progression of the disease.

According to WHO, nearly 35.6 million people around the world live with dementia. With population ageing and no widely effective prevention options, this number is expected to double by 2030 (65.7 million) and more than triple by 2050 (115.4 million) (WHO and Alzheimer Disease International, 2012).

In 2009, there were an estimated 14 million people aged 60 years and over suffering from dementia in OECD countries, accounting for more than 5% of the population in that age group, according to estimates by Wimo et al. (2010) (Figure 8.4.1). France, Italy, Switzerland, Spain, Sweden and Norway had the highest prevalence rate, with 6.3% to 6.5% of the population aged 60 years and over estimated as having dementia. The prevalence rate was only about half these rates in some emerging economies including South Africa, Indonesia and India, although this in part reflects fewer detected cases.

Clinical symptoms of dementia usually begin after the age of 65, and the prevalence increases markedly with age (Figure 8.4.2). The disease affects more women than men. In Europe, 14% of men and 16% of women aged 80-84 years were estimated as having dementia in 2009, compared to less than 4% among those under 75 years of age (Alzheimer Europe, 2009). For people aged 90 years and over, the figures rise to 31% of men and 47% of women. A similar pattern is observed in Australia (AIHW, 2012c). Early-onset dementia among people aged younger than 65 years is rare; they comprise less than 2% of the total number of people with dementia.

The direct costs of dementia account for a significant share of total health expenditure in OECD countries, greater than the direct costs related to depression and other mental disorders such as schizophrenia (Figure 8.4.3). In the Netherlands, dementia accounted for nearly 6% of overall health spending in 2007. Most of these costs were related to caring for people with dementia in nursing homes, but part of the costs were also related to home-based care and a smaller proportion for hospital-based care (Slobbe et al., 2011). In Germany, dementia accounted for 3.7% of total health expenditure in 2008, with most of the costs also allocated for care in nursing homes (Federal Statistical Office, 2013). In Korea, nearly 3% of total health expenditure was devoted to dementia care in 2009, but with most of the costs in this country related to care provided in hospital (unpublished data submitted to the OECD).

With a growing number of older persons suffering from the disease, dementia has become a health policy priority in many countries. National policies in Australia, Austria, Canada, France, the United States and other countries typically involve measures to improve early diagnosis, promote quality of care for people with dementia, and support informal caregivers (Wortmann, 2009; Juva, 2009; Ersek et al., 2009; Kenigsberg, 2009; Alzheimer Europe, 2012; OECD and European Commission, 2013).

Definition and comparability

Dementia prevalence rates are based on estimates of the total number of persons aged 60 years and over living with dementia divided by the size of the corresponding population. Estimates on prevalence by Wimo et al. (2010) are based on previous national epidemiological studies and meta-analyses which used the following age-specific dementia percentages: 1% for ages 60-64, 1,5% for ages 65-69, 3% for ages 70-74, 6% for ages 75-79, 13% for ages 80-84, 24% for ages 85-89, 34% for ages 90-94 and 45% for ages 95+.

In Figure 8.4.3, depression refers to mood disorders and schizophrenia includes schizophrenia, schizotypical and delusional disorders.

8.4.1. Prevalence of dementia among the population aged 60 years and over, 2009

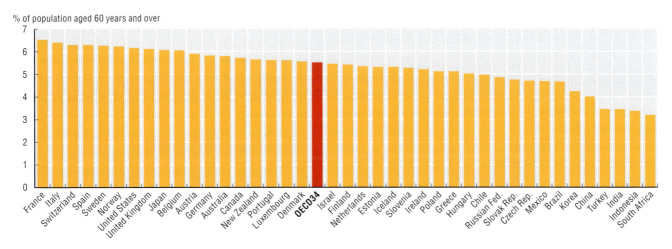

Source: Wimo et al. (2010).

StatLink ⬛️🖳 http://dx.doi.org/10.1787/888932919270

8.4.2. Age- and gender- specific prevalence of dementia in Europe and Australia, 2009

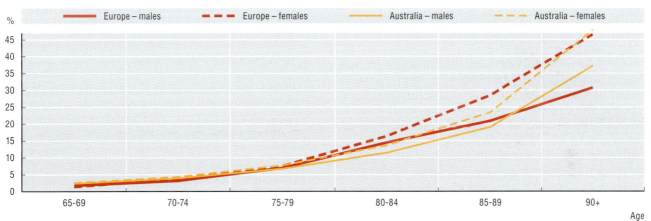

Source: Alzheimer Europe (2009); AIHW (2012).

StatLink ⬛️🖳 http://dx.doi.org/10.1787/888932919289

8.4.3. Share of total health expenditure allocated to dementia and other mental disorders, selected OECD countries, 2009 (or nearest year)

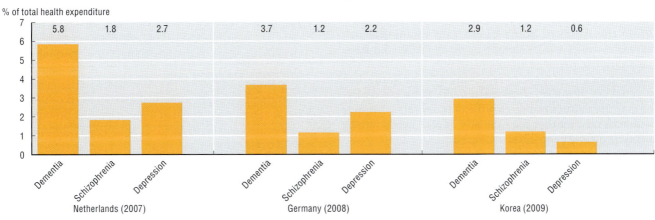

Source: OECD Project on Expenditure by Disease, Age and Gender (unpublished).

StatLink ⬛️🖳 http://dx.doi.org/10.1787/888932919308

8.5. Recipients of long-term care

The number of people receiving long-term care (LTC) services in OECD countries is rising, mainly due to population ageing and the growing number of elderly dependent persons, as well as the development of services and facilities in many countries.

Although long-term care services are delivered both to elderly people and younger disabled groups, the vast majority of LTC recipients are over 65 years of age. Among all LTC recipients, around 60% are women because of their higher life expectancy combined with a higher prevalence of disabilities and functional limitations in old age.

On average across OECD countries, over 12% of the population aged 65 and over were receiving some long-term care services at home or in institutions in 2011 (Figure 8.5.1). The number of LTC recipients as a share of the population aged 65 and over was the highest in Israel and Switzerland, with more than one-fifth of the population in that age group receiving long-term care. On the other hand, only about 1% of the population aged 65 and over in Poland receives formal LTC services, with most of them receiving them in institutions, although many more may receive informal care from family members at home. The use of long-term care services increases sharply with age. On average across OECD countries, 30% of the people aged 80 and over receive LTC services.

In response to most people's preference to receive LTC services at home, an important trend in many OECD countries over the past decade has been the implementation of programmes and benefits to support home-based care. In most countries for which trend data are available, the share of people aged 65 and over receiving long-term care at home in the total number of LTC recipients has increased over the past ten years (Figure 8.5.2). The proportion of LTC recipients at home is the highest in Japan and Hungary, with about 75% of LTC recipients receiving care at home. In Hungary, LTC in institutions has been restricted by budgetary constraints and stricter admission criteria. The share of home-based care recipients has also increased markedly in Sweden, Korea, France and Luxembourg. The share of home care recipients in France has increased from 40% to over 60%, as part of a multi-year plan to increase home nursing care capacity to 230 000 by 2025 (Colombo et al., 2011).

While the share of home-based care recipients has increased over the past decade in many OECD countries, the share has declined from 69% to 60% in Finland. The actual number of people receiving LTC at home has remained fairly stable, while the number of people receiving care in institutions has grown at a faster rate. This may be due to the fact that the intensity of care needs among the more elderly people has increased.

In the Unites States, only around 40% of LTC recipients receive care at home in 2009 (latest year available). This may partly reflect a traditional bias in supporting institutional-based care. Financial support to promote home-based care has only been implemented by certain states. Additional support or changes in incentives may be needed in the United States and in other countries to further encourage home-based care (Colombo et al., 2011).

Definition and comparability

LTC recipients are defined as persons receiving long-term care by paid providers, including non-professionals receiving cash payments under a social programme. They also include recipients of cash benefits such as consumer-choice programmes, care allowances or other social benefits which are granted with the primary goal of supporting people with long-term care needs. LTC institutions refer to nursing and residential care facilities which provide accommodation and long-term care as a package. LTC at home is defined as people with functional restrictions who receive most of their care at home. Home care also applies to the use of institutions on a temporary basis, community care and day-care centres and specially designed living arrangements. Concerning the number of people aged 65 and over receiving LTC in institutions, the estimate for Ireland is under-reported. Data for Japan underestimate the number of recipients in institutions because hospitals also provide LTC. In the Czech Republic, LTC recipients refer to recipients of the care allowance (i.e., cash allowance paid to eligible dependent persons). Data for Poland only refer to services in nursing homes. Data in Spain only refer to a partial coverage of facilities or services. In Australia, the data do not include recipients who access the Veterans' Home Care Program and those who access services under the National Disability Agreement, as it is currently unknown how many of these people could be included in LTC recipients. Australia does not directly collect data on whether clients or consumers of health and aged care services are receiving LTC and data are therefore estimated. With regard to the age threshold, data for Austria, Belgium, France and Poland refer to people aged over 60, while they refer to people over 62 in the Slovak Republic. This is resulting in a slight under-estimation of the share in these countries, given that a much smaller proportion of people aged 60-65 or 62-65 receive LTC compared with older age groups.

8.5.1. Population aged 65 years and over receiving long-term care, 2011 (or nearest year)

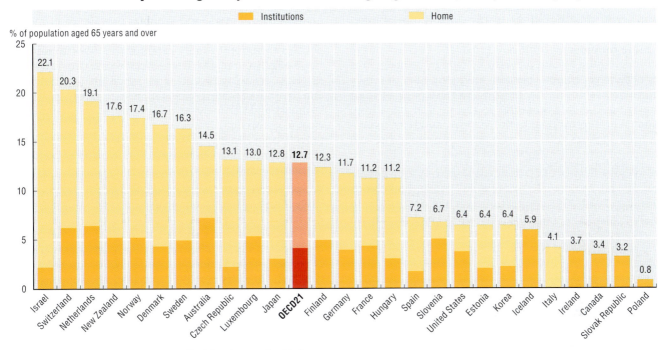

Source: OECD Health Statistics 2013, http://dx.doi.org/10.1787/health-data-en.

StatLink ᴍ⬛ᴸ http://dx.doi.org/10.1787/888932919327

8.5.2. Share of long-term care recipients aged 65 years and over receiving care at home, 2000 and 2011 (or nearest year)

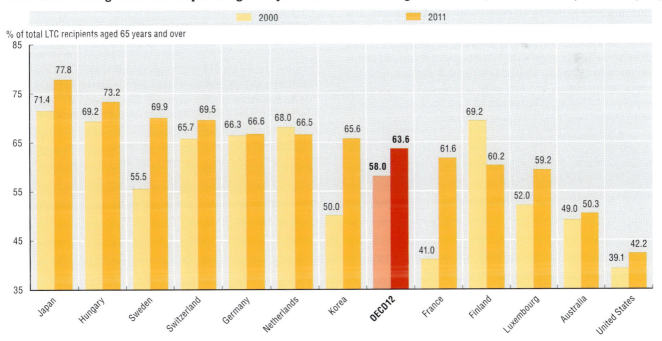

Source: OECD Health Statistics 2013, http://dx.doi.org/10.1787/health-data-en.

StatLink ᴍ⬛ᴸ http://dx.doi.org/10.1787/888932919346

8.6. Informal carers

Family carers are the backbone of long-term care systems in all OECD countries, although there are substantial variations across countries in the relative importance of informal caregiving by family members compared with the use of more formal long-term care providers. Because of the informal nature of care provided by family members, it is not easy to get comparable data on the number of family carers across countries, nor on the frequency of their caregiving. The data presented in this section come from national or international health surveys, and refer to people aged 50 years and over who report providing care and assistance to family members and friends.

On average across OECD countries, over 15% of people aged 50 and over provided care for a dependent relative or friend in 2010. This proportion reaches about 20% in Belgium and Italy (Figure 8.6.1). In Italy, the high proportion of people who provide care to a family member is associated with relatively few formal (paid) LTC workers (see Indicator 8.7).

Most informal carers are women. On average across countries, more than 60% of carers are women. This ranges from a high of 71% in Hungary to a low of 54% in Denmark (Figure 8.6.2).

On average across OECD countries, 66% of informal carers provide care on a daily basis, while the remaining 34% provide care only on a weekly basis. However, there is wide variation across countries in the intensity in caregiving (Figure 8.6.3). In some southern European countries (Portugal, Spain and Italy), Poland and Slovenia where there is a strong culture of family members providing care for their elderly parents, three-quarter or more of informal carers report providing care on a daily basis. By contrast, in countries such as Sweden, Switzerland and Denmark where a greater share of LTC services is provided by paid workers, the proportion of people providing care on a daily basis is much lower.

Intensive caregiving is associated with a reduction in labour force attachment for caregivers of working age, higher poverty rates, and a higher prevalence of mental health problems. Many OECD countries have implemented policies to support family carers with a view to mitigate these negative impacts. These include paid care leave (e.g., Belgium), allowing flexible work schedules (e.g., Australia and the United States), providing respite care (e.g., Austria, Denmark and Germany) as well as counselling/training services (e.g., Sweden). Moreover, a number of OECD countries provide cash benefits to family caregivers or cash-for-care allowances for recipients which can be used to pay informal caregivers (Colombo et al., 2011).

The potential pool of working-age and older family carers is likely to shrink in the coming decades as a result of declining family size, changes in residential patterns of people with disabilities, and rising participation rates of women in the labour market. Therefore, it is likely that a greater share of people providing informal care may be required to provide high-intensity care. Without adequate support, informal caregiving might exacerbate employment and health inequalities (Colombo et al., 2011).

Definition and comparability

Family carers are defined as people providing daily or weekly help to family members, friends and people in their social network living in their household or outside of the household who require help for Activities of Daily Living (ADL) and Instrumental Activities of Daily Living (IADL). The data relate only to the population aged 50 and over, and are based on national or international health surveys. Survey results may be affected by reporting biases or recall problems.

8.6.1. Population aged 50 and over reporting to be informal carers, 2010 (or nearest year)

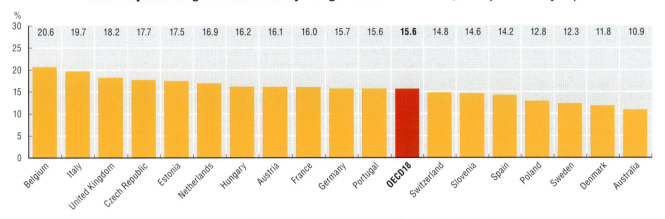

Source: OECD estimates based on 2011 HILDA survey for Australia, 2009 BHPS survey for the United Kingdom and 2010 SHARE survey for other European countries.

StatLink 🔗 *http://dx.doi.org/10.1787/888932919365*

8.6.2. Share of women among all informal carers aged 50 and over, 2010 (or nearest year)

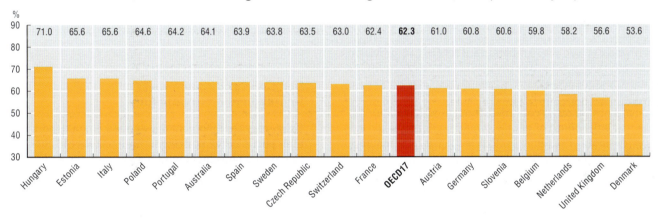

Source: OECD estimates based on 2011 HILDA survey for Australia, 2009 BHPS survey for the United Kingdom and 2010 SHARE survey for other European countries.

StatLink 🔗 *http://dx.doi.org/10.1787/888932919384*

8.6.3. Frequency of care provided by informal carers, 2010 (or nearest year)

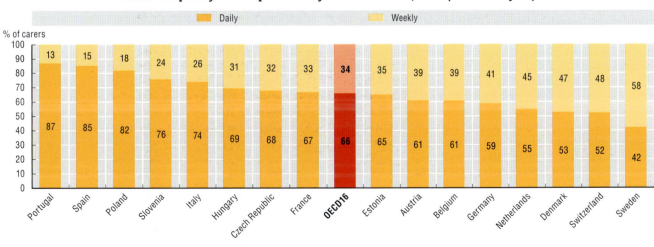

Source: OECD estimates based on the 2010 SHARE survey.

StatLink 🔗 *http://dx.doi.org/10.1787/888932919403*

The provision of long-term care (LTC) is a labour-intensive activity. Formal LTC workers are defined as paid workers, typically nurses and personal carers, providing care and/or assistance to people limited in their daily activities at home or in institutions. Formal long-term care is complemented by informal, usually unpaid, care by family and friends, which accounts for a large part of care for older people in all OECD countries (see Indicator 8.6).

Relative to the population aged 65 and over, Norway and Sweden have the largest number of LTC workers, and Italy the lowest share (Figure 8.7.1). The organisation of formal care also varies across OECD countries. Care providers work mainly in institutions in the United States, Denmark, Switzerland, Canada and the Czech Republic, even though most recipients may receive care at home in some of these countries (see Indicator 8.5). People working in LTC institutions often attend to people with more severe limitations. Conversely, most formal LTC workers provide care at home in Estonia, Israel, Korea and Japan.

Most LTC workers are women and work part-time. Over 90% of LTC workers are women in Canada, Denmark, the Czech Republic, Ireland, Korea, New Zealand, the Slovak Republic, the Netherlands, Norway and Sweden. Foreign-born workers also play an important role in LTC provision, although their presence is uneven across OECD countries. While Germany has very few foreign-born LTC workers, in the United States nearly one in every four care workers is foreign-born. In other countries, foreign-born workers represent a large share of people providing home-based services, including LTC services. This is the case, for instance, in Italy where about 70% of people providing services at home are foreign-born (Colombo et al., 2011). The recruitment of foreign-born workers to provide LTC at home or in institutions can help respond to growing demand, often at a relatively low cost. But the growing inflows of LTC workers coming from other countries have raised some issues in certain countries, such as the management of irregular migration inflows and paid work which is undeclared for tax and social security purposes.

Employment in the LTC sector still represents only a small share of total employment in OECD countries, averaging just over 2% across all OECD countries. However, this share has increased over the past decade in many countries, with the broadening of public protection against LTC risks and increased demand stemming from population ageing. In Japan, the number of LTC workers has more than doubled since the implementation of the universal LTC insurance programme in 2000, while there was a slight decrease in total employment in the economy over this period. Employment has also increased in the LTC sector in Germany and, to lesser extent, in Denmark and Norway (Figure 8.7.2).

On average, close to 30% of formal LTC providers are nurses, while the other 70% are personal care workers (who may be called under different names in different countries – nursing aides, health assistants in institutions, home-based care assistants, etc.). Many countries are looking at possibilities to delegate some of the tasks currently provided by nurses to lower-skilled providers to increase the supply of services and reduce costs, while ensuring at the same time that minimum standards of quality of care are maintained. One of the common approaches to ensure quality of services in OECD countries has been to set educational and training requirements for personal care workers. Still, these requirements vary substantially across OECD countries resulting in various qualifications level among personal care workers, especially where home-based care is concerned (OECD/European Commission, 2013).

Given population ageing and the expected decline in the availability of family caregivers, the demand for LTC workers as a share of the working population is expected to at least double by 2050. A combination of policies is needed to respond to this, including policies to improve recruitment (e.g., encouraging more unemployed people to consider training and working in the LTC sector); to improve retention (e.g., enhancing pay and work conditions); and to increase productivity (e.g., through reorganisation of work processes and more effective use of new technologies) (Colombo et al., 2011; European Commission, 2013).

Definition and comparability

Long-term care workers are defined as paid workers who provide care at home or in institutions (outside hospitals). They include qualified nurses (see definition under Indicator 3.7) and personal care workers providing assistance with ADL and other personal support. Personal care workers include different categories of workers who may have some recognised qualification or not. Because they may not be part of recognised occupations, it is more difficult to collect comparable data for this category of LTC workers. LTC workers also include family members or friends who are employed under a formal contract either by the care recipient, an agency, or public and private care service companies. The numbers are expressed as head counts, not full-time equivalent.

The data for Germany exclude elderly care nurses, and persons declared to social security systems as caregivers, resulting in a substantial under-estimation. The data for Italy exclude workers in semi-residential long-term care facilities. The data for Japan involve double-counting (as some workers may work in more than one home). The data for Ireland refer only to the public sector. The data for Australia are estimates drawn from the 2011 National Aged Care Workforce Census and Survey, and underrepresent the numbers of people who could be considered LTC workers.

8.7.1. Long-term care workers as share of population aged 65 and over, 2011 (or nearest year)

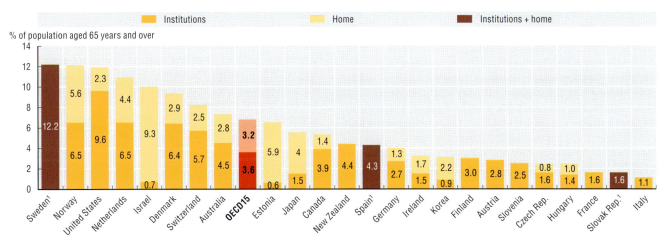

1. In Sweden, Spain and the Slovak Republic, it is not possible to distinguish LTC workers in institutions and at home.
Source: OECD Health Statistics 2013, http://dx.doi.org/10.1787/health-data-en.

StatLink http://dx.doi.org/10.1787/888932919422

8.7.2. Trends in long-term care employment and total employment, selected OECD countries, 2000-11 (or nearest year)

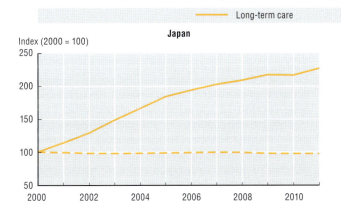
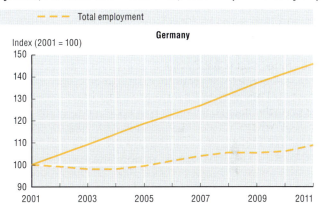

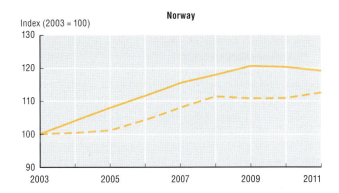

Source: OECD Health Statistics 2013, http://dx.doi.org/10.1787/health-data-en.

StatLink http://dx.doi.org/10.1787/888932919441

8.8. Long-term care beds in institutions and hospitals

The number of beds in long-term care (LTC) institutions and in LTC departments in hospitals provides a measure of the resources available for delivering LTC services to individuals outside of their home.

On average across OECD countries, there were 44 beds in LTC institutions and five beds in LTC departments in hospitals per 1 000 people aged 65 and over in 2011 (Figure 8.8.1). Luxembourg had the highest number of LTC beds in 2011, with almost 80 beds per 1 000 people aged 65 and over in LTC institutions. On the other hand, there were fewer than 20 beds per 1 000 people aged 65 and over in LTC institutions or in hospitals in Italy and Poland.

While most countries allocate very few beds for LTC in hospitals, others still use hospital beds quite extensively for LTC purposes. Although the number of beds in LTC institutions in Korea has increased strongly following the implementation of a public LTC insurance programme for the elderly in 2008, many beds in hospitals are still dedicated to LTC services. Similarly, in Japan many hospital beds have been traditionally used for long-term care, even if the number of beds in LTC institutions has also recently increased. Among European countries, Finland and Hungary have maintained a fairly large number of LTC beds in hospitals. Finland has, however, developed institutional facilities while reducing the use of hospital beds for long-term care, similar to what is occurring in countries such as Iceland and France (Figure 8.8.2).

Many other OECD countries have expanded capacity in LTC institutions to provide care to patients who no longer need acute care in hospitals and to free up costly hospital beds. In most OECD countries, the number of LTC beds in institutions has increased more rapidly than the number of LTC beds in hospitals, Korea, Estonia and Hungary being the exceptions (Figure 8.8.2). Available LTC beds in institutions have increased substantially in Korea and Spain since 2000. In Sweden, the reduction in both hospital and institutional beds reflects the implementation of policies designed to promote home-based care (Colombo et al., 2011).

Providing LTC in institutions is generally more expensive than providing home-based care, if only because of the additional cost of board and lodging and also because of higher staffing ratios. LTC users generally prefer to remain at home. However, depending on individual circumstances, a move to LTC institutions may be the most appropriate option, for example for people living alone and requiring round the clock care and supervision (Wiener et al., 2009) or people living in remote areas with limited home-care support.

Definition and comparability

Long-term care institutions refer to nursing and residential care facilities which provide accommodation and long-term care as a package. They include specially designed institutions or hospital-like settings where the predominant service component is long-term care for people with moderate to severe functional restrictions. Beds in adapted living arrangements for persons who require help while guaranteeing a high degree of autonomy and self control are not included. For international comparisons, they should not include beds in rehabilitation centers.

However, there are variations in data coverage across countries. Several countries only include beds in publicly-funded LTC institutions, while others also include private institutions (both profit and non-for-profit). Some countries also include beds in treatment centers for addicted people, psychiatric units of general or specialised hospitals, and rehabilitation centers. Australia does not collect data on the numbers of beds provided for LTC. Data on Australian LTC beds in institutions are estimated from the aged care database.

8.8.1. Long-term care beds in institutions and hospitals, 2011 (or nearest year)

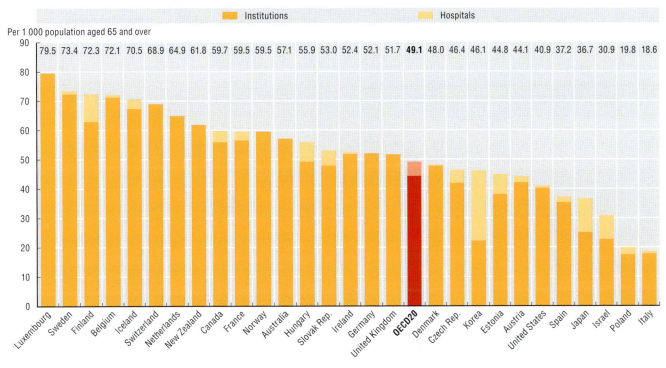

Source: OECD Health Statistics 2013, http://dx.doi.org/10.1787/health-data-en.

StatLink ⫘ http://dx.doi.org/10.1787/888932919460

8.8.2. Trends in long-term care beds in institutions and in hospitals, 2000-11 (or nearest year)

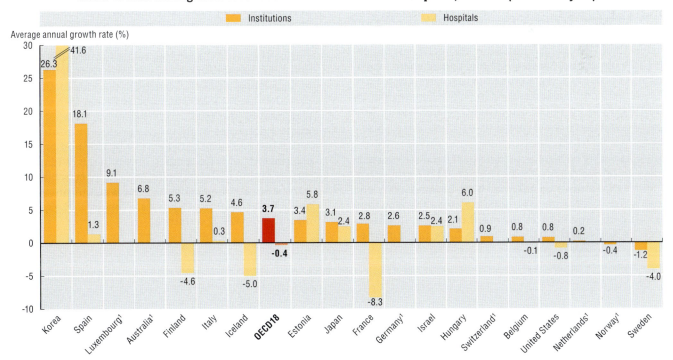

Note: The OECD average excludes Korea (due to the extremely high growth rate).
1. Australia, Germany, Luxembourg, the Netherlands, Norway and Switzerland do not report any long-term care beds in hospital.
Source: OECD Health Statistics 2013, http://dx.doi.org/10.1787/health-data-en.

StatLink ⫘ http://dx.doi.org/10.1787/888932919479

8.9. Long-term care expenditure

Long-term care (LTC) expenditure has risen over the past few decades in most OECD countries and is expected to rise further in the coming years due mainly to population ageing and a growing number of people requiring health and social care services on an on-going basis.

A significant share of LTC services is funded from public sources. Total public spending on LTC (including both the health and social care components) accounted for 1.6% of GDP on average across OECD countries in 2011 (Figure 8.9.1). The highest spenders are the Netherlands and Sweden, where public expenditure on long-term care was two-times greater than the OECD average (at 3.7% and 3.6% of GDP). On the contrary, Greece, Portugal, Estonia, Hungary, the Czech Republic and Poland allocated less than 0.5% of their GDP to public spending on long-term care. This variation reflects both differences in population structure but especially the development of formal long-term care systems, as opposed to more informal arrangements based mainly on care provided by unpaid family members. Despite the problems of under-reporting, privately-funded LTC expenditure plays a relatively large role in Switzerland (0.8% of GDP), Germany, the United States, Finland and Spain (about 0.4% of GDP). Most of the private spending comes from out-of-pocket spending, since private health insurance for long-term care does not play an important role in any country.

The boundaries between health and social LTC spending are not fully consistent across countries (see box on "Definition and comparability"), with some reporting particular components of LTC as health care, while others view it as social spending. The Netherlands, Denmark and Norway spent over 2% of GDP on the health part of LTC, which is double the OECD average. Regarding the social part of public LTC expenditure, Sweden has the highest share, reaching 3% of GDP, much higher than the OECD average of 0.7%. The Netherlands, Finland and Japan reported more than 1% of GDP on this spending component. Poland, Spain, New Zealand and Korea reported less than 0.1% of GDP on social public LTC spending.

Public spending on LTC has grown rapidly in recent years in some countries (Figure 8.9.2). The annual growth rate in public expenditures on LTC was 4.8% between 2005 and 2011 across OECD countries, which is above the growth in health care expenditures during this period. Countries such as Korea and Portugal, which have implemented

measures to expand the coverage of their LTC systems in recent years, have had the highest public spending growth rates between 2005 and 2011. On the other hand, countries with high spending levels and those with a longer history of public LTC coverage tend to record below-average growth rates in recent years.

Although a high proportion of LTC expenditure continues to be allocated for institutional care, many OECD countries have expanded the availability of home care services. Between 2005 and 2011, the annual growth rate of public spending on home care was about 5% compared with 4% for institutional care (Figure 8.9.3). There were significant increases in home care spending in Korea, Estonia and Spain, while public spending on institutional care was reduced in Finland and Hungary.

Projection scenarios suggest that public resources allocated to LTC as a share of GDP may double or more by 2060 (Colombo et al., 2011; De La Maisonneuve and Oliveira Martins, 2013). One of the main challenges in many OECD countries in the future will be to strike the right balance between providing appropriate LTC protection and ensuring that this protection is fiscally sustainable in the long run.

Definition and comparability

LTC spending comprises both health and social support services to people with chronic conditions and disabilities needing care on an on-going basis. Based on the System of Health Accounts (SHA), the health component of LTC spending relates to nursing and personal care services (i.e. assistance with activities of daily living, ADL). It covers palliative care and care provided in LTC institutions or at home. LTC social expenditure primarily covers assistance with instrumental activities of daily living (IADL). Countries' reporting practices between the health and social components of LTC spending may differ. In addition, publicly-funded LTC expenditure is more suitable for international comparisons as there is significant variation in the reporting of privately-funded LTC expenditure across OECD countries.

8.9.1. Long-term care public expenditure (health and social components), as share of GDP, 2011 (or nearest year)

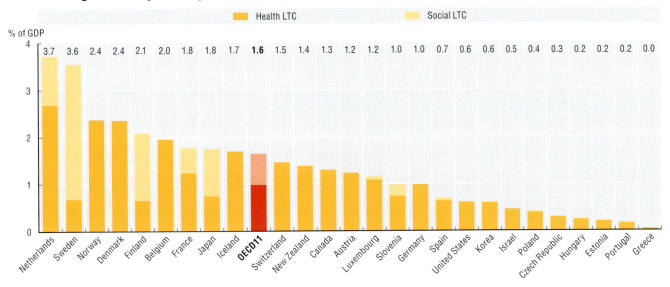

Note: The OECD average only includes the 11 countries that report health and social LTC.
Source: OECD Health Statistics 2013, http://dx.doi.org/10.1787/health-data-en.

StatLink ⟶ http://dx.doi.org/10.1787/888932919498

8.9.2. Annual growth rate in public expenditure on long-term care (health and social), in real terms, 2005-11 (or nearest year)

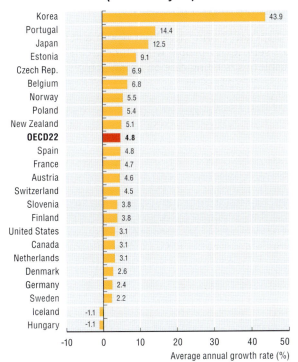

Note: The OECD average excludes Korea (due to the extremely high growth rate).
Source: OECD Health Statistics 2013, http://dx.doi.org/10.1787/health-data-en.

StatLink ⟶ http://dx.doi.org/10.1787/888932919517

8.9.3. Annual growth rate in public expenditure on long-term care in institutions and at home, in real terms, 2005-11 (or nearest year)

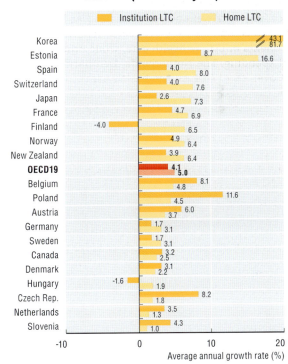

Note: The OECD average excludes Korea (due to the extremely high growth rate).
Source: OECD Health Statistics 2013, http://dx.doi.org/10.1787/health-data-en.

StatLink ⟶ http://dx.doi.org/10.1787/888932919536

Bibliography

ACMMP – Advisory Committee on Medical Manpower Planning (2010), "Capacity Plan", Vol. 2, *General Medicine*, Utrecht.

Adriaenssens, N. et al. (2011), "European Surveillance of Antimicrobial Consumption (ESAC): Disease Specific Quality Indicators for Outpatient Antibiotic Prescribing", *Quality and Safety in Health Care*, Vol. 20, pp. 764-772.

ADA – American Diabetes Association (2013), *Economic Costs of Diabetes in the US in 2012.*

AHRQ – Agency for Health Research and Quality (2006), *Patient Safety Indicators Overview: AHRQ Quality Indicators – February 2006*, AHRQ, Rockville, MD.

AHRQ (2011a), *2010 National Healthcare Quality Report*, AHRQ, Rockville, MD.

AHRQ (2011b), *2010 National Healthcare Disparities Report*, AHRQ, Rockville, MD.

AIHW – Australian Institute of Health and Welfare (2011), *The Health and Welfare of Australia's Aboriginal and Torres Strait Islander People: An Overview 2011*, Cat. No. IHW 42, AIHW, Canberra.

AIHW (2012a), *Australia's Health 2012*, Australia's Health Series No. 13, Cat. No. AUS 156, AIHW, Canberra.

AIHW (2012b), *Mental Health Services in Brief 2012*, AIHW, Canberra.

AIHW (2012c), *Dementia in Australia*, Cat. No. AGE 70, AIHW, Canberra.

AIHW (2013), *Stroke and its Management in Australia: An Update,* Cardiovascular Disease Series No. 37, Cat. No. CVD 61, AIHW, Canberra.

Aiken, L. and R. Cheung (2008), "Nurse Workforce Challenges in the United States: Implications for Policy", *OECD Health Working Paper No. 35*, OECD Publishing, *http://dx.doi.org/10.1787/236153608331.*

Akkerman, A.E. et al. (2005), "Prescribing Antibiotics for Respiratory Tract Infections by GP's: Management and Prescriber Characteristics", *British Journal of General Practice*, Vol. 55, pp. 114-118.

Allepuz, A. et al. (2009), "Hip and Knee Replacement in the Spanish National Health System", *Revista Española de Cirugía Ortopédica y Traumatología*, Vol. 53, No. 5, pp. 290-299.

Alzheimer's Australia (2009), "Keeping Dementia Front of Mind: Incidence and Prevalence 2009-2050", *Access Economics Reports*, available at *www.alzheimers.org.au/research-publications/access-economics-reports.aspx.*

Alzheimer Europe (2009), "Prevalence of Dementia in Europe", available at *www.alzheimer-europe.org/EN/Research/European-Collaboration-on-Dementia/Prevalence-of-dementia2/Prevalence-of-dementia-in-Europe.*

Alzheimer Europe (2012), *Dementia in Europe Yearbook 2012*, Luxembourg.

Anand, P. et al. (2008), "Cancer is a Preventable Disease that Requires Major Lifestyle Changes", *Pharmaceutical Research*, Vol. 25, No. 9, pp. 2097-2116.

Arah, O. et al. (2006), "A Conceptual Framework for the OECD Health Care Quality Indicators Project", *International Journal for Quality in Health Care*, Vol. 18, Supplement No. 1, pp. 5-13.

Babor, T., R. Caetano, S. Casswell et al. (2010), *Alcohol: No Ordinary Commodity – Research and Public Policy*, Oxford University Press, Oxford.

Baghestan, E. et al. (2007), "A Validation of the Diagnosis of Obstetric Sphincter Tears in Two Norwegian Databases, the Medical Birth Registry and the Patient Administration System", *Acta Obstetricia et Gynecologica*, Vol. 86, pp. 205-209.

Baker, L., S.W. Atlas and C.C. Afendulis (2008), "Expanded Use of Imaging Technology and the Challenge of Measuring Value", *Health Affairs*, Vol. 27, No. 6, pp. 1467-1478.

Banthin, J.S., P. Cunningham and D.M. Bernard (2008), "Financial Burden of Health Care, 2001-2004", *Health Affairs*, Vol. 27, pp. 188-195.

Bateman, B.T. et al. (2010), "Temporal Trends in the Epidemiology of Severe Postoperative Sepsis After Elective Surgery", *Anaesthesiology*, Vol. 112, No. 4, pp. 917-925.

Bellanger, M. and Z. Or (2008), "What Can We Learn From a Cross-Country Comparison of the Costs of Child Delivery?", *Health Economics*, Vol. 17, pp. S47-S57.

Bewley, S. and J. Cockburn (2002), "The Unethics of 'Request' Caesarean Section", *British Journal of Obstetrics and Gynaecology*, Vol. 109, pp. 593-596.

Björkenstam, E. et al. (2012), "Quality of Medical Care and Excess Mortality in Psychiatric Patients – A Nationwide Register-based Study in Sweden", *BMJ Open 2012*, Vol. 2, e000778, *http://dx.doi.org/10.1136/bmjopen-2011-000778*.

Bond, J. et al. (2006), "Self-rated Health Status as a Predictor of Death, Functional and Cognitive Impairments: A Longitudinal Cohort Study", *European Journal of Ageing*, Vol. 3, pp. 193-206.

Borghans, I. et al. (2012), "Fifty Ways to Reduce Length of Stay: An Inventory of How Hospital Staff Would Reduce the Length of Stay in their Hospital", *Health Policy*, Vol. 104, pp. 222-233.

Borraccino, A. et al. (2009), "Socioeconomic Effects on Meeting Physical Activity Guidelines: Comparisons Among 32 Countries", *Medicine and Science in Sports and Exercise*, Vol. 41, pp. 749-756.

Bouchery, E.E. et al. (2011), "Economic Costs of Excessive Alcohol Consumption in the US, 2006", *American Journal of Preventive Medicine*, Vol. 41, No. 5, pp. 516-524.

Bourgueil, Y., A. Marek and J. Mousquès (2006), "Vers une Coopération entre Médecins et Infirmières – L'apport d'expériences européennes et canadiennes", *Série études*, No. 57, DREES, Paris, March.

Brekke, M. and B. Gjelsvik (2009), "Secondary Cardiovascular Risk Prevention – We Can Do Better", *The Lancet*, Vol. 373, No. 9667, pp. 873-875.

Brotherton, J.M, M. Fridman and C.L. May et al. (2011), "Early Effect of the HPV Vaccination Programme on Cervical Abnormalities in Victoria, Australia: An Ecological Study", *The Lancet*, Vol. 377, No. 9783, pp. 2085-2092.

Bronzwaer S., O. Cars, U. Buchholz et al. (2002), "A European Study on the Relationship between Antimicrobial use and Antimicrobial Resistance", *Emerging Infectious Diseases*, Vol. 8, pp. 278-282.

Buchan, J. and S. Black (2011), "The Impact of Pay Increases on Nurses' Labour Market: A Review of Evidence from four OECD Countries", *OECD Health Working Papers*, No. 57, OECD Publishing, *http://dx.doi.org/10.1787/5kg6jwn16tjd-en*.

Butler, C.C., F. Dunstan, M. Heginbothom et al. (2007), "Containing Antibiotic Resistance: Decreased Antibiotic-resistant Coliform Urinary Tract Infections with Reduction in Antibiotic Prescribing by General Practices", *British Journal of General Practice*, Vol. 57, pp. 785-792.

CIHI – Canadian Institute for Health Information (2012), *Drug Expenditure in Canada, 1985 to 2011*, CIHI, Ottawa.

Castoro, C. et al. (2007), *Policy Brief-Day Surgery: Making it Happen*, World Health Organization on behalf of the European Observatory on Health Systems and Policies, Copenhagen.

CDC – Centers for Disease Control and Prevention (2012), *Alcohol and Public Health: Alcohol-related Disease Impact* (ARDI), Atlanta, available at *http://apps.nccd.cdc.gov/DACH_ARDI/default/default.aspx* (accessed 1 June 2012).

Ceccherini-Nelli, A. and S. Priebe (2011), "Economic Factors and Suicide Rates: Associations over Time in Four Countries", *Social Psychiatry and Psychiatric Epidemiology*, Vol. 46, No. 10, pp. 975-982.

CfWI – Centre for Workforce Intelligence (2012), *A Strategic Review of the Future Healthcare Workforce: Informing Medical and Dental Student Intakes*, London.

Chia, S.K. et al. (2007), "The Impact of New Chemotherapeutic and Hormone Agents on Survival in a Population-based Cohort of Women with Metastatic Breast Cancer", *Cancer*, Vol. 110, No. 5, pp. 973-979.

Classen, T.J. and R A. Dunn (2012). "The Effect of Job Loss and Unemployment Duration on Suicide Risk in the United States: A New Look Using Mass-Layoffs and Unemployment Duration", *Health Economics*, Vol. 21, No. 3, pp. 338-350.

Cochrane Collaboration (2013), *The Cochrane Acute Respiratory Infections Group*, available at *www.ari.cochrane.org* (accessed 10 July 2013).

Coenen, S. et al. (2007), "European Surveillance of Antimicrobial Consumption (EASC): Quality Indicators for Outpatient Antibiotic Use in Europe", *Quality & Safety in Health Care*, Vol. 16, pp. 440-445.

Cole, T.J. et al. (2000), "Establishing a Standard Definition for Child Overweight and Obesity Worldwide: International Survey", *British Medical Journal*, Vol. 320, pp. 1-6.

Colombo, F. et al. (2011), *Help Wanted? Providing and Paying for Long-Term Care*, OECD Publishing, *http://dx.doi.org/10.1787/9789264097759-en*.

Commonwealth Fund (2004), *2004 Commonwealth Fund International Health Policy Survey of Adults' Experiences with Primary Care*, Chartpack, Commonwealth Fund, New York.

Commonwealth Fund (2007), *2007 International Health Policy Survey in Seven Countries*, Chartpack, Commonwealth Fund, New York.

Commonwealth Fund (2010), *2010 International Health Policy Survey in Eleven Countries*, Chartpack, Commonwealth Fund, New York.

Corazziari I., M. Quinn and R. Capocaccia (2004), "Standard Patient Population for Age Standardising Survival Ratios", *European Journal of Cancer*, Vol. 40, No. 15, pp. 2307-2316.

Corsini, V. (2010), "Highly Educated Men and Women Likely to Live Longer: Life Expectancy by Educational Attainment", *Eurostat Statistics in Focus 24/2010*, European Commission, Luxembourg.

Currie, C. et al. (eds.) (2004), *Young People's Health in Context: International Report from the HBSC 2001/2002 Survey*, WHO Regional Office for Europe, Copenhagen.

Currie, C. et al. (eds.) (2008), *Inequalities in Young People's Health: Health Behaviour in School-aged Children (HBSC) International Report from the 2005/2006 Survey*, WHO Regional Office for Europe, Copenhagen.

Currie, C. et al. (eds.) (2012), *Social Determinants of Health and Well-being Among Young People. Health Behaviour in School-aged Children (HBSC) Study: International Report from the 2009/2010 Survey*, WHO Regional Office for Europe, Copenhagen.

Cutler, D. and E.L. Glaeser (2006), "Why do Europeans Smoke More Than Americans?", *Working Paper* No. 12124, National Bureau of Economic Research, Cambridge.

Crump, C., et al. (2013), "Sociodemographic, Psychiatric and Somatic Risk Factors for Suicide: A Swedish National Cohort Study", *Psychological Medicine*, pp. 1-11.

Dartmouth Institute (2010), *Trends and Regional Variation in Hip, Knee and Shoulder Replacement*, Dartmouth Atlas Surgery Report, 6 April.

de Jong, J.D. et al. (2006), "Variation in Hospital Length of Stay: Do Physicians Adapt their Length of Stay Decisions to What Is Usual in the Hospital Where They Work?, *Health Services Research*, Vol. 41, No. 2.

de Hert, M. et al. (2011), "Physical Illness in Patients with Severe Mental Disorders. I. Prevalence, Impact of Medications and Disparities in Health Care", *World Psychiatry*, Vol. 10, No. 1, pp. 52-77, February.

Department of Health (2011), "The Operating Framework for the NHS in England 2012/13", England.

Delamaire, M.-L. and G. Lafortune (2010), "Nurses in Advanced Roles: A Description and Evaluation of Experiences in 12 Developed Countries", *OECD Health Working Paper*, No. 54, OECD Publishing, *http://dx.doi.org/10.1787/5kmbrcfms5g7-en*.

De La Maisonneuve, C. and J.O. Martins (2013), "Public Spending on Health and Long-term Care: A New Set of Projections", *OECD Economic Policy Papers*, No. 6, OECD Publishing, *http://dx.doi.org/10.1787/5k44t7jwwr9x-en*.

DeSalvo, K.B., V.S. Fan, M.B. McDonell and S.D. Fihn (2005), "Predicting Mortality and Healthcare Utilization with a Single Question", *Health Services Research*, Vol. 40, pp. 1234-1246.

Devaux, M. and M. de Looper (2012), "Income-related Inequalities in Health Service Utilisation in 19 OECD countries", *OECD Health Working Papers*, No. 58, OECD Publishing, *http://dx.doi.org/10.1787/5k95xd6stnxt-en*.

Devaux, M. and F. Sassi (forthcoming), "Alcohol Consumption and Harmful Drinking: Trends and Social Disparities across OECD Countries", *OECD Health Working Paper*, OECD Publishing.

Devaux, M., F. Sassi, J. Church et al. (2011), "Exploring the Relationship between Education and Obesity", *OECD Journal: Economic Studies*, Issue No. 1, OECD Publishing, *http://dx.doi.org/10.1787/eco_studies-2011-5kg5825v1k23*.

Di Mario, S. et al. (2005), *What is the Effectiveness of Antenatal Care? (Supplement)*, WHO Regional Office for Europe (Health Evidence Network Report), Copenhagen.

Diabetes Care (2013), Vol. 36, pp. 1033-1046, April.

Dickman, P.W. and H.O. Adami (2006), "Interpreting Trends in Cancer Patient Survival", *Journal of Internal Medicine*, No. 260, pp. 103-117.

Dormont, B. and H. Huber (2006), "Causes of Health Expenditure Growth: The Predominance of Changes in Medical Practices Over Population Ageing", *Annales d'Économie et de Statistique*, No. 83/84, pp. 187-217.

DREES – Direction de la recherche, des études, de l'évaluation et des statistiques (2013), "Les médecins en France au 1er janvier 2013", *Document de travail, Série statistiques*, No. 179, DREES, Paris, April.

Drösler, S.E., P.S. Romano, et al. (2011), "International Comparability of Patient Safety Indicators in 15 OECD Member Countries: A Methodological Approach of Adjustment by Secondary Diagnoses", *Health Services Research*, *http://dx.doi.org/10.1111/j.1475-6773.2011.01290.x*.

Eagle, K.A. et al. (2005), "Guideline-Based Standardized Care is Associated with Substantially Lower Mortality in Medicare Patients with Acute Myocardial Infarction: The American College of Cardiology's Guidelines Applied in Practice (GAP)", *Journal of the American College of Cardiology*, Vol. 46, pp. 1242-1248.

Echevarría-Zuno, S., J.M. Mejía-Aranguré, A.J. Mar-Obeso et al. (2010), "Infection and Death from Influenza A H1N1 Virus in Mexico: A Retrospective Analysis", *The Lancet*, Vol. 374, No. 9707, pp. 2072-2079.

Elmadfa, I. (ed.) (2009), *European Nutrition and Health Report 2009*, Karger, Basel, Switzerland.

Elliman, D. and H. Bedford (2013), "Should the UK Introduce Compulsory Vaccination?", *The Lancet*, Vol. 381, No. 9876, pp. 1434-1436.

Epstein, A. et al. (2011), "Coronary Revascularization Trends in the United States, 2001-2008", *Journal of the American Medical Association*, Vol. 305, No. 17, pp. 1769-1775, 4 May.

Ersek, K. et al. (2009), "Parallel Sessions-Dementia Policies: Epidemiology and Disease Burden of Dementia in Hungary", *Alzheimer Europe*, available at *www.alzheimer-europe.org/Conferences/Previous-conferences/2009-Brussels/Abstracts-and-presentations/Dementia-policies*.

European Commission (2006), *European Guidelines for Quality Assurance in Breast Cancer Screening and Diagnosis*, 4th edition, Luxembourg.

European Commission (2008a), *Hospital Data Project Phase 2, Final Report*, Luxembourg.

European Commission (2008b), *Major and Chronic Diseases – Report 2007*, EC Directorate-General for Health and Consumers, Luxembourg.

European Commission (2013), "Long-term Care in Ageing Societies – Challenges and Policy Options", Commission Staff Working Document, SWD 41, Brussels.

Euro-Peristat (2013), *European Perinatal Health Report: The Health and Care of Pregnant Women and their Babies in 2010*, Luxembourg.

Federal Joint Committee (2012), *Planning guideline of the Federal Joint Committee*, Federal Ministry of Justice.

Fedorowicz, Z., D. Lawrence and P. Gutierrez (2004), "Day Care versus In-Patient Surgery for Age-related Cataract", *Cochrane Database of Systematic Reviews*, Vol. 25, No. CD004242.

FHF – Fédération hospitalière de France (2008), *Étude sur les césariennes*, FHF, Paris.

Forde, I. (forthcoming), "Hospital Length of Stay: Trends and Drivers", *OECD Health Working Paper*, OECD Publishing.

Foresight (2007), "Tackling Obesities: Future Choices", Government Office for Science, available at *www.foresight.gov.uk/Obesity/17.pdf*.

Franco, E.L., T.E. Rohan and L.L. Villa (1999), "Epidemiologic Evidence and Human Papillomavirus Infection as a Necessary Cause of Cervical Cancer", *Journal of the National Cancer Institute*, Vol. 91, No. 6, pp. 506-511.

Friðfinnsdóttir, E. and J. Jónsson (2010), *The Impact of the Economic Recession on Nurses and Nursing in Iceland*, International Centre for Human Resources in Nursing (ICHRN), Geneva.

Fujisawa, R. and G. Lafortune (2008), "The Remuneration of General Practitioners and Specialists in 14 OECD Countries: What are the Factors Explaining Variations across Countries?", *OECD Health Working Paper*, No. 41, OECD Publishing, *http://dx.doi.org/10.1787/228632341330*.

Gakidou, E., S. Nordhagen and Z. Obermeyer (2008), "Coverage of Cervical Cancer Screening in 57 Countries: Low Average Levels and Large Inequalities", *PLoS Medicine*, Vol. 5, No. 6, pp. 0863-0868.

Gardete-Correia L., J.M. Boavida, J.F. Raposo et al (2011), "First Diabetes Prevalence Study in Portugal: PREVADIAB Study", *Diabetic Medicine*, Vol. 27, pp. 879-881.

Gawande, A.A., D.M. Studdert, E.J. Orav et al. (2003), "Risk Factors for Retained Instruments and Sponges after Surgery", *New England Journal of Medicine*, Vol. 348, No. 3, pp. 229-235.

Germany Federal Statistical Office (2013), "Cost-of-Illness Accounts", available at *www.kostenvanziekten.nl*.

Gili, M. et al. (2012), "The Mental Health Risks of Economic Crisis in Spain: Evidence from Primary Care Centres, 2006 and 2010", *European Journal of Public Health*, Vol. 1-5, April 19.

Goldhaber-Fiebert, J.D. et al. (2008), "Cost-effectiveness of Cervical Cancer Screening with Human Papillomavirus DNA Testing and HPV-16, 18 Vaccination", *Journal of the National Cancer Institute*, Vol. 100, No. 5, pp. 308-320.

Goossens, H., M. Ferech, R. Vander Stichele et al. (2005), "Outpatient Antibiotic Use in Europe and Association with Resistance: A Cross-national Database Study", *The Lancet*, Vol. 365, pp. 579-587.

Government of Western Australia (2013), "Diagnostic Imaging Pathways: A Clinical Decision Support Tool and Educational Resource for Diagnostic Imaging", available at *www.imagingpathways.health.wa.gov.au*.

Grignon, M., J. Hurley, L. Wang and S. Allin, (2010), "Inequality in a Market-Based Health System: Evidence from Canada's Dental Sector", *Health Policy*, Vol. 98, pp. 81-90.

Grigoryan, L et al. (2006), "Self-medication with Antimicrobial Drugs in Europe", *Emerging Infectious Diseases*, Vol. 12, No 3, pp. 452-459.

Guariguata, L., Whiting, D., Weil, C. and Unwin, N. (2011), "The International Diabetes Federation Diabetes Atlas Methodology for Estimating Global and National Prevalence of Diabetes in Adults", *Diabetes Research and Clinical Practice*, Vol. 94, No. 3, pp. 322-332.

Guize, L. et al. (2008), "Diabetes and Socio-economic Deprivation. A Study in a Large French Population", *Bulletin de l'Académie nationale de médecine,* Vol. 192, No. 9, p. 1707.

Hacke, W. et al. (1995), "Intravenous Thrombolysis with Recombinant Tissue Plasminogen Activator for Acute Hemispheric Stroke. The European Co-operative Acute Stroke Study (ECASS)", *Journal of the American Medical Association*, Vol. 274, No. 13, pp. 1017-1025.

Hallal, P.C. et al. (2006), "Adolescent Physical Activity and Health: A Systematic Review", *Sports Medicine*, Vol. 36, No. 12, pp. 1019-1030.

Hallal, P.C. et al. (2012), "Global Physical Activity Levels: Surveillance Progress, Pitfalls, and Prospects", *The Lancet*, Vol. 380, No. 9838, pp. 247-257.

Hals, E. et al. (2010), "A Multicenter Interventional Program to Reduce the Incidence of Anal Sphincter Tears", *Obstetrics and Gynecology*, Vol. 116, No. 4, pp. 901-908.

Happell, B., C. Palmer and R. Tennent (2010), "Mental Health Nurse Incentive Program: Contributing to Positive Client Outcomes", *International Journal of Mental Health Nursing*, Vol. 19, pp. 331-339.

Hatem, M., J. Sandall, D. Devane et al. (2008), "Midwife-led Versus Other Models of Care for Childbearing Women", *Cochrane Database Systematic Review*, Vol. 4:CD004667, Oct. 8.

Hawton, K., K.E. Saunders and R.C. O'Connor, (2012), "Self-Harm and Suicide in Adolescents", *The Lancet*, Vol. 379, No. 9834, pp. 2373-2382.

Heijink, R., M.A. Koopmanschap and J.J. Polder (2006), *International Comparison of Cost of Illness*, RIVM, Bilthoven.

Health Workforce Australia (2012), *Health Workforce 2025 - Doctors, Nurses and Midwives*, Vol. 1 and 2, Adelaide, available at *www.hwa.gov.au/sites/uploads/FinalReport_Volume1_FINAL-20120424.pdf*.

Heit, J.A. (2012), "Estimating the Incidence of Symptomatic Postoperative Venous Thromboembolisms", *Journal of American Medical Association*, Vol. 307, No. 3, pp. 306-307.

Hollingworth, S. et al. (2010), "Affective and Anxiety Disorders: Prevalence, Treatment and Antidepressant Medication Use", *Australian and New Zealand Journal of Psychiatry*, Vol. 44, pp. 513-519.

Hoot, N.R. and D. Aronsky (2008), "Systematic Review of Emergency Department Crowding: Causes, Effects, and Solutions", *Annals of Emergency Medicine*, Vol. 52, No. 2, pp. 126-136.

Huttner, B. et al. (2010), "Characteristics and Outcomes of Public Campaigns Aimed at Improving the Use of Antibiotics in Outpatients in High-income Countries", *The Lancet Infectious Diseases*, Vol. 10, pp. 17-31.

IARC Working Group on the Evaluation of Carcinogenic Risks to Humans (1995), *Human Papillomaviruses*, Monographs on the Evaluation of Carcinogenic Risks to Humans, Vol. 64, International Agency for Research on Cancer, Lyon.

IDF – International Diabetes Federation (2011), *Diabetes Atlas*, 5th edition, Brussels.

Indredavik, B. (2009), "Stroke Unit Care Is Beneficial Both for the Patient and for the Health Service and Should Be Widely Implemented", *Stroke*, Vol. 40, No. 1, pp. 1-2.

Institute of Alcohol Studies (2007), "Binge Drinking-Nature, Prevalence and Causes", *IAS Fact Sheet*, available at *www.ias.org.uk/resources/factsheets/binge_drinking.pdf*.

International Association for the Study of Obesity (2011), "Overweight Children around the World", available at *www.iaso.org*.

Iversen, H.H., Ø.A. Bjertæs, G. Groven and G. Bukholm (2010), "Usefulness of a National Patient Experience Survey in Quality Improvement: Views of Paediatric Department Employees", *Quality and Safety in Health Care*, Vol. 19, No. 5, BMJ Publishing Group Limited, London.

Januel, J.M. et al. (2012), "Symptomatic In-hospital Deep Vein Thrombosis and Pulmonary Embolism Following Hip and Knee Arthroplasty Among Patients Receiving Recommended Prophylaxis", *Journal of American Medical Association,* Vol. 307, No. 3, pp. 294-303.

Jefferson, T.C., J. Di Pietrantoni, L.A. Al-Ansary et al. (2010), "Vaccines for Preventing Influenza in the Elderly", *Cochrane Database Syst Review*, Vol. 2, CD004876.

Jemal, A., F. Bray, M.M. Center et al. (2011), "Global Cancer Statistics", *A Cancer Journal for Clinicians*, Vol. 61, No. 2, pp. 69-90.

Jeon, Hong Jin (2011), "Depression and Suicide", *Journal of the Korean Medical Association*, Vol. 54, No. 4, pp. 370-375.

Jha, P. et al. (2006), "Social Inequalities in Male Mortality, and in Male Mortality from Smoking: Indirect Estimation from National Death Rates in England and Wales, Poland, and North America", *The Lancet*, Vol. 368, No. 9533, pp. 367-370.

Jhun, Hyung-Joon, Ho Kim and Sung-Il Cho (2011), "Time Trend and Age-Period-Cohort Effects on Acute Myocardial Infarction Mortality in Korean Adults from 1988 to 2007", *Journal of Korean Medical Science*, Vol. 26, No. 5, pp. 637-641.

Jonsson, P.M. et al. (2013), "Finland", Part II, Chapter 7 in *Waiting Time Policies in the Health Sector: What Works*, OECD publishing, *http://dx.doi.org/10.1787/9789264179080-en*.

Joseph, K.S. et al. (2012), "Influence of Definition Based Versus Pragmatic Registration on International Comparisons of Perinatal and Infant Mortality: Population Based Retrospective study", *British Medical Journal*, Vol. 344, e746.

Juva, M. (2009), "Parallel Sessions-Dementia Policies: From National Dementia Plan to Local Reality", *Alzheimer Europe*, available at *www.alzheimer-europe.org/Conferences/Previous-conferences/2009-Brussels/Abstracts-and-presentations/Dementia-policies*.

Kapral, M.K., R. Hall, M. Stamplecoski et al. (2011), "Registry of the Canadian Stroke Network – Report on the 2008/09 Ontario Stroke Audit", Institute for Clinical Evaluative Sciences, Toronto.

Kelley, E. and J. Hurst (2006), "Health Care Quality Indicators Project: Conceptual Framework", *OECD Health Working Paper*, No. 23, OECD Publishing, *http://dx.doi.org/10.1787/440134737301*.

Kelly, H. et al. (2011), "The Age-Specific Cumulative Incidence of Infection with Pandemic Influenza H1N1 2009 Was Similar in Various Countries Prior to Vaccination", *PLoS One,* Vol. 6, No. 8, e21828, *http://dx.doi.org/10.1371/journal.pone.0021828*.

Kenigsberg, P.A. (2009), "Parallel Sessions-Dementia Policies: The Changing Economic Environment of Alzheimer's Disease in France", Alzheimer Europe, available at *www.alzheimer-europe.org/Conferences/Previous-conferences/2009-Brussels/Abstracts-and-presentations/Dementia-policies*.

Khush, K.K., E. Rapaport and D. Waters (2005), "The History of the Coronary Care Unit", *Canadian Journal of Cardiology*, Vol. 21, pp. 1041-1045.

Kiely, J., K. Brett, S. Yu and D. Rowley (1995), "Low Birth Weight and Intrauterine Growth Retardation", in L. Wilcox and J. Marks (eds.), *From Data to Action: CDC's Public Health Surveillance for Women, Infants, and Children*, Center for Disease Control and Preventions, Atlanta, pp. 185-202.

Koechlin, F., L. Lorenzoni and P. Schreyer (2010), "Comparing Price Levels of Hospital Services across Countries: Results of a Pilot Study", *OECD Health Working Paper*, No. 53, OECD Publishing, *http://dx.doi.org/10.1787/5km4k7mrnnjb-en*.

Kohlhammer, Y. et al. (2007), "Determinants of Influenza and Pneumococcal Vaccination in Elderly People: A Systematic Review", *Public Health*, Vol. 121, pp. 742-751.

Kohn, L.T., J.M. Corrigan and M.S. Donaldson (eds.) (2000), *To Err is Human: Building a Safer Health System*, Institute of Medicine, National Academy Press, Washington, DC.

Koller, D. et al (2013), "Variation in Antibiotic Prescriptions: Is Area Deprivation an Explanation? Analysis of 1.2 Million Children in Germany", *Infection*, Vol. 41, No. 1, pp. 121-127.

Kotseva, K. et al. (2009), "UROASPIRE III: A Survey on the Lifestyle, Risk Factors and Use of Cardioprotective Drug Therapies in Coronary Patients from 22 European Countries", *European Journal of Cardiovascular Prevention and Rehabilitation*, Vol. 16, pp. 121-137.

Kovess-Masfety, V. et al. (2007), "Differences in Lifetime Use of Services for Mental Health Problems in Six European Countries", *Psychiatric Services*, Vol. 58, No. 2, pp. 213-220.

Kringos, D. et al. (2010), "The Breadth of Primary Care: A Systematic Literature Review of its Core Dimensions", *BMC Health Services Research*, Vol. 10, No. 65, *http://dx.doi.org/10.1186/1472-6963-10-65*.

Kroneman, M. et al. (2003), "Influenza Vaccination Uptake in Europe: An Inventory of Strategies to Reach Target Populations and Optimise Vaccination Uptake", *Eurosurveillance*, Vol. 8, No. 6.

Kumar, A. and M. Schoenstein (2013), "Managing Hospital Volumes: Germany and Experiences from OECD Countries", *OECD Health Working Papers*, No. 64, OECD Publishing, *http://dx.doi.org/10.1787/5k3xwtg2szzr-en*.

Kunze, U. et al. (2007), "Influenza Vaccination in Austria, 1982-2003", *Wien Med Wochenschr*, Vol. 157, No. 5-6, pp. 98-101.

Lang, P.O., A. Mendes, J. Socquet, N. Assir, S. Govind and R. Aspinall (2012), "Effectiveness of Influenza Vaccine in Aging and Older Adults: Comprehensive Analysis of the Evidence", *Clinical Interventions in Aging,* Vol. 7, No. 55.

Lansdorp-Vogelaar, I., A.B. Knudsen and H. Brenner (2010), "Cost-Effectiveness of Colorectal Cancer Screening – An Overview", *Best Practice & Research Clinical Gastroenterology*, Vol. 24, pp. 439-449.

Lee, Hye Ah and Hyesook Park (2012), "Trends in Ischemic Heart Disease Mortality in Korea, 1985-2009: An Age-period-cohort Analysis", *Journal of Preventive Medicine and Public Health*, Vol. 45, No. 5, pp. 323-328.

Listl, S. (2011), "Income-Related Inequalities in Dental Service Utilization by Europeans Aged 50+", *Journal of Dental Research*, Vol. 90, No. 6, pp. 717-723.

Lobstein T. (2010), "The Size and Risks of the International Epidemic of Child Obesity", in F. Sassi (eds.), *Obesity and the Economics of Prevention: Fit Not Fat*, OECD Publishing, pp. 107-114, *http://dx.doi.org/10.1787/9789264084865-en*.

Lozano, R., M. Naghavi and K. Foreman (2012), "Global and Regional Mortality from 235 Causes of Death for 20 Age Groups in 1990 and 2010: A Systematic Analysis for the Global Burden of Disease Study 2010 ", *The Lancet*, Vol. 380, No. 9859, pp. 2095-2128.

Lundström, M. et al. (2012), "Evidence-based Guidelines for Cataract Surgery: Guidelines Based on Data in the European Registry of Quality Outcomes for Cataract and Refractive Surgery Database", *Journal of Cataract and Refractive Surgery*.

Mackenbach, J.P. et al. (2008), "Socio-economic Inequalities in Health in 22 European Countries", *New England Journal of Medicine,* Vol. 358, pp. 2468-2481.

Mackie, C.O. et al. (2009), "Hepatitis B Immunisation Strategies: Timing is Everything", *Canadian Medical Association Journal*, Vol. 18, No. 2, pp. 196-202.

Maiorova, T., F. Stevens, L. van der Velden et al. (2007), "Gender Shift in Realisation of Preferred Type of GP Practice: Longitudinal Survey over the Last 25 Years", *BMC Health Services Research*, Vol. 7, No. 111.

Mariotto, A.B., K.R. Yabroff, Y. Shao et al. (2011), "Projections of the Cost of Cancer Care in the United States: 2010-2020", *Journal of the National Cancer Institute*, available at *jnci.oxfordjournals.org/content/early/2011/01/12/jnci.djq495.abstract*.

Mathers, C. et al. (2005), "Counting the Dead and What They Died From: An Assessment of the Global Status of Cause of Death Data", *Bulletin of the World Health Organization*, Vol. 83, No. 3, pp. 171-177.

Mauri, D., N.P. Polyzos, G. Salanti et al. (2008), "Multiple-treatments Meta-analysis of Chemotherapy and Targeted Therapies in Advanced Breast Cancer", *Journal of the National Cancer Institute*, Vol. 100, No. 24, pp. 1780-1791.

McGuire, A. et al. (2010), "Technology Diffusion and Health Care Productivity: Angioplasty in the UK", *Working Paper* No. 17/2010, London School of Economics, London.

McKinsey Global Institute (2008), "Accounting for the Cost of US Health Care: A New Look at Why Americans Spend More", available at *www.mckinsey.com/mgi/reports/pdfs/healthcare/US_healthcare_report.pdf*.

McPherson, K., G. Gon and M. Scott (2013), "International Variations in a Selected Number of Surgical Procedures", *OECD Health Working Papers* No. 61, OECD publishing, *http://dx.doi.org/10.1787/5k49h4p5g9mw-en*.

Mercier, A. et al. (2011), "Understanding the Prescription of Antidepressants: A Qualitative Study among French GPs", *BMC Family Practice*, Vol. 12, No. 99.

Mereckiene, J. et al. (2008), "Low Coverage of Seasonal Influenza Vaccination in the Elderly in Many European Countries", *Eurosurveillance*, Vol. 13, No. 41.

Mereckiene, J. et al. (2012), "Influenza A(H1N1)pdm09 Vaccination Policies and Coverage in Europe", *Eurosurveillance*, Vol. 17, No. 4.

Minkoff, H. and F.A. Chervenak (2003), "Elective Primary Cesarean Section", *New England Journal of Medicine*, Vol. 348, pp. 946-950.

Ministry of Health (2012), *Rising to the Challenge: The Mental Health and Addiction Service Development Plan 2012-2017*, Ministry of Health, Wellington.

Moïse, P. et al. (2003), "OECD Study of Cross-national Differences in the Treatment, Costs and Outcomes for Ischaemic Heart Disease", *OECD Health Working Paper*, No. 3, OECD Publishing, *http://dx.doi.org/10.1787/230112362071*.

Morgan, D. and R. Astolfi (2013), "Health Spending Growth at Zero: Which Countries, Which Sectors Are Most Affected?", *OECD Health Working Papers*, No. 60, OECD Publishing, *http://dx.doi.org/10.1787/5k4dd1st95xv-en*.

Murray, C.J.L et al. (2013), "Disability-adjusted Life Years (DALYs) for 291 Diseases and Injuries in 21 Regions, 1990–2010: a Systematic Analysis for the Global Burden of Disease Study 2010", *The Lancet*, Vol. 380, No. 9859, pp. 2197-2223.

Myers, M. and P. Zimmet (2008), "Halting the Accelerating Epidemic of Type 1 Diabetes", *The Lancet*, Vol. 371, No. 9626, pp. 1730-1731.

National Research Council and Institute of Medicine, S. Woolf and L. Aron (eds.) (2013), *US Health in International Perspective: Shorter Lives, Poorer Health*, Panel on Understanding Cross-National Health Differences Among High-Income Countries, National Academies Press, Washington, DC.

NCHS – National Center for Health Statistics (2011), *Health, United States, 2010: With Special Feature on Death and Dying*, NCHS, Hyattsville, MD.

NCHS (2013), *Health, United States, 2012: With Special Feature on Emergency Care*, NCHS, Hyattsville, MD.

Neufeld, M. and J. Rehm (2013), "Alcohol Consumption and Mortality in Russia Since 2000: Are There any Changes Following the Alcohol Policy Changes Starting in 2006?", *Alcohol and Alcoholism*, Vol. 48, No. 2, pp. 222-230.

Nghiem, H., L. Connelly and S. Gargett (2013), "Are Road Traffic Crash Fatality Rates Converging among OECD Countries?", *Accident Analysis & Prevention*, Vol. 52, pp. 162-170.

Nguyen, T. et al. (2011), "Acceptance of A Pandemic Influenza Vaccine: a Systematic Review of Surveys of the General Public", *Infection and Drug Resistance*, Vol. 4, pp. 197-207.

NICE – National Institute for Health and Clinical Excellence (2012), "Published Diagnostics guidance", NICE, London and Manchester, available at *guidance.nice.org.uk/DT/Published*.

Nock, M.K. et al. (2008), "Suicide and Suicidal Behavior", *Epidemiologic Reviews*, Vol. 30, pp. 133-154.

Nolting, H.-D. et al. (2012), *Healthcare Fact Check: Regional Variations in German Healthcare*, Bertelsmann Stiftung, Gutersloh.

NOMESCO – Nordic Medico-Statistical Committee (2010), *Medicines Consumption in the Nordic Countries 2004-2008*, NOMESCO, Copenhagen.

Nordentoft, M. et al. (2013), "Excess Mortality, Causes of Death and Life Expectancy in 270,770 Patients with Recent Onset of Mental Disorders in Denmark, Finland and Sweden", *PLoS One*. Vol. 8, No. 1, *http://dx.doi.org/10.1371/journal.pone.0055176*.

Norhammar, A. et al. (2007), "Improved but Still High Short-and Long-term Mortality Rates after Myocardial Infarction in Patients with Diabetes Mellitus: A Time-trend Report from the Swedish Register of Information and Knowledge about Swedish Heart Intensive Care Admission", *Heart*, Vol. 93, No. 12, pp. 1577-1583.

OECD (2000), *A System of Health Accounts*, OECD Publishing, *http://dx.doi.org/10.1787/9789264181809-en*.

OECD (2003), *A Disease-based Comparison of Health Systems: What is Best and at What Cost?*, OECD Publishing, *http://dx.doi.org/10.1787/9789264100053-en*.

OECD (2004a), *Towards High-performing Health Systems*, OECD Publishing, *http://dx.doi.org/10.1787/9789264015562-en*.

OECD (2004b), *Private Health Insurance in OECD Countries*, OECD Publishing, *http://dx.doi.org/10.1787/9789264007451-en*.

OECD (2008a), *The Looming Crisis in the Health Workforce: How Can OECD Countries Respond?*, OECD Publishing, *http://dx.doi.org/10.1787/9789264050440-en*.

OECD (2008b), *Pharmaceutical Pricing Policies in a Global Market*, OECD Publishing, *http://dx.doi.org/10.1787/9789264044159-en*.

OECD (2010a), *Health Care Systems: Efficiency and Policy Settings*, OECD Publishing, *http://dx.doi.org/10.1787/9789264094901-en*.

OECD (2010b), *Value for Money in Health Spending*, OECD Health Policy Studies, OECD Publishing, *http://dx.doi.org/10.1787/9789264088818-en*.

OECD (2011a), *OECD Regions at a Glance 2011*, OECD Publishing, *http://dx.doi.org/10.1787/reg_glance-2011-en*.

OECD (2011b), *Society at a Glance 2011 – OECD Social Indicators*, OECD Publishing, *http://dx.doi.org/10.1787/soc_glance-2011-en*.

OECD (2012a), *OECD Reviews of Health Care Quality: Israel – Raising Standards*, OECD Publishing, *http://dx.doi.org/10.1787/9789264029941-en*.

OECD (2012b), *OECD Reviews of Health Care Quality: Korea – Raising Standards*, OECD Publishing, *http://dx.doi.org/10.1787/9789264173446-en*.

OECD (2012c), *OECD Reviews of Health Systems: Russian Federation*, OECD Publishing, *http://dx.doi.org/10.1787/9789264168091-en*.

OECD (2013a), *OECD Health Statistics 2013*, Online database, OECD Publishing, *http://dx.doi.org/10.1787/health-data-en*.

OECD (2013b), *OECD Reviews of Health Care Quality: Turkey – Raising Standards*, OECD Publishing, *http://dx.doi.org/10.1787/9789264202054-en*.

OECD (2013c), *OECD Pensions at a Glance*, OECD Publishing, forthcoming.

OECD (2013d), *OECD Reviews of Health Care Quality: Denmark – Raising Standards*, OECD Publishing, *http://dx.doi.org/10.1787/9789264191136-en*.

OECD (2013e), *Cancer Care: Assuring Quality to Improve Survival*, OECD Publishing, *http://dx.doi.org/10.1787/9789264181052-en*.

OECD (2013f), *OECD Regions at a Glance*, OECD Publishing.

OECD (forthcoming), *Mental Health Services in OECD Countries* (provisional title), OECD Publishing.

OECD and European Commission (2013), *A Good Life in Old Age? Monitoring and Improving Quality in Long-term Care*, OECD Health Policy Studies, OECD Publishing, *http://dx.doi.org/10.1787/9789264194564-en*.

OECD and WHO (2011), *OECD Reviews of Health Systems: Switzerland*, OECD Publishing, *http://dx.doi.org/ 10.1787/9789264120914-en*.

OECD, Eurostat and WHO (2011), *A System of Health Accounts, 2011 Edition*, OECD Publishing, *http:// dx.doi.org/10.1787/9789264116016-en*.

OECD/ITF (2011), *IRTAD Road Safety 2010 Annual Report*, OECD Publishing.

OECD/ITF (2013), *IRTAD Road Safety 2013 Annual Report*, OECD Publishing.

OFSP – Office fédéral de la santé publique (2013), *Accouchements par césarienne en Suisse* [Births by Caesareans in Switzerland], OFSP, Bern, 27 February.

Ono, T., G. Lafortune and M. Schoenstein (2013), "Health Workforce Planning in OECD Countries: A Review of 26 Projection Models from 18 Countries", *OECD Health Working Papers*, No. 62, OECD Publishing, *http://dx.doi.org/10.1787/5k44t787zcwb-en*.

Ono, T., M. Schoenstein and J. Buchan (forthcoming), "Geographic Imbalances in Doctor Supply and Policy Responses" (provisional title), *OECD Health Working Papers*, OECD Publishing.

Or, Z. (2000), "Exploring the Effects of Health Care on Mortality across OECD Countries", *OECD Labour Market and Social Policy Occasional Paper*, No. 46, OECD Publishing, *http://dx.doi.org/10.1787/ 716472585704*.

Or, Z., F. Jusot and E. Yilmaz (2008), "Impact of Health Care System on Socioeconomic Inequalities in Doctor Use", *IRDES Working Paper* No. 17, IRDES, Paris.

Ouhoummane, N. et al. (2010), "Trends in Postacute Myocardial Infarction Management and Mortality in Patients with Diabetes. A Population-based Study from 1995 to 2001", *Canadian Journal of Cardiology*, Vol. 26, No. 10, pp. 523-531.

OXERA (2001), *Fundamental Review of the Generic Drugs Market*, Report prepared for the Department of Health, OXERA, Oxford.

Palència, L. et al. (2010), "Socioeconomic Inequalities in Breast and Cervical Cancer Screening Practices in Europe: Influence of the Type of Screening Program", *International Journal of Epidemiology*, Vol. 39, pp. 757-765.

Paris, V., M. Devaux and L. Wei (2010), "Health Systems Institutional Characteristics: A Survey of 29 OECD Countries", *OECD Health Working Paper*, No. 50, OECD Publishing, *http://dx.doi.org/10.1787/ 5kmfxfq9qbnr-en*.

Patterson, C.C., G.G. Dahlquist, E. Gyürüs, et al. and the EURODIAB Study Group (2009), "Incidence Trends for Childhood Type 1 Diabetes in Europe During 1989-2003 and Predicted New Cases 2005-20: A Multicentre Prospective Registration Study", *The Lancet*, Vol. 373, No. 9680, pp. 2027-2033.

Peralta, L.M.P. (2006), "The Prehospital Emergency Care System in Mexico City: A System's Performance Evaluation", *Prehospital and Disaster Medicine*, Vol. 21, No. 2, pp. 104-111.

Pitman, R.J., A. Melegaro, D. Gelb et al. (2006), "Assessing the Burden of Influenza and Other Respiratory Infections in England and Wales", *Journal of Infection*, Vol. 54, No. 6, pp. 530-538.

Poland, G. (2011), "The 2009-2010 Influenza Pandemic: Effects on Pandemic and Seasonal Vaccine Uptake and Lessons Learned for Seasonal Vaccination Campaigns", *Vaccine*, Vol. 28S, pp. D3-D13.

Pong, R.W. (2011), "Putting Up the Stethoscope for Good?", Canadian Institute for Health Information (CIHI), available at *www.cihi.ca*.

Public Health Agency of Canada (2009), "Publicly-funded Immunization Programs in Canada – Routine Schedule for Infants and Children", available at *www.phac-aspc.gc.ca/im/ptimprog-progimpt/table-1-eng.php*.

Public Health Agency of Canada (2013), *Economic Burden of Illness in Canada, 2005-2008*.

Qin, P., E. Agerbo and P.B. Mortensen (2003), "Suicide Risk in Relation to Socioeconomic, Demographic, Psychiatric, and Familial Factors: A National Register-based Study of All Suicides in Denmark, 1981–1997", *American Journal of Psychiatry*, Vol. 160, No. 4, pp. 765-772, April.

Rasmussen, M. et al. (2006), "Determinants of Fruit and Vegetable Consumption among Children and Adolescents: A Review of the Literature. Part 1: Quantitative Studies", *International Journal of Behavioural Nutrition and Physical Activity*, Vol. 3, No. 22.

Rehm, J. et al. (2009), "Global Burden of Disease and Injury and Economic Cost Attributable to Alcohol Use and Alcohol-use Disorder", *The Lancet*, Vol. 373, pp. 2223-2233.

Retzlaff-Roberts, D., C. Chang and R. Rubin (2004), "Technical Efficiency in the Use of Health Care Resources: A Comparison of OECD Countries", *Health Policy*, Vol. 69, pp. 55-72.

Rosso, S., A. Gondos, R. Zanetti et al. and EUNICE Survival Working Group (2010), "Up-to-date Estimates of Breast Cancer Survival for the Years 2000-2004 in 11 European Countries: The Role of Screening and a Comparison with Data from the United States", *European Journal of Cancer*, Vol. 46, No. 18, pp. 3351-3357.

Saha, S., D. Chant and J. McGrath (2007), "A Systematic Review of Mortality in Schizophrenia Is the Differential Mortality Gap Worsening Over Time?", *Archives of General Psychiatry*, Vol. 64, No. 10, pp. 1123-1131, *http://dx.doi.org/10.1001/archpsyc.64.10.112*.

Sandvik, C. et al. (2005), "Personal, Social and Environmental Factors Regarding Fruit and Vegetable Consumption Intake Among Schoolchildren in Nine European Countries", *Annals of Nutrition and Metabolism*, Vol. 49, No. 4, pp. 255-266.

Sassi, F. (2010), *Obesity and the Economics of Prevention – Fit not Fat*, OECD Publishing, *http://dx.doi.org/10.1787/9789264084865-en*.

Sassi, F., M. Devaux, J. Church et al. (2009), "Education and Obesity in Four OECD Countries", *OECD Health Working Paper*, No. 46, OECD Publishing, *http://dx.doi.org/10.1787/5km4psmtn8zx-en*.

Schiele, F. et al. (2005), "Compliance with Guidelines and 1-year Mortality in Patients with Acute Myocardial Infarction: A Prospective Study", *European Heart Journal*, Vol. 26, pp. 873-880.

Schoen, C. et al. (2010), "How Health Insurance Design Affects Access to Care and Costs, by Income, in Eleven Countries", *Health Affairs*, Vol. 29, No. 12, pp. 2323-2334.

Schull, M.J., M.M. Mamdani and J. Fang (2004), "Community Influenza Outbreaks and Emergency Department Ambulance Diversion", *Annals of Emergency Medicine*, Vol. 44, pp. 61-67.

Seenan, P., M. Long and P. Langhorne (2007), "Stroke Units in Their Natural Habitat: Systematic Review of Observational Studies", *Stroke*, Vol. 38, pp. 1886-1892.

Sengupta, N. et al. (2004), "Does the MMR Triple Vaccine Cause Autism? ", *Evidence-based Healthcare and Public Health*, Vol. 8, No. 5, pp. 239-245, October.

Siciliani, L., M. Borowitz and V. Moran (2013), *Waiting Time Policies in the Health Sector: What Works?*, OECD Health Policy Studies, OECD Publishing, *http://dx.doi.org/10.1787/9789264179080-en*.

Sirven, N. and Z. Or (2010), "Disparities in Regular Health Care Utilisation in Europe", *IRDES Working Paper* No. 37, IRDES, Paris.

Slobbe, L.C.J, J.M. Smit, J. Groen et al. (2011), *Trends in Cost of Illness in the Netherlands, 1999- 2010*, National Institute for Public Health and the Environment (RIVM), available at *www.costofillness.nl*.

Smith-Bindman, R., D.L. Miglioretti and E.B. Larson (2008), "Rising Use of Diagnostic Medical Imaging in a Large Integrated Health System", *Health Affairs*, Vol. 27, No. 6, pp. 1491-1502.

Society of Obstetricians and Gynaecologists of Canada et al. (2008), "Joint Policy Statement on Normal Childbirth", *Journal of Obstetrics and Gynaecology Canada*, Vol. 30, No. 12, pp. 1163-1165.

Sonnenberg, A. et al. (2000), "Cost-Effectiveness of Colonoscopy in Screening for Colorectal Cancer", *Annals of Internal Medicine*, Vol. 133, No. 8, pp. 573-584.

Soriguer, F., A. Goday, A. Bosch-Comas et al. (2012), "Prevalence of Diabetes Mellitus and Impaired Glucose Regulation in Spain: the Di@ bet.es Study", *Diabetologia*, Vol. 55, No. 1, pp. 88-93.

Starfield, B. et al. (2005), "Contribution of Primary Care to Health Systems and Health", *The Milbank Quarterly*, Vol. 83, No. 3, pp. 457-502.

Strong, W.B. et al. (2005), "Evidence Based Physical Activity for School-Age Youth", *Journal of Pediatrics*, Vol. 146, pp. 732-737.

Sullivan, D.F. (1971), "A Single Index of Mortality and Morbidity", *Health Services Mental Health Administration Health Reports*, Vol. 86, pp. 347-354.

Sundquist, J. (2012), "Long-Term Outcome after Obstetric Injury: A Retrospective Study", *Acta Obstetricia et Gynecologica Scandinavica*, Vol. 91, No. 6, pp. 715-718.

Swedish Association of Local Authorities and Regions and National Board of Health and Welfare (2010), *Quality and Efficiency in Swedish Health Care – Regional Comparisons 2009*, Stockholm.

Szalay, T. et al. (2011), "Slovakia: Health System Review", *Health Systems in Transition*, Vol. 13, No. 2, pp. 1-200.

Taggart, D. (2009), "PCI or CABG in Coronary Artery Disease?", *The Lancet*, Vol. 373, pp. 1190-1197.

Tidemalm, D. et al. (2008), "Excess Mortality in Persons with Severe Mental Disorder in Sweden: A Cohort Study of 12 103 Individuals with and without Contact with Psychiatric Services", *Clinical Practice and Epidemiology in Mental Health* 2008, Vol. 4, No. 23, *http://dx.doi.org/10.1186/1745-0179-4-2.*

Unicef and WHO (2004), *Low Birthweight: Country, Regional and Global Estimates*, UNICEF, New York.

Valenciano. M. et al. (2011), "Estimates of Pandemic Influenza Vaccine Effectiveness in Europe, 2009-2010: Results of Influenza Monitoring Vaccine Effectiveness in Europe (I-MOVE) Multicentre Case-Control Study", *PLoS Med*, Vol. 8, No. 1.

Van Doorslaer, E. et al. (2004), "Income-related Inequality in the Use of Medical Care in 21 OECD Countries", *OECD Health Working Paper*, No. 14, OECD Publishing, *http://dx.doi.org/10.1787/687501760705.*

Verdecchia, A. et al. (2007), "Recent Cancer Survival in Europe: A 2000-02 Period Analysis of EUROCARE-4 Data", *The Lancet Oncology*, Vol. 8, pp. 784-796.

Villar, J. et al. (2006), "Caesarean Delivery Rates and Pregnancy Outcomes: the 2005 WHO Global Survey on Maternal and Perinatal Health in Latin America", *The Lancet*, Vol. 367, pp. 1819-1829.

Vogel, T.R. et al. (2010), "Postoperative Sepsis in the United States", *The Annals of Surgery*, Vol. 252, No 6, pp. 1065-1071.

Vogler, S. (2012), "The Impact of Pharmaceutical Pricing and Reimbursement Policies on Generic Uptake: Implementation of Policy Options on Generics in 29 European Countries – An Overview", *Generics and Biosimilars Initiative Journal*, Vol. 1, No. 2, pp. 44-51.

Walls, H.C.et al. (2012), "Reductions in Transport Mortality in Australia: Evidence of a Public Health Success", *Accident Analysis & Prevention*, Vol. 49.

Westert, G.P. et al. (eds.) (2010), *Dutch Health Care Performance Report 2010*, National Institute for Public Health and the Environment, Bilthoven, The Netherlands.

Westert, G. and N. Klazinga (2011), *The Dutch Health Care System, 2011*, Report prepared for the Commonwealth Fund, available at *www.commonwealthfund.org/Topics/International-Health-Policy/Countries/The-Netherlands.aspx.*

Wahlbeck, K. et al. (2011), "Outcomes of Nordic Mental Health Systems: Life Expectancy of Patients with Mental Disorders", *The British Journal of Psychiatry*, Vol. 199, No. 6, pp. 453-458.

Wheeler, C.M. et al. (2009), "Human Papillomavirus Genotype Distributions: Implications for Vaccination and Cervical Cancer Screening in the United States", *Journal of the National Cancer Institute*, Vol. 101, No. 7, pp. 1-13.

WHA – World Health Assembly (2003), *Prevention and Control of Influenza Pandemics and Annual Epidemics*, 56th World Health Assembly, World Health Organization, Geneva.

WHO – World Health Organization (2000), *Obesity: Preventing and Managing the Global Epidemic. Report of a WHO Consultation*, WHO Technical Report Series No. 894, WHO, Geneva.

WHO (2001), *World Health Report 2001 – Mental Health: New Understanding, New Hope*, WHO, Geneva.

WHO (2009a), *Global Status Report on Road Safety: Time for Action*, WHO, Geneva.

WHO (2009b), *Hepatitis B WHO Fact Sheet* No. 204, WHO, Geneva.

WHO (2009c), *Vaccines for Pandemic Influenza A (H1N1)*, available at *www.who.int/csr/disease/swineflu/frequently_asked_questions/vaccine_preparedness/en/index.html.*

WHO (2009d), "Weekly epidemiological record", No. 40, pp. 405-420, available at *www.who.int/wer/2009/wer8440.pdf* (accessed 10 July 2013).

WHO (2010a), *Global Strategy to Reduce the Harmful Use of Alcohol*, WHO, Geneva.

WHO (2010b), *Chronic Rheumatic Conditions*, Fact Sheet, available at *www.who.int/chp/topics/rheumatic/en.*

WHO (2010c), *The World Health Report: Health Systems Financing: The Path to Universal Coverage*, WHO, Geneva.

WHO (2011a), *Global Information System on Alcohol and Health*, WHO, Geneva, available at *www.apps.who.int/ghodata.*

WHO (2011b), "Asthma", *Fact Sheet No. 307*, WHO, Geneva, available at *www.who.int/mediacentre/factsheets/fs307/en/index.html.*

WHO (2011c), "Chronic Obstructive Pulmonary Disease (COPD)", *Fact Sheet No. 315*, WHO, Geneva, available at *www.who.int/mediacentre/factsheets/fs315/en/index.html*.

WHO (2011d), *Global Status Report on Alcohol and Health*, WHO, Geneva.

WHO (2011e), *Mental Health Atlas 2011*, WHO, Geneva.

WHO (2012), *World Health Statistics 2012*, WHO, Geneva.

WHO (2013), "Tobacco", *Fact Sheet No. 339*, WHO Geneva, available at *www.who.int/mediacentre/factsheets/fs339/en/index.html* (accessed 15 July 2013).

WHO/Unicef (2013), "Immunization Schedule – June 2013 Update", available at *www.who.int/immunization_monitoring/data/data_subject/en/index.html* (accessed 9 July 2013).

WHO and Alzheimer Disease International (2012), *Dementia: A Public Health Priority*, Geneva.

Wiegers, T. and C. Hukkelhoven (2010), "The Role of Hospital Midwives in the Netherlands", *BMC Pregnancy and Childbirth*, Vol. 10, No. 80, available at *www.biomedcentral.com/1471-2393/10/80*.

Wiener, J. et al. (2009), "Why Are Nursing Home Utilization Rates Declining?", Real Choice System Change Grant Program, US Department of Health and Human Services, Centres for Medicare and Medicaid Services, available at *www.hcbs.org/files/160/7990/SCGNursing.pdf*.

Wimo, A., B. Winblad and L. Jonsson (2010), "The Worldwide Societal Costs of Dementia: Estimates for 2009", *Alzheimer's & Dementia*, Vol. 6, pp. 98-103.

Woods, L.M., B. Rachet and M.P. Coleman (2006), "Origins of Socio-economic Inequalities in Cancer Survival: A Review", *Annals of Oncology*, Vol. 17, No. 1, pp. 5-19.

Wortmann, M. (2009), "Parallel Sessions-Dementia Policies: The Role of Alzheimer Associations in Campaigning for Change", *Alzheimer Europe*, available at *www.alzheimer-europe.org/Conferences/Previous-conferences/2009-Brussels/Abstracts-and-presentations/Dementia-policies*.

Wübker, A. (2013), "Explaining Variations in Breast Cancer Screening Across European Countries", *European Journal of Health Economics*, *http://dx.doi.org/10.1007/s10198-013-0490-3*.

Yan, R.T. et al. (2006), "Under-use of Evidence-based Treatment Partly Explains the Worse Clinical Outcome in Diabetic Patients with Acute Coronary Syndromes", *American Heart Journal*, Vol. 152, No. 4, pp. 676-683.

Zaridze, D. et al. (2009), "Alcohol and Cause-specific Mortality in Russia: A Retrospective Case–control Study of 48 557 Adult Deaths", *The Lancet*, Vol. 373, No. 9682, pp. 2201-2214.

Zivin, K., M. Paczkowski and S. Galea (2011), "Economic Downturns and Population Mental Health: Research Findings, Gaps, Challenges and Priorities", *Psychological Medicine*, Vol. 41, No. 07, pp. 1343-1348.

DATABASE REFERENCES

OECD Health Data: Health status, *http://dx.doi.org/10.1787/data-00540-en* (accessed 15 October 2013).

OECD Health Data: Non-medical determinants of health, *http://dx.doi.org/10.1787/data-00546-en* (accessed 15 October 2013).

OECD Health Data: Health care resources, *http://dx.doi.org/10.1787/data-00541-en* (accessed 15 October 2013).

OECD Health Data: Health care utilisation, *http://dx.doi.org/10.1787/data-00542-en* (accessed 15 October 2013).

OECD Health Data: Health Care Quality Indicators, *http://dx.doi.org/10.1787/data-00592-en* (accessed 15 October 2013).

OECD Health Data: Pharmaceutical market, *http://dx.doi.org/10.1787/data-00545-en* (accessed 15 October 2013).

OECD Health Data: Long-term care resources and utilisation, *http://dx.doi.org/10.1787/data-00543-en* (accessed 15 October 2013).

OECD Health Data: Health expenditure and financing, *http://dx.doi.org/10.1787/data-00349-en* (accessed 15 October 2013).

OECD Health Data: Social protection, *http://dx.doi.org/10.1787/data-00544-en* (accessed 15 October 2013).

OECD Health Data: Demographic references, *http://dx.doi.org/10.1787/data-00547-en* (accessed 15 October 2013).

OECD Health Data: Economic references, *http://dx.doi.org/10.1787/data-00548-en* (accessed 15 October 2013).

ANNEX A

Additional information on demographic and economic context, and health expenditure and financing

Table A.1. **Total population, mid-year, 1960 to 2011**

Thousands

	1960	1970	1980	1990	2000	2010	2011
Australia	10 275	12 507	14 695	17 065	19 153	22 065	22 323
Austria	7 048	7 467	7 549	7 678	8 012	8 390	8 421
Belgium	9 153	9 656	9 859	9 967	10 251	10 920	11 048
Canada	18 178	21 745	24 518	27 690	30 688	34 120	34 484
Chile	7 643	9 570	11 174	13 179	15 398	17 094	17 248
Czech Republic	9 602	9 858	10 304	10 333	10 272	10 497	10 496
Denmark	4 580	4 929	5 123	5 141	5 340	5 548	5 571
Estonia	1 211	1 359	1 477	1 569	1 369	1 340	1 340
Finland	4 430	4 606	4 780	4 986	5 176	5 363	5 388
France	45 684	50 772	53 880	56 709	59 062	62 927	63 249
Germany[1]	55 608	61 098	61 549	62 679	82 212	81 777	81 373
Greece	8 322	8 793	9 643	10 157	10 917	11 308	11 300
Hungary	9 984	10 338	10 711	10 374	10 211	10 000	9 993
Iceland	176	204	228	255	281	318	319
Ireland	2 829	2 957	3 413	3 514	3 805	4 520	4 575
Israel	2 150	2 958	3 878	4 660	6 289	7 624	7 749
Italy	50 200	53 822	56 434	56 719	56 942	60 483	60 724
Japan	93 419	103 721	117 061	123 613	126 927	128 058	127 799
Korea	25 012	32 241	38 124	42 869	47 008	49 410	49 779
Luxembourg	314	339	364	382	436	507	518
Mexico	37 877	50 785	67 384	83 971	98 439	108 396	109 220
Netherlands	11 487	13 039	14 150	14 952	15 926	16 615	16 718
New Zealand	2 382	2 828	3 170	3 390	3 858	4 366	4 404
Norway	3 581	3 876	4 086	4 241	4 491	4 889	4 952
Poland	29 561	32 526	35 578	38 031	38 256	38 517	38 526
Portugal	8 858	8 680	9 766	9 983	10 226	10 605	10 557
Slovak Republic	4 068	4 538	4 980	5 299	5 389	5 409	5 398
Slovenia	1 580	1 670	1 884	1998	1990	2049	2052
Spain	30 455	33 815	37 439	38 850	40 263	46 071	44 835
Sweden	7 485	8 043	8 311	8 559	8 872	9 378	9 447
Switzerland	5 328	6 181	6 319	6 712	7 184	7 828	7 912
Turkey	27 438	35 294	44 522	55 120	64 252	73 328	74 165
United Kingdom	52 371	55 633	56 331	57 238	58 888	61 344	61 760
United States	180 671	205 052	227 225	249 623	282 162	309 326	311 588
OECD (total)	**768 959**	**870 899**	**965 909**	**1 047 508**	**1 149 946**	**1 230 391**	**1 235 233**

1. Population figures for Germany prior to 1991 refer to West Germany.
Source: OECD Health Statistics 2013, http://dx.doi.org/10.1787/health-data-en.

StatLink ᵐˢ᪑ *http://dx.doi.org/10.1787/888932919555*

Table A.2. **Share of the population aged 65 and over, 1960 to 2011**

	1960	1970	1980	1990	2000	2010	2011
Australia	8.5	8.3	9.6	11.1	12.4	13.5	13.7
Austria	12.2	14.1	15.4	14.9	15.4	17.6	17.7
Belgium	12	13.4	14.3	14.9	16.8	17.2	17.3
Canada	7.5	7.9	9.4	11.3	12.6	14.2	14.7
Chile	4.8	5	5.5	6.1	7.2	9	9.3
Czech Republic	9.5	12.1	13.5	12.6	13.8	15.4	16.2
Denmark	10.6	12.3	14.4	15.6	14.8	16.6	17.1
Estonia	10.6	11.7	12.5	11.6	15.1	17	17.2
Finland	7.3	9.2	12	13.4	14.9	17.3	17.8
France	11.6	12.9	13.9	14	16.1	16.8	17.1
Germany	10.8	13.1	15.5	15.5	16.4	20.6	20.7
Greece	8.2	11.1	13.1	13.7	16.6	19.1	19.5
Hungary	9	11.6	13.4	13.3	15.1	16.7	16.8
Iceland	8.1	8.8	9.9	10.6	11.6	12.1	12.9
Ireland	11.1	11.1	10.7	11.4	11.2	11.6	12.2
Israel	5	6.7	8.6	9.1	9.8	9.9	10
Italy	9.3	10.9	13.1	14.9	18.3	20.3	21
Japan	5.7	7.1	9.1	12.1	17.4	23.2	23.3
Korea	2.9	3.1	3.8	5.1	7.2	11	11.4
Luxembourg	10.9	12.5	13.6	13.4	14.1	13.9	13.9
Mexico	3.4	4.6	4.3	4.1	4.7	5.8	6.1
Netherlands	9	10.2	11.5	12.8	13.6	15.4	15.9
New Zealand	8.7	8.4	9.7	11.2	11.8	13	13.3
Norway	11	12.9	14.8	16.3	15.2	15	15.2
Poland	5.8	8.2	10.1	10.1	12.2	13.6	13.9
Portugal	7.9	9.4	11.3	13.4	16.2	18.4	19
Slovak Republic	6.9	9.1	10.5	10.3	11.4	12.4	12.7
Slovenia	7.8	9.9	11.7	10.7	14	16.6	16.8
Spain	8.2	9.6	11	13.6	16.8	17	17.6
Sweden	11.8	13.7	16.3	17.8	17.3	18.3	19.3
Switzerland	10.2	11.4	13.8	14.6	15.3	17.4	17.1
Turkey	3.6	4.4	4.7	5.2	6.5	7.7	7.9
United Kingdom	11.7	13	15	15.7	15.8	15.8	16.2
United States	9.2	9.8	11.3	12.5	12.4	13.1	13.2
OECD34	**8.6**	**9.9**	**11.4**	**12.1**	**13.5**	**15.1**	**15.4**

Source: OECD Health Statistics 2013, http://dx.doi.org/10.1787/health-data-en.

StatLink ᴍˢᴾ http://dx.doi.org/10.1787/888932919574

Table A.3. **GDP per capita in 2011 and average annual growth rates, 1970 to 2011**

	GDP per capita in USD PPP	Average annual growth rate per capita, in real terms				
	2011	1970-80	1980-90	1990-2000	2000-10	2010-11
Australia	44 201	1.3	1.5	2.4	1.7	2.2
Austria	42 186	3.5	2.1	2.2	1.1	2.3
Belgium	38 629	3.2	1.9	1.9	0.8	0.6
Canada	40 449	2.8	1.6	1.9	0.8	1.5
Chile	20 855	..	..	4.8	3.1	5.0
Czech Republic	26 209	..	..	0.6	3.2	1.8
Denmark	40 933	1.9	2.0	2.2	0.2	0.7
Estonia[1]	21 998	..	..	..	3.8	8.3
Finland	37 479	3.4	2.6	1.7	1.4	2.3
France	35 395	3.0	1.9	1.5	0.5	1.2
Germany[2, 3]	39 662	2.8	2.1	1.3	1.0	3.5
Greece	25 859	3.6	0.2	1.6	1.7	-7.0
Hungary[2]	21 409	..	..	..	2.2	1.7
Iceland	36 611	5.2	1.6	1.5	0.9	2.6
Ireland	41 548	3.2	3.3	6.6	0.9	0.2
Israel	28 958	2.4	1.9	2.7	1.3	2.9
Italy	32 648	3.3	2.3	1.6	-0.2	0.0
Japan	33 843	3.2	4.1	0.9	0.7	-0.4
Korea	29 833	7.2	8.4	5.6	3.6	2.9
Luxembourg	88 781	1.9	4.5	3.6	1.2	-0.6
Mexico	17 446	3.6	-0.4	1.8	0.8	3.1
Netherlands	42 716	2.3	1.7	2.5	0.9	0.4
New Zealand	30 942	0.6	1.3	1.7	1.1	0.2
Norway	61 060	4.2	1.0	3.9	1.3	4.0
Poland	21 138	..	..	3.7	3.8	4.5
Portugal	25 588	3.5	3.0	2.7	0.3	-1.1
Slovak Republic[4]	24 112	..	..	..	4.7	3.4
Slovenia	27 351	..	..	1.9	2.4	0.4
Spain	33 045	2.6	2.6	2.4	0.7	3.2
Sweden	41 461	1.6	1.9	1.7	1.6	2.9
Switzerland	51 227	1.0	1.6	0.4	0.9	0.8
Turkey	16 984	1.7	3.0	2.1	2.5	7.5
United Kingdom	36 158	1.8	2.6	2.5	1.3	0.3
United States	48 113	2.2	2.3	2.2	0.6	1.1
OECD	**35 436**	**2.9**	**2.3**	**2.4**	**1.5**	**1.8**

1. First year available 1993.
2. First year available 1991.
3. Data prior to 1991 refer to Western Germany.
4. First year available 1992.
Source: OECD Health Statistics 2013, http://dx.doi.org/10.1787/health-data-en.

StatLink ⟨⟩ *http://dx.doi.org/10.1787/888932919593*

Table A.4. **Total expenditure on health per capita in 2011,
average annual growth rates, 2000 to 2011**

	Total health expenditure per capita in USD PPP	Annual growth rate per capita in real terms[1]				
	2011	2007/08	2008/09	2009/10	2010/11	2000-11
Australia[2]	3 800	2.2	3.6	0.0	..	2.7
Austria	4 546	3.2	2.1	0.5	0.0	1.8
Belgium[3]	4 061	4.3	3.1	0.4	0.7	3.1
Canada	4 522	1.8	6.8	1.8	-0.3	3.0
Chile[4]	1 568	3.0	12.2	4.3	6.6	7.1
Czech Republic	1 966	6.9	10.7	-4.3	2.8	4.7
Denmark	4 448	0.6	5.7	-2.4	-1.2	2.3
Estonia	1 303	12.6	-0.1	-6.9	1.2	5.3
Finland	3 374	3.1	0.5	0.8	2.5	3.5
France	4 118	0.7	2.6	0.7	0.8	1.8
Germany	4 495	3.5	4.4	2.5	1.6	2.1
Greece	2 361	2.6	-2.9	-11.4	-10.9	2.1
Hungary	1 689	-1.7	-3.2	5.4	-0.1	3.0
Iceland	3 305	-0.9	-1.4	-7.2	-0.4	0.6
Ireland	3 700	10.5	3.7	-9.0	-4.2	4.4
Israel	2 239	3.3	-1.6	3.2	3.5	1.7
Italy	3 012	2.6	-0.6	1.3	-2.0	1.2
Japan[2]	3 213	3.5	4.7	4.9	..	3.0
Korea	2 198	4.7	7.7	8.6	4.0	8.7
Luxembourg[5]	4 246	-3.4	4.0	..	..	0.7
Mexico[2]	977	1.6	2.2	0.7	..	2.8
Netherlands	5 099	3.5	3.6	2.7	-0.7	4.7
New Zealand[3]	3 182	6.6	7.9	0.6	1.0	3.8
Norway	5 669	2.7	1.6	-1.4	2.5	2.4
Poland	1 452	14.3	6.3	0.2	2.2	6.0
Portugal	2 619	2.1	2.6	2.0	-6.3	1.1
Slovak Republic[2]	1 915	9.2	8.2	2.8	..	10.0
Slovenia	2 421	9.6	0.6	-2.6	0.2	2.9
Spain	3 072	4.7	2.8	-0.8	-0.1	3.3
Sweden	3 925	2.1	1.4	0.7	2.9	3.1
Switzerland	5 643	1.7	3.5	0.8	2.1	1.8
Turkey[6]	906	-0.7	..	..	..	5.6
United Kingdom	3 405	3.6	5.6	-2.5	-1.1	4.0
United States	8 508	1.5	2.1	1.7	1.0	3.0
OECD	**3 322**	**3.9**	**3.2**	**-0.2**	**0.3**	**3.4**

1. Using national currency units at 2005 GDP price level.
2. Most recent year 2010.
3. Excluding investment.
4. CPI is used as deflator.
5. Most recent year 2009.
6. Most recent year 2008.
Source: OECD Health Statistics 2013, http://dx.doi.org/10.1787/health-data-en.

StatLink http://dx.doi.org/10.1787/888932919612

Table A.5. **Public expenditure on health per capita in 2011, average annual growth rates, 2000 to 2011**

	Public health expenditure per capita in USD PPP	Annual growth rate per capita in real terms[1]				
	2011	2007/08	2008/09	2009/10	2010/11	2000-11
Australia[2]	2 578	2.7	4.6	-1.0	..	2.9
Austria	3 466	3.9	2.0	-0.1	0.5	1.9
Belgium[3]	3 083	6.5	4.7	-0.9	1.8	3.3
Canada	3 183	2.2	7.4	1.6	-0.8	3.0
Chile[4]	735	5.0	21.3	3.4	5.8	6.1
Czech Republic	1 655	3.5	12.6	-4.5	3.3	4.0
Denmark	3 795	0.9	6.2	-2.3	-1.0	2.5
Estonia	1 033	15.9	-3.4	-2.5	1.8	5.6
Finland	2 545	3.3	1.4	0.2	3.4	4.0
France	3 161	0.1	2.8	0.6	0.6	1.5
Germany	3 436	3.6	4.9	2.5	1.2	1.7
Greece	1 536	1.9	10.8	-13.4	-13.3	2.9
Hungary	1 098	-2.0	-5.2	4.0	0.3	2.2
Iceland	2 656	-0.8	-2.1	-8.9	-0.4	0.5
Ireland	2 477	10.0	-0.1	-12.7	-7.7	3.3
Israel	1 362	4.4	-0.2	1.7	3.3	1.4
Italy	2 345	3.5	-0.7	0.8	-2.8	1.7
Japan[2]	2 638	4.8	4.9	5.6	..	3.2
Korea	1 217	4.3	11.4	8.1	1.9	9.6
Luxembourg[5]	3 596	-3.4	7.7	..	..	0.9
Mexico[2]	462	5.0	5.1	-1.2	..	3.0
Netherlands[6]	4 055	4.4	4.5	2.8	-0.8	6.9
New Zealand[3]	2 631	7.2	8.1	0.8	0.5	4.4
Norway	4 813	3.0	1.8	-1.2	2.7	2.7
Poland	1 021	16.5	6.1	-0.3	0.9	6.0
Portugal	1 703	0.0	4.6	1.1	-7.6	0.9
Slovak Republic [2]	1 358	10.7	4.9	0.9	..	6.5
Slovenia	1 784	12.8	0.2	-2.3	-0.2	2.8
Spain	2 244	6.4	5.2	-1.5	-1.7	3.4
Sweden	3 204	2.2	1.4	0.7	3.1	2.7
Switzerland	3 661	12.1	4.2	0.4	1.5	3.3
Turkey[7]	661	6.9	..	..	..	7.6
United Kingdom	2 821	4.7	7.6	-1.4	-1.9	4.4
United States	4 066	3.4	4.8	2.4	1.5	4.0
OECD	**2 414**	**5.1**	**4.4**	**-0.7**	**-0.1**	**3.5**

1. Using national currency units at 2005 GDP price level.
2. Most recent year 2010.
3. Excluding investment.
4. CPI is used as deflator.
5. Most recent year 2009.
6. Data refer to public current expenditure.
7. Most recent year 2008.
Source: OECD Health Statistics 2013, http://dx.doi.org/10.1787/health-data-en.

StatLink 🔗📈 *http://dx.doi.org/10.1787/888932919631*

Table A.6. **Total expenditure on health, percentage of GDP, 1980 to 2011**

	1980	1990	1995	2000	2005	2009	2010	2011
Australia	6.1	6.8	7.3	8.1	8.5	9.0	8.9	..
Austria	7.5		8.4	9.6	10.0	10.4	11.2	11.0	10.8
Belgium[1]	6.3	7.2		7.6	8.1		10.0	10.6	10.5	10.5
Canada	7.0	8.9	9.0	8.8	9.8	11.4	11.4	11.2
Chile	..	..	5.2	6.4	6.6	7.9	7.4	7.5
Czech Republic	..	4.4		6.7		6.3		6.9	8.0	7.4	7.5
Denmark	8.9	8.3	8.1	8.7		9.8	11.5	11.1	10.9
Estonia	..	..	..	5.3	5.0	7.0	6.3	5.9
Finland	6.3	7.7		7.8	7.2	8.4	9.2	9.0e	9.0e
France	7.0	8.4		10.4	10.1		11.0	11.7	11.7	11.6
Germany	8.4	8.3		10.1	10.4	10.8	11.8	11.5	11.3
Greece	5.9	6.7	8.7	8.0	9.7	10.2	9.5	9.1
Hungary	..	7.1 1991	7.3		7.2		8.4	7.7	8.0	7.9
Iceland	6.3	7.8	8.2	9.5	9.4	9.6	9.3	9.0
Ireland	8.1	6.0	6.6	6.1	7.6	10.0	9.3	8.9
Israel	7.7	7.1	7.6	7.5	7.9	7.7	7.7	7.7
Italy	..	7.7	7.1	7.9	8.7	9.4	9.4	9.2
Japan	6.4	5.8		6.8	7.6	8.2	9.5	9.6	..
Korea	3.6	3.9	3.7	4.3	5.6	7.1	7.3	7.4
Luxembourg	5.2	5.4		5.6		7.5	7.9	8.0	7.2	6.6
Mexico	..	4.4	5.1		5.1		5.9	6.4e	6.2e	..
Netherlands	7.4	8.0	8.3		8.0		10.9	11.9	12.1	11.9
New Zealand[1]	5.8	6.8	7.1	7.6	8.4	10.0	10.2	10.3
Norway	7.0	7.6		7.9		8.4		9.0	9.7	9.4	9.3
Poland	..	4.8	5.5	5.5		6.2	7.2	7.0	6.9
Portugal	5.1	5.7		7.5		9.3	10.4	10.8	10.8	10.2
Slovak Republic	..	..	5.8 1997	5.5		7.0	9.2	9.0		7.9
Slovenia	..	..	7.5	8.3		8.4	9.2	8.9	8.9
Spain	5.3	6.5	7.4		7.2		8.3	9.6	9.6	9.3
Sweden	8.9	8.2		8.0	8.2	9.1	9.9	9.5	9.5
Switzerland	7.2	8.0		9.3	9.9	10.9	11.0	10.9	11.0
Turkey	2.4	2.7	2.5		4.9	5.4	6.1 2008	..	..
United Kingdom	5.6	5.8	6.8	7.0	8.3	9.9	9.6	9.4
United States	9.0	12.4	13.7	13.7	15.8	17.7	17.7	17.7
OECD[2]	**6.6**	**6.9**	**7.5**	**7.8**	**8.7**	**9.6[2]**	**9.4[2]**	**9.3[2]**
Brasil	..	..	6.7	7.2	8.2	8.8	9.0	8.9
China	..	..	3.5	4.6	4.7	5.1	5.0	5.2
India	..	..	4.0	4.3	4.2	3.9	3.7	3.9
Indonesia	..	..	2.0	2.0	2.8	2.9	2.8	2.7
Russia	..	..	5.4	5.4	5.2	6.2	6.5	6.2
South Africa	..	..	7.4	8.3	8.8	8.7	8.7	8.5

| Break in the series.
e: Preliminary estimate
1. Excluding investment.
2. OECD average calculated with the most recent data available.
Source: OECD Health Statistics 2013, http://dx.doi.org/10.1787/health-data-en; WHO Global Health Expenditure Database.

StatLink ᵐˢᵖ *http://dx.doi.org/10.1787/888932919650*

ORGANISATION FOR ECONOMIC CO-OPERATION AND DEVELOPMENT

The OECD is a unique forum where governments work together to address the economic, social and environmental challenges of globalisation. The OECD is also at the forefront of efforts to understand and to help governments respond to new developments and concerns, such as corporate governance, the information economy and the challenges of an ageing population. The Organisation provides a setting where governments can compare policy experiences, seek answers to common problems, identify good practice and work to co-ordinate domestic and international policies.

The OECD member countries are: Australia, Austria, Belgium, Canada, Chile, the Czech Republic, Denmark, Estonia, Finland, France, Germany, Greece, Hungary, Iceland, Ireland, Israel, Italy, Japan, Korea, Luxembourg, Mexico, the Netherlands, New Zealand, Norway, Poland, Portugal, the Slovak Republic, Slovenia, Spain, Sweden, Switzerland, Turkey, the United Kingdom and the United States. The European Union takes part in the work of the OECD.

OECD Publishing disseminates widely the results of the Organisation's statistics gathering and research on economic, social and environmental issues, as well as the conventions, guidelines and standards agreed by its members.

OECD PUBLISHING, 2, rue André-Pascal, 75775 PARIS CEDEX 16
(81 2013 16 1 P) ISBN 978-92-64-20071-5 – No. 60937 2013-08